Inner Mysteries of the Western

At last in a clear and intellectually re
about the deepest levels of the history of the Western Magical Tradition. Magic is a technology of the imagination— and once this is understood, not only in the theoretical realm, but also once it is seen and demonstrated in the historical context of actual practices and practitioners throughout the history of the Western World, this technology becomes all the more usable to the modern magician.

This book is written by one of the world's leading authorities on practical magic and is therefore highly useful in its insights into the historical aspects of the tradition. At the same time, the author makes use of clear and precise methods of scholarship and has written a fine piece of authoritative history not only of certain ideas but also of the imagination.

Magic And The Western Mind forms a complete and authentic collection of the major trends in mainstream magical thought in the West. It is an ideal book to be read by the intellectuals who want to satisfy their curiosity about the history of magical thought, or by practicing magicians who want to deepen their understanding of the roots and branches of their work.

Magic is a middle path between religion and science—all three are needed. But magic has been the most neglected in recent centuries. The Western mind developed magic originally as one of the noblest arts and sciences, and now needs that magic as never before. This book can tell you why intelligent and responsible people are turning back to magic as a radical way of finding not only meaning in modern life—but as a means of survival in it.

About the Author

Gareth Knight has spent close to four decades actively investigating and writing about the Western Magical Tradition and the Qabalistic symbolism. He is one of the world's foremost authorities on magic and the active use of symbolism. In 1976 he was awarded an honorary doctorate for his work in the field, and he has acted as a consultant for Jungian analysts and for television producers in the area of archetypal symbolism.

Mr. Knight now lives in his native Essex in England.

To Write to the Author

We cannot guarantee that every letter written to the author will be answered, but all will be forwarded. Both the author and the publisher appreciate hearing from readers, learning of your enjoyment and benefit from the book. Llewellyn also publishes a bi-monthly news magazine with news and reviews of practical esoteric studies and articles helpful to the student, and some readers' questions and comments to the author may be answered through this magazine's columns if permission to do so is included in the original letter. The author sometimes participates in seminars and workshops, and dates and places are announced in *The Llewellyn New Times*. To write to the author, or to ask a question, write to:

Gareth Knight
c/o THE LLEWELLYN NEW TIMES
P. O. BOX 64383-374, St. Paul, MN 55164-0383, U.S.A.
Please enclose a self-addressed, stamped envelope for reply, or
$1.00 to cover costs.

Llewellyn's Western Magick Historical Series

Magic and the Western Mind

Ancient Knowledge and the Transformation of Consciousness

Gareth Knight

1991
Llewellyn Publications
St. Paul, Minnesota, 55164-0383, U.S.A.

FIRST LLEWELLYN EDITION
Originally published as *A History of White Magic,* A. R. Mowbray & Co. Ltd., Oxford, UK, 1978

Library of Congress Cataloging-in-Publication Data

Knight, Gareth.
   Magic and the western mind: ancient knowledge and the transformation of consciousness / Gareth Knight. —1st Llewellyn ed., Rev.
        p.   ca.   — (Llewellyn's western magick historical series)
   Rev. ed. of: A history of white magic. 1978.
   Includes index.
   ISBN 0–87542–374–4 : $12.95
   1. Magic—history.   I. Knight, Gareth. History of white magic.
   II. Title.   III. Series.
BF1589.K48   1991
133.4'3'09—dc20   90–27860
                                                              CIP

Llewellyn Publications
A Division of Llewellyn Worldwide, Ltd.,
P.O. Box 64383, St. Paul, MN 55164–0383

Llewellyn's Western Magick Historical Series

Weird shadows flicker over the figure of the Cro-Magnon shaman as he dances around the primitive campfire clad in deerskin and antlers. Sumerian magi study the sky and wonder. Greek nobles sacrifice sheep in attempts to speak with the wise who are no longer living, while their philosophers formulate ideas of mysticism that will dominate Western thought for two thousand years. In the Renaissance, an alchemist works his spiritual advancement through chemical analogs; a magus studies navigation and mechanics along with angelic communication; a member of the old religion, still called "witch" and thought to be evil by the established church, tends her healing herbs. Later, secret fraternities plot the overthrow of oppressive monarchies — and succeed in the French and American revolutions. Men and women band together in societies to practice magick or study unknown philosophies. The Age of Aquarius dawns as attention is focused on the deeper realities. In an unbroken stream from that primordial campfire to the modern magickal awakening, a deeper reality continues to assert itself.

Historians have tended to ignore magick and the occult as unworthy of serious study, yet how much of world history has been molded by the beliefs and practices of shamans, wise men, magi, astrologers, witches, alchemists, and adepts? From its roots in tribal practices, through the stargazing of the Chaldeans and the esoteric mathematics of Pythagoras, the mysteries of the *I Ching*, and the secrets of yogis and tantrists, magick became one of the noblest of the arts and sciences. Occult thought and philosophy were one and the same. The mystic ideas of the Greek philosophers, mixed with the qabala and other secret traditions, fed the Renaissance revival and led directly to modern scientific thought as well as New Age occultism. Only within the last two centuries has science become the religion of rationalism and sought vainly to divorce itself from its roots — roots that continually appear in new guises such as quantum physics and cosmology.

Llewellyn's Western Magick Historical Series will attempt to trace the myriad pathways that began with shamans and seers before recorded history and that lead in branching but continuous trails to the occult revival of the last decade of the our own century. The roots and the realities will not go unrecorded nor be forgotten.

Other books by Gareth Knight

A Practical Guide to Qabalistic Symbolism
The Occult: An Introduction
Experience of the Inner Worlds
The Secret Tradition in Arthurian Legend
The Rose Cross and the Goddess
The Treasure House of Images/Tarot Magic (USA edition)
The Magical World of the Inklings

Forthcoming:

The Magical World of the Tarot
Stars, Crystals and Heroes

A system, the first principle of which it is to render the mind intuitive of the *spiritual* in man (i.e. of that which lies *on the other side* of our natural consciousness) must needs have a great obscurity for those, who have never disciplined and strengthened this ulterior consciousness.

S. T. Coleridge
Biographia Literaria.

To Roma, Richard and Rebecca,
for putting up so well with having
a magician in the house.

Table of Contents

FOREWORD

Every civilization rests upon certain assumptions and its achievements, for better and for worse, realize whatever potentialities these assumptions contain in themselves. But no civilization can grow beyond the limits inherent in its premises; or, in the words of W. B. Yeats, "things thought too long can be no longer thought." There is a widespread feeling at this time that, for all its impressive technological achievement, the assumptions upon which our powerful but soul-destroying materialist civilization rests are not so unquestionable as they once seemed. Materialism, in the seventeenth century the "progressive" thought of liberal learning, rose to intellectual dominance in the eighteenth, and in the nineteenth showed its power to transform the environment in which mankind lives. But to increasing numbers at this time the Utopia of materialism has come to seem a hell of the spirit and the current belief in what many call a "new age" is accompanied by the rejection of the materialist premises: not matter, but spirit is once more coming to be seen as the ground of what we call "reality."

Teilhard de Chardin has pointed out that beginnings are seldom discernible: only when some new theme has developed do we begin to look for its origins. Gareth Knight's eminently well-balanced history of "white magic" traces some of the sources of a movement that seems destined to work a transformation no less long lasting and fundamental than the rise of materialism. It was when the power of Imperial Rome seemed supreme that the seed of Christian civilization began to germinate in the obscurity of the catacombs; now the *hybris* of materialism seems boundless; but the opposite principle, preserved underground in the Western esoteric tradition, is again seen at work.

"Magic" is a word whose associations are both glamorous and sinister; Gareth Knight, well known to his readers as the most down-to-earth and pragmatic of magicians, by seeking to show what magic really is and to what body of thought it belongs, dissipates both these illusions. At the same time he shows how real is the world upon whose laws the operations of "magic" (and of prayer for that matter) depend. It is the world of "imagination." Consciousness itself the secret *prima materia* of the alchemists. Imagination (he uses the word in Coleridge's sense and in

Blake's) is none the less real because it cannot be quantified. It is a radical fallacy of materialism that there are in the world differences only of degree; but between the quantifiable world of matter and the world of consciousness there is a difference in kind; the one can never be described or understood in terms of the other. What Coleridge calls "facts of mind" constitute no part of quantifiable scientific knowledge; but they are none the less real. Alchemy, discarded by science as primitive chemistry, has another meaning for Jungian psychology; psychical phenomena are now no longer something to be explained away by some Sherlock Holmes, secure in his assurance that rationalist materialism can explain all. Now these are rather something demanding explanation; and so with a whole miscellaneous body of belief and practice covered by the word "magic." The soul has too long been crushed between the upper millstone of the Church's abstract discursive theology (based upon the philosophy of Aristotle) and the nether millstone of scientific materialism. A renewed attention to the world of Imagination (the soul's native and proper element) is an important aspect of what Yeats foresaw as "the rise of soul against intellect now beginning in the world."

—Kathleen Raine

PREFACE

I am grateful to Richard Mulkern for his vision in wanting to publish a history of white magic; and to the Reverend Anthony Duncan for suggesting that I do it.

Having completed it, I am only too aware of the vast size of the subject and of the amount of material that has had to be left out. I am not a professional scholar but I have tried to be reasonably academically sound in a subject area that has not only been incompletely covered in itself, but which demands a certain acquaintance with subjects as diverse as the history of science, analytical psychology, the literary arts and comparative theology, in order to place it in its proper context.

Apart from much reading, some of which is recorded in the Bibliographical Index, I am indebted to Anthony Duncan for guidance in theological matters and to conversations over the years with the poet and scholar Kathleen Raine, and Bernard Nesfield Cookson of Hawkwood College, particularly in relation to the magical importance of the Romantic poets.

Needless to say they are not necessarily to be associated with all the views I express.

Brenda Bartholomew showed unflagging enthusiasm and personal loyalty in typing a difficult manuscript.

Whatever the faults of the book may be, I hope it will at least serve a purpose in being an attempt by one who knows the subject from "the inside" and who practices what he tries to preach.

—Gareth Knight

Postscript to this Edition

For this new edition, my special thanks to Carl Weschcke and Morris Kahn, who, as it happens, were also responsible for introducing me to authorship and publishing in the springtime of my days—thus holders of light to my path in the most practical of ways.

G.K.

Experience of the Inner Worlds. A Renaissance view of the vision of angelic wheels and vortices that awaits anyone who succeeds in breaking through the outer world of sense impressions into the inner space that is its subtle foundation. Note that the seeker is upon a hill of vision beside a prominent Tree, and also the polarity of the sun and the moon in the sky against a background of stars. These are all common elements in the search for transformative vision.

Chapter 1
The Magical Imagination

There is a certain fascination about the word MAGIC. It conjures half forgotten memories of childhood tales. Of Arabian nights of mystery and splendor, of carpets that waft their owners to adventures in strange lands, of rings that grant wishes, of bottles containing genie, of strange trees with wonderful fruit, of quests and dragons, of seventh sons of seventh sons, of enchantments and winning hands of fair princesses.

The world of magic is one of high imagination. Etymologists trace it back to the Persian *Magi*—whom they baldly describe as "fire worshippers"—but the word has obvious connections with *imagination*. It certainly has much to do with *images*, for images are the stuff of both imagination and of magic.

The ability to work creatively with images is the gift of the creative artist. It is the hallmark of the creative scientist and technologist too, for besides the painstaking learning, the observation and experiment, it is the flight of the imagination that leads to new insights, new experiments and new achievements. In its true sense magic is a high art and science itself that should release the powers of the imagination for the benefit of any other part of life. Just as mathematics is a universal tool of intellect, so should magic be a universal tool of the imagination. Both mathematics and magic have wide application, they are behind all descriptions of phenomena. It has been claimed that God is a great mathematician. It might also be said that God is a great magician.

Why then is magic held in disrepute? The scientifically minded class it as superstition; the religious regard it as a sinister area of dark forces and dubious motives. Yet it seems significant that the views that science and religion have of magic are very much like the distorted carica-

1

tures that each in the past has held of the other! In the nineteenth century there was tedious and acrimonious debate between "science" and "religion." In fact in some unenlightened areas it still smolders on, but it is magic that now provides a mutual whipping boy. This might well be expected if magic is found to be a middle ground of both science and religion; if it forms a common ground so close to each that it falls into their mutual shadow.

Is it a part of religion which, because it is so like science, seems to threaten the authority of science? And is it also a part of science which, because it is so like religion, threatens to trespass on the preserves of religion?

This has certainly happened with mathematics. In its time mathematics has been derided from both a "rational," and a "religious" viewpoint. The Alexandrian mathematics of conic sections by Appolonius of Perga were regarded as superfluous until Kepler, nineteen hundred years later, discovered them to apply to planetary orbits. And under Protector Somerset mathematical books of the library of the University of Oxford were burned on account of their "Magical and Papistical diagrams."

As with mathematics yesterday—is it so with magic today?

Let us first differentiate between "magic" in particular and its background "the occult." Magic today is a particular specialized branch of a vast range of learning and speculation known as the occult.

Like magic, the occult falls between religion and science. It is in fact a great rubbish heap of discarded fragments of unwanted religion and science. Some of these fragments, perhaps most, have been discarded for good reason. However, some have been thrown there simply because at some time they went out of fashion and subsequent generations have passed them by. Fashion and custom rule in even the most disciplined areas of thought, from experimental science to theology. A journey of historical investigation therefore seems worthwhile to see if any treasures much prized by our forefathers have been thrown into the discard for inadequate reason.

The quest goes back to remote antiquity, to the beliefs and practices of primitive man—which can also be studied in the anthropology of primitive tribes today. It also takes us to the great mystery religions of the ancient world, from Egypt of the pyramids through to post-Christian Greece and Alexandria. The thread then leads to Islam and Europe of the High Middle Ages, and thence to Renaissance Italy, the seventeenth- and eighteenth-century secret societies and finally in a strange underground course through the nineteenth century to the present day.

Our study must also include alchemy, which was magic using the terminology of science. The alchemists said that their *prima materia* could be found anywhere, rejected as useless by the common man, but capable of being distilled and transformed into purest gold. So it is with the imagination. It is there for any to use, free to all, yet few realize its true potential or try to distill it to a precious quintessence.

Spiritual alchemists were not primitive chemical prospectors seeking for metallic gold. The gold they sought was an altogether higher principle, yet capable of transforming common matter, of rejuvenating organisms and promising immortal life.

First it will be necessary to define the nature of the subject of our investigation, the *prima materia* of the human imagination. For this we can turn to Samuel Taylor Coleridge. Coleridge formulated a theory of the imagination and moreover, through his own poetry and that of his friend William Wordsworth, showed that the theory could work. Coleridge himself, though more of a thinker than a poet, wrote as a result some of the most evocative symbolic poetry in the English language.

Coleridge's theory of the imagination, which produced such a rich literary harvest, categorized the imagination into three functions—the *primary imagination,* the *secondary imagination* and the *fancy.*

The *primary imagination* is almost completely automatic to us. It is the part of the mind that selects and interprets the teeming production of sense impressions into meaning and order. The microscope's eye view of the external world is of an attenuated system of electromagnetic forces and probability fields, in which tiny charges of energy exist in an enormous vacuum. This is the world of atoms, molecules, quanta, electrons, nuclei, quarks, neutrons, neutrinos, positrons and so forth. Through organisms consisting of the same basic material, we, as conscious beings, perceive this attenuated electromagnetic force field as the world around us of sights, sounds, colors, shapes, loved ones, works of art, chairs, tables, telephones, mountains, fields, streets, whiskey and soda, symphony orchestras, dogs, mosquitoes, hamburger-stalls, and so on. This complex multi-colored world of sight, sound and sensation in which we live and move and have our being is a construct of the *primary imagination.* We use it all our lives without realizing it—just as Molière's "Bourgeois Gentilhomme" discovered he had been speaking prose all his life without knowing it.

Perhaps we can only realize the existence of what we so easily take for granted if we are involved in the rare case of recovering the use of sight after a period of blindness. The eyes do not immediately register the common world we know—the brain has to take time to interpret the images in a meaningful way. Thus the world takes shape through the eye of the beholder.

Coleridge went so far as to liken this faculty of the mind to the equivalent of the creative word of God first formulating the universe. The eye and the other sense organs range out over the electromagnetic sea as the Spirit of God, in Genesis, is poetically described as going forth over the waters. We use the imaginative faculty in another, more conscious way however. This is in the subjective pictures and ideas that, in common parlance, we usually refer to as the imagination. Coleridge, however, split this type of mind working into two—the *fancy*, and the *secondary imagination*.

The fancy is a simple association of ideas. Thus we may contrive to think of a blue lobster with a green straw hat riding a yellow bicycle. This would be derived from our experienced ideas of blue, green, yellow, lobsters, straw, hats, people and bicycles. This does not necessarily have any deeper meaning than superficial juxtaposition, though in less apparently ridiculous examples we have the processes of rational thought and ideation.

Beyond this level of obvious or accidental connection Coleridge posited the *secondary imagination* wherein a transformation takes place amongst the images. They are not merely juxtaposed but fused, distilled or otherwise processed so as to give a meaning and experience that is totality far greater than that which comprises their constituent parts. This is the stuff of great poetry or literature—and indeed of all the arts. It is the difference between a rhyming jingle and a poem, between a pop-tune and a symphony, between a government report and a page of living prose.

It is evident that there is a higher, or deeper, level of consciousness, that can create with the images of the mind in this way, and communicate at a profound level with others, whose experience and consciousness is thereby enriched and deepened.

In parallel with these concepts of fancy and the primary and secondary imagination Coleridge formulated a more ratiocinative function, divided into two, which he called the *understanding* and the *reason*.

The *understanding* he used in the sense of the way we intellectually grasp an idea of daily life whether it be the contents of the daily newspaper or the adding of a shopping list. The *reason* he saw as a higher faculty, that we today might prefer to call the intuition, in which a synthesising leap can be made, transcending the logical steps of the understanding.

This may be a more direct approach to truth, and, like the secondary imagination, reveal a higher reach of human nature and psychology.

This concept of reason was first developed in philosophical terms by Immanuel Kant in *The Critique of Pure Reason,* though Coleridge goes somewhat beyond the constraints of philosophy. The concept of secondary imagination was also poetically explored by Wordsworth, and in his collected works, arranged by himself, one will find certain poems grouped together as "Poems of Fancy" and others grouped as "Poems of Imagination."

In their early work together, (a kind of manifesto for which was published in the preface to their *Lyrical Ballads* of 1798), they agreed each to write a particular type of poetry. Coleridge was to write poems whereby the supernatural broke into ordinary life to reveal another level of reality beyond the obvious daily round. Wordsworth was to write poems that described the everyday world about us in such a way that the underlying supernatural splendor should be seen shining through the dust of over-familiarity.

Wordsworth once stated that the key to understanding his whole poetry lay in the poem of imagination commencing: "I wandered lonely as a cloud." This, like much of Wordsworth, has been hackneyed to the point of banality by anthologists under the title of *The Daffodils.*

It may seem that there is little hidden knowledge that could be culled from such a simple poem of nature. But let us look more closely at it. Wordsworth was not a simple dauber of poetic landscapes as many of his Victorian admirers thought. He was describing the use of certain faculties of the mind in a way which, in other contexts, could validly be described as "magic." And it was this "magic" that gave impetus to the whole Romantic movement.

Let us examine this deceptively simple poem.

I wandered lonely as a cloud
That floats on high o'er vales and hills . . .

This wandering lonely as a cloud, floating on high o'er vales and hills, is not a decorated way of stating that he was merely walking along. Wordsworth, as a poet of high genius, made every word and syllable count—there are no superfluities, no padding. He is indicating a state of abstracted meditation, where he is drawn in upon himself, in touch with the higher levels of consciousness. We know he was not physically alone on this occasion for his sister Dorothy records the same event in her diary.

No doubt the daffodils were an impressive sight. Dorothy was impelled to record the fact in her diary, just as a modern tourist might record the occasion with a camera. Wordsworth described it poetically in four lines:

> When all at once I saw a crowd,
> A host, of golden daffodils;
> Beside the lake, beneath the trees,
> Fluttering and dancing in the breeze.

The following stanzas describe the effect of the conjunction of the higher faculties of the reason and secondary imagination with this unusual sight of nature. The fluttering crowd of daffodils becomes transformed into a unified vision of the whole of nature as a dance measure. A vision of unified motion that pertains throughout the universe from the depths of inter-stellar space to the vegetation of the countryside and the rippling of lake water in the wind and sunlight.

> Continuous as the stars that shine
> And twinkle on the milky way,
> They stretched in never ending line
> Along the margin of a bay:
> Ten thousand saw I at a glance,
> Tossing their heads in sprightly dance.
>
> The waves beside them danced, but they
> Out-did the sparkling waves in glee:
> A poet could not be but gay,
> In such a jocund company . . .

The conjunction of nature and the higher faculties of man thus brings man into a closer emotional rapport with the created world about him, and brings about a realization of the living, joyful, cooperative life of even seemingly inanimate matter.

But there is more to be gained than a temporary flash of vision. The actual vision is an immediate thing, and described by the extended use of the verb "gazing."

> I gazed—and gazed—but little thought
> What wealth the show to me had brought:

And it is in the final stanza that the nature of this wealth—this alchemical gold—is described.

> For oft, when on my couch I lie
> In vacant or in pensive mood,
> They flash upon that inward eye
> Which is the bliss of solitude;

And then my heart with pleasure fills,
And dances with the daffodils.

Again we have the description of what might nowadays be described as meditation, wherein the fancy and the lower understanding are stilled. And now as a result of this way of mind working, the whole original higher experience and realization can be relived, further enriching the soul and developing the use of the reason and secondary imagination.

This is very close to what a contemporary practitioner of magic, Dion Fortune, has defined the aim of magic to be: "to effect changes in consciousness in conformity with will." In other words there is a well-tried and defined technique whereby man may rise above his workaday consciousness and go some way to fulfilling his spiritual potential. And one of these ways, or at any rate one of the names by which this technique goes, is Magic.

We are talking in terms of techniques, and techniques in themselves are neither good nor bad in a moral sense. They are to be judged simply in terms of their efficiency.

All techniques, like all technologies, can be put to good use or bad, and in our field of inquiry this constitutes a division of the subject into White Magic and Black. The former is a use of techniques of the imagination to expand consciousness and improve the common good; the latter is their use for selfish or squalid ends. In the former people are healed or helped, in the latter they may be cheated, dominated or degraded.

As long as good uses outweigh the abuses there is no good case for banning a technology—and this applies to magic. It is a technology as old as mankind and will last as long as mankind. This is because it is the science and art of the human imagination, and as long as we have imagination, we shall have magic. The right use of the imagination can bring many deep and lasting benefits, and might even prove a key to our survival.

Early magic, like the rest of early science, technology and religion, is lost in the mists of antiquity. In our efforts to build a picture of what life was like for our remote ancestors we must not assume that they thought and felt as we do. It is highly unlikely that early religion, magic and technology (aspects of early civilization inextricably entwined) were the result of primitive man intellectually questioning the reason for various phenomena of nature.

To assume that early man looked at nature, and raised philosophical questions about it is analogous to assuming that a small child views the world with the same ratiocination as an adolescent or an adult.

Primitive man's beliefs are not logically formulated. They are an instinctual and intuitive grasp of nature through being virtually at one with it.

Modern man, (and woman), has become individualized; separated out to a great degree from the group consciousness that characterized the tribe and close-knit family group.

Primitive man is not so individualized, so isolated in the shell of his own psyche. He is at one with his fellows and also with his environment, harsh and cruel though it might often be. In a similar way the young child is at one with its mother and immediate surroundings.

The evolution of consciousness might be described as a development to self-consciousness. Just as the process of biological evolution is recapitulated in the womb, so is psychic evolution broadly recapitulated in childhood and adolescence (though some may find difficulty in attaining maturity until a comparatively late physical age).

One way forward in the evolution of consciousness was by the practice of magic, or training the imagination.

The anthropologist Lévy-Bruhl described the mode of awareness of primitive man as a *participation mystique.* It is difficult for us as modern men and women, accustomed to an analytical and individualized mode of consciousness, to come to an appreciation of such a condition. We are apt to regard primitive ritual, whether it be of initiation to adulthood, or a rain dance, or series of animal rock paintings, from a detached, even patronizing point of view. Such an attitude is no more justifiable than an adolescent feeling superior to an infant. A difference in point of growth in consciousness is a quantitative, not a qualitative gap, although their modes of action may seem as different as a larva from a butterfly.

Primitive man is very much a part of nature. His consciousness is not only rooted in it, as is ours, but is barely throwing individualized shoots above the surface.

He sees things differently from us. In the adoption of a tribal "totem," say a particular bird, to the primitive consciousness the bird *is* the spirit of the tribe, the spirit of the tribe *is* the totem, the totem *is* the bird. It is not a matter of pious belief or social convention, it is a matter of observable fact.

The world view and pattern of perception of the environment is thus a very different thing if viewed through the sensoria of primitive as opposed to modern man. This may even extend to the perception of color. There is evidence that early man, even as late as the ancient Greeks, was unable to distinguish between blue and green. (For detailed treatment of this see Owen Barfield: *Saving the Appearances.*)

It is also an interesting exercise to speculate just how accurate is our construction of the primeval world. In the patient reconstructions based on analysis of fossils we tend to build this world as through our own eyes. But in fact how would it have appeared to the unity of consciousness living in it? How did it really appear to the dinosaur? This may seem a far-fetched and even flippant question, but are we likely to construct a more accurate picture of historical events through our own appropriate stage of consciousness and perception? Much depends on the relative position and mode of observation of the observer. So far as we can judge, early man had a highly developed imaginative and intuitive faculty. In modern man this has given place to a strongly developed rational mind. We think *about* things, standing off from them, making them objects, rather than participating in a mutual subjectivity with them.

Such considerations are important to our study because magic deals with the very stuff of consciousness as its raw material. We are not simply dealing with the history of ideas. We have to take into account the development of consciousness as well. We are rather in the position of Alice in Wonderland trying to play croquet, not with simple inanimate mallets and balls, but with flamingos and curled up hedgehogs, that have a consciousness and will of their own.

So when we look at magical theory and practice we need to take account of the phase in the development of consciousness with which the magic is concerned. Primitive magical ideas superficially may appear similar to later ones but may in fact have very different aims and applications in a modern or a medieval context.

We are apt to forget that an element of group consciousness plays a major part in all perception. We have grown used to the terminology of analytical psychology and have come to accept and understand, at any rate to some degree, a concept such as the "collective unconscious." One hears very little however about an even more important concept simply because it is taken for granted: this is what could be called the "collective consciousness." It is our ordinary "common-sense" view of the world, and we are apt to regard it as self-evident. However, every era of man thinks its own collective consciousness to be self-evident although they may in fact be very different.

We are apt, for instance, to look back upon medieval art as simple and crude. This is something of a short-sighted arrogance on our part. A medieval painting simply does not use scale and perspective as we have come to take them for granted. But this may be not merely a matter of medieval painters being naive and incapable of perspective. Early manuscript illumination shows technique of a very high order. It is more a matter of the medieval collective consciousness regarding each thing as important in itself, equal in the eyes of God, and of an easy intercourse between levels of reality. Perspective was not discovered because it was not needed!

Furthermore, the biblical story of Elijah drawn up to Heaven would be depicted in contemporary dress and the mode of transport as a horse and cart. It would be unthinkable for us today to depict Elijah in modern dress traveling skywards in a motorcar or even in a rocket. We would want to follow a convention of draperies and tricks of perspective and light. This shows that we today would consider such a translation to be in symbolic terms, whereas the medieval saw it in real and contemporary terms.

To modern man symbolism can be an important road to self-understanding and to other modes of consciousness. But symbolism can also be a veil between us and reality. Earlier phases of man's development found no need for symbolism, at any rate in this same sense. To early man the symbols of gods and natural forces were real and immediate; to us they are representational and remote from actuality.

This is what we must bear in mind in any analysis of magic. Starting points, motivations and *modus operandi* in the manipulation of the imagination were by no means exactly the same as may seem apparent today. In our more individualized cocoons, an act of faith, or willing suspension of disbelief, may be necessary to appreciate the things that appeared self-evident to early man.

This is not because we are superior; we are simply at a different stage of growth. The individualized consciousness of man had to be striven for and might be considered in the famous analogy of the life cycle of a butterfly. The mass of grubs eating a leaf is like a collective tribe of early man; their subsequent individual enfoldment into an isolated cocoon is like the conscious state of modern man; and we might look forward, if the analogy holds, to a consequent higher mode of consciousness where, coming forth from the cocoon of isolation, we do not revert to the mass but become more individualized, less isolated, with freedom of another element and with the ability to create new life.

This process is enshrined in various religious beliefs. It is the hoped for event of "rebirth"—which is not necessarily just a sublimated desire for prolonged physical existence. The terms of such rebirth will be found to differ in various stages of man's conscious growth. At a primitive level it may be a desire to join a community of deceased ancestors, and this is an idealized reversion to the group, seen as a larger and greater thing than the individual. Later, as individualization becomes stronger, the urge is more in terms of survival of the self by the knowledge of various pass-words and routes through the underworld. This is particularly evident in ancient Egyptian belief, supported by attempts to preserve the actual physical corpse as long as possible. At a later stage of development we find the desire to become face to face with God, in the participation in a higher collective life in the Kingdom of Heaven. This in turn may give place to a desire for a maintenance of the individual in expansion of con-sciousness, so that the whole can be contained in consciousness—an identification or union with God, which is a higher collectivism. The wheel come full spiral.

In this development we find much of the history of religion, at any rate in the West, where there is a clearly discernible thread of evolution, as opposed to the more static and contemplative East. A remarkable syn-thesis of ancient pagan religions under Alexander the Great was eventu-ally undermined by a small and insignificant nation, who developed a pure monotheism built on a moral foundation that they called the Law, and which is preserved in what we now call the Old Testament.

This Jewish nation approached monotheism through an elevation of their own tribal deity to universal status rather than through a syncretic amalgamation with other local gods. This gives the appearance of intoler-ance, racial ambition and sectarian pride compared to which the growth towards a monotheistic idea of God by amalgamation of local pagan gods and goddesses seems much more liberal and civilized.

However, there is another side to this. The pagan monotheism de-veloped into a number of mystery religions in which "salvation" or "re-birth" might be gained by an elect band of the initiated. The Jewish vision catered for all—at any rate within the tribe—and in St. Paul's Christian teaching this was extended to all humanity. We have an ironic paradox in that Greek philosophical liberalism degenerated in the end to Roman Imperial decadence, whilst Jewish theological exclusiveness led the way to a new religious vision, the Christian, combining universalism with a view that the individual soul is sacrosanct.

In terms of the evolution of consciousness the Christian religion marks a specific step away from the collective. In pagan terms the rever-ence for the collective common denominator of consciousness was usu-ally expressed in terms of the Great Mother; the evolution from depend-ence on the group tended towards religions of a Sky Father, who is be-yond nature.

As in childhood development, which recapitulates human historical development in consciousness, the psychic detachment from the mother towards the father is intimately bound up with the growth of individuality. Consciousness strives to become separate from the maternal involvement, and aspires toward the outside world represented by the father.

One of the central teachings of Jesus was that of the loving Father who cared for every single one of his children, but in an individual way in response to a personal commitment by the individual. And in subsequent Christian theology of the Incarnation we have not merely the idea of Godhead descending into humanity, but humanity being taken up into Godhead.

In terms of spiritual evolution of consciousness this might be phrased as the gaining of spiritual adulthood. The key of the door that the young adult traditionally receives being, in a sense, the keys of heaven held by Peter the Apostle!

The whole picture is complicated by the various stages at which different sections and individuals of the human race may be. There are many cross-currents and eddies in the historical process.

The general view of the evolution of consciousness is as follows. It has been developed at length by Dr. Erich Neumann in his *History and Origins of Consciousness.* Early man, like a baby, becomes conscious of creation by at first being one with it. Gradually he becomes aware of nature as a great mother, who may perhaps be propitiated in some way, and who can give nourishment and comfort. The growing away from dependence upon the mother is reflected in legends and myths of the Hero. The hero is indeed a pattern of man himself a focus of aspiration. There comes a stage however when projections of idealized fantasies must cease, and the environment be seen for what it is.

This growth to appreciation of reality is the attainment of spiritual maturity. This is the assumption of individual responsibility for all one's actions and an aspiration of service to the whole. This may in turn lead to a profound personal religious experience, which may be expressed in the terms of any religion and which in analytical psychological terms has been called the identification with the Self. It is an expansion of consciousness which completely transcends the conscious ego.

This religious experience may occur to anyone, regardless of their religious belief or lack of it, for it is less a matter of intellectual content than evolution of spiritual will. It is one of the aims of White Magic to bring about this experience, and it is an aim shared by some psychotherapies. Indeed C. G. Jung stated that most of his cures were achieved in religious terms.

It is in this light that we shall pursue our history of Magic and the Western Mind. It may be seen as the techniques surrounding the growing point of the evolution of consciousness in any particular age. It is expressed in ways most acceptable to the prevailing culture and in accordance with the stage in consciousness that is appropriate for the time. This will run from blood sacrifice and orgy in primitive times (efforts to come to terms with the existential gates of birth and death), through initiation rites that achieve through the ages a high degree of intellectual and spiritual sophistication, to an eventual explosion into popular consciousness in our own day. Magic thus has a continuing relevance from ancient times to the present day, and with important implications for our future.

Chapter 2
The Ancient Mysteries

Western religious philosophy is built upon a dual polarity which is always at a point of tension: the influence of Jerusalem and the influence of Athens.

Athens, the intellectual center of the ancient world, resumed in its culture the highest philosophical ideas of pagan civilization. Jerusalem, a small town in a petty kingdom, was the center of the Jewish heritage, and the focus for the biblical tradition of a revealed religion.

We can approach early magic either through the evidence of the Old Testament, or through the Dialogues of Plato, Pythagorean mathematics and the Mysteries of Delphi or Eleusis. Both Hebrew and Greek sources are rich in wisdom, but the precious metal has to be smelted from them. Too literal an interpretation of either can be misleading.

The geometry of astronomy was wrong until Kepler and Newton in the seventeenth century because it was assumed, from Plato and Aristotle, that all heavenly bodies must move in a perfect circle. In like fashion Old Testament chronology was accorded literal acceptance until it was refuted by nineteenth century geology. Such facile assumptions caused much of the needless and indeed meaningless confrontation between "science" and "religion".

The study of periods of confrontation can, however, be informative. They throw issues into sharp relief. We have such a period of conflict in the Old Testament history of the Jews when a qualitative change took place in their religious consciousness. The more primitive reliance on the

Great Mother, represented by various vegetation gods and goddesses, was challenged by a Sky Father, represented by the Jahweh of the prophets. The books of the Old Testament portray this long struggle. The oldest books of the Old Testament, Genesis, Exodus, Leviticus, Numbers and Deuteronomy, were put into writing at a comparatively late date. They are called the books of Moses, to whose authorship they are traditionally attributed, and to the Jews they constitute the *Torah*, or *Law*.

Genesis and Exodus are based on the interweaving of two old documents, one deriving from the Southern Kingdom of Judah in the ninth century B.C. and the other from the Northern Kingdom of Israel in the eighth century. The first source is referred to by scholars as J because it refers to God as Jehovah, and the second is called E because it refers to God as Elohim. They were amalgamated into a framework of priestly ideas with a third book, found in the Temple, dating from about 700 B.C. The third book is called D, because it forms much of the Book of Deuteronomy, and the priestly framework is called P. This amalgamation of four strands of tradition took place at the end of the Babylonian exile, about 440 B.C. Between them they embody oral traditions, however, which go back to the time of Abraham (c. 1800 B.C.) and beyond. Some of the stories are told twice or three times, such as that of Abraham's wife posing as his sister before the Pharaoh, and there are two separate versions of the creation and fall of man. The first is the more popular story of Adam and Eve in the Garden of Eden (Gen. 1); the second the story of angels coming from heaven and mating with the creatures of earth (Gen. 3).

There are mythical elements in some of the stories. The act of one of the sons of Noah discovering his father's nakedness when the latter was drunk carries a horror with it and subsequent punishment that are beyond all proportion. This suggests that a crucial part of the story has been excised. In fact it is very similar to the Greek myth of the castration of Uranus by his son Zeus. (The theme is developed and further examples given by Robert Graves and R. Patai in *Hebrew Myths*.) The later religious beliefs of the Jews caused them to try to eradicate or disguise all such pagan mythology.

Other early stories are legendary, that is, based on reasonably identifiable historical fact. Noah's Flood falls into this category in that the legend is shared with many other peoples of this geographical area. The Jews were a nomadic people who originated from Chaldea, near the outflow of the two great rivers, the Tigris and Euphrates. There is archaeological evidence of catastrophic inundation of this great tract of land in about

4000 B.C.

The Jewish assimilation of this event into their legendary tradition is characteristic and shows their difference from their neighbors. They saw it as the act of a single Creator God rather than the chance result of some quarrel between the gods. They also believed in a covenant between God and man, to the effect that whatever the evil, and however richly it might be deserved, God would not destroy all life again. The token of this divine covenant was the rainbow.

A covenant between God and man was held to originate from the Fall, and the prophecy of Eve eventually bruising the head of the Serpent with her heel. It also is developed in later times with God's promises to the patriarch Abraham who led his people forth from Chaldea (c. 1750 B.C.) and subsequently in the great events under Moses at Mount Sinai following the exodus from Egypt (c. 1250 B.C.).

The difference in religious attitude between the Jews and their neighbors was no easy cut-and-dried affair. The Jews' biblical history is a long struggle to consolidate their faith in a new and covenanted revelation with a *super*-natural God, and to avoid reverting to the worship of the gods of nature.

They interpreted their history in these terms, and regarded any national misfortunes as a punishment for their falling away from this faith. The struggle is epitomized by the story of Moses descending Mount Sinai where he has been communing with God to discover the people reverting to Egyptian Apis worship and dancing round a golden calf.

In the books of the prophets there is consistent fulmination against the despised nature gods of the surrounding Canaanites—the Baalim and the Ashtoroth. The depth of invective is occasioned because these vegetation gods and goddesses were attractive— particularly to a nomadic race settling down to an agricultural existence. Many Jews did prefer them to the Jehovah who had his roots in a nomadic tribal culture. But it is instructive to note that the ten northern tribes who did revert to natural religion were assimilated into the local nations and vanished without a trace. The history of the Jews is then continued by just two tribes of the original twelve, those comprising the Southern Kingdom.

The Baalim and Ashtoroth deserve a better press than they have received, and we are now able to take a more objective and charitable view of them. The suffixes -im and -oth are simply the masculine and feminine plural forms of the Hebrew language and so we are talking of the various local Baals and Ishtars, the gods and goddesses of fertility and vegetation, who were usually worshipped at hilltop shrines. They were thus not so much evil as atavistic as far as developing Jewish religious consciousness was concerned, but it is a natural tendency to condemn vociferously that to which one is afraid of succumbing.

The Jewish attitude persisted into post-biblical times with riots against the Greek rule by Judas Maccabeus, and later against the Romans, when these great pagan powers attempted to compromise the Jewish religion.

From this religious cultural heritage so closely guarded by the Jews there eventually swept the new Christian religion which in the space of three hundred years dominated the known world and replaced or absorbed the old pagan formulations. Revealed religion had finally replaced natural religion.

The natural religion continued in an unofficial, even underground way, and still persists today. It will continue to do so as long as there are those who have a spiritual or psychic need for it. This natural religion also has an historical development of its own. There is a considerable distance between the tribal fetishes of primitive man and the sophisticated gods of Olympus.

However, the pattern of their pantheons is similar. Parallels can be traced between one nation's gods and another's. This is because gods and goddesses are projections of man's own psychic needs. Mankind projects an image of himself onto the backdrop of the unknown, and peoples the natural world of earth and sky with images of his own characteristics.

The ancients themselves realized this degree of similarity when given the opportunity. This opportunity came with the rule of Alexander the Great, whose conquests in the fourth century B.C. unified the known world. Alexander's empire had two important effects. It gave an era of political and economic stability which encouraged travel and trade; and it broke down language barriers through the spread of a common language—demotic Greek.

This interchange of culture promoted a great pagan religious tolerance. Similarities were seen between one local god and another and amalgamations took place. This accelerated a process that had begun in earlier times as a result of conquest or tribal migration.

In course of time some gods and goddesses absorbed so many others that they became internationally revered. Particularly important examples are those of Isis, who resumed in herself most characteristics of femininity. So universal did she become in fact that she even began to be worshipped in different aspects of herself: the Isis of Nature, Isis of the Heavens, Isis the Mother, Isis the Virgin, Isis the Bride and so on.

Isis, the Mother of the Mysteries. An eighteenth-century engraving, from Lenoir's *La Franche-Maçonnerie,* of the goddess Isis. Originally an Egyptian goddess, in the course of time she took over the attributes of most other goddesses so that she embodied the attributes of all things feminine. In particular she was mistress of the sea and of the moon. Here, although clad in classical draperies, she carries the Egyptian temple sistrum and wears a headress deriving from the winged sun-disk of the Egyptians, surrounded by serpents of wisdom. In a basket she carries the fruits of the earth. In a sense, she is the Soul of the World, the great Being that is organic nature, yet she also has a cosmic aspect as Isis Urania and is then shown winged. The Cult of the Blessed Virgin Mary has taken over much of the old Isiac attributions and festivals.

This kind of development led naturally in time to a kind of monotheism, whereby all the many gods and goddesses would be seen, at least philosophically, as aspects of one God.

An important pagan god-form that is relevant to our study is Thoth/Hermes/Mercury—the "thrice greatest"—who in ancient Egypt, Greece and Rome was lord of magic, of trade, of books and of learning. A corpus of writings attributed to Hermes formed the core of European magical practice and theory from early post-Christian times until beyond the Renaissance.

In spite of the subsequent tension of ideas between Athens and Jerusalem, if we go back to ancient Egypt we find a common link between them. This is because the Jewish tribes spent some generations under Egyptian influence, from the time of Joseph and his brothers until led forth by Moses in search of a land of their own. Egypt had much influence on Greece not only because of the similarities noted between Greek and Egyptian pantheons but because the Egyptian religious system, with its impressive pyramids, temples and statuary, including the Sphinx, ancient and awe-inspiring then as now, helped to give Egypt an especial reputation of great magical power and secret mysteries.

The ancient Egyptian civilization was a very static one, largely for geographical reasons. It existed virtually unchanged for millennia, its origins going back beyond 3000 B.C. The forms of its gods and goddesses reflect this great antiquity in that, while some of them have human forms, many of them, and the important ones at that, have animal heads. Thus Horus, the son of Osiris and Isis, was hawk-headed. The Opener of the Ways, called Anubis, was dog headed. The evil Set had the head of a jackal. There was a goddess Sekhmet with the head of a cat. And Thoth, the Lord of Books and Learning, had the head of an ibis.

There was much more than primitive animal fetishes in the Egyptian conception however—although their origins may well have been as tribal totems. Anubis, for example, as guardian of the threshold between the dead and the living, had many of the attributes of an intelligent watchdog and thus the dog head was very appropriate. The rest of the god-form was human, which to a Greek would suggest that he combined the functions of the Greek three-headed dog Cerberus who guarded the gates of the Underworld and the ferryman who transported souls across the river between life and death.

The long beak and neck of the ibis-headed Thoth were also appropriate for a Lord of Books and Learning, showing the discerning perceptiveness of knowledge and wisdom, able to pick out the relevant and useful in just the way that an ibis detected and plucked its food from the bed of the sacred river Nile.

The hawk head of Horus represented the human spirit in one sense, the savior god in another—and the hovering hawk, still and silent on the air at high altitude, is an evocative symbol of these qualities. (See, for example, Gerard Manley Hopkins' poem *The Windhover*.)

There was a particularly important cycle in Egyptian religious tradition based on the story of a king-god Osiris and his queen Isis. Osiris ruled well until tricked and betrayed by his adversary, the evil Set. Set persuaded Osiris to lie in a beautiful mummy casket that he had prepared for him. When Osiris did so, Set slammed down the lid and threw it into the river Nile. The weeping Isis searched the land for her lost Lord and eventually found the coffin lodged in a tree where it became the architrave of an important temple. She then conceived a child Horus, of the dead Osiris, whom she revived for the purpose by magical means. Set, however, seized the body of Osiris and cut it into a thousand pieces and scattered them throughout the land. The mourning Isis wandered the land again seeking to collect together the dismembered fragments, and subsequently collected them all save one the organ of generation. Horus grew from a child, sitting upon a lotus making a gesture of silence, to an avenging hawk-like warrior, and avenged himself, his father and mother by destroying the evil Set.

In this story one finds parallels with many other pagan accounts for the origin of evil and the human condition. There are similarities in Greek myth with the mourning mother Demeter, searching the land for her lost daughter Persephone who had been seized by the god of the Underworld, Pluto, and subsequently kept for six months of each year, during which time the grief of Demeter causes the months of Winter. Or there is the story of the Babylonian Ishtar, going down into the seven hells in search of her lover Tammuz, discarding a veil each time until she stands naked before the god of the Underworld. This is the origin of the dance of the seven veils—originally a deep religious parable rather than an erotic cabaret.

In earlier times these religious stories were no doubt believed literally by the Egyptian priesthood and populace. In later more philosophically minded times they were interpreted in terms of allegory. Osiris could thus be seen as representative of the human race, free spirits tricked into incarnating into physical bodies as Osiris was tricked and nailed into his coffin. The subsequent chopping into pieces signified the dispersion of the peoples and the loss of primal unity. The final restoration awaited the dual works of the adored wife and mother goddess Isis, seeking and treasuring every divided piece or individual human soul; and Horus, the divine savior-son who would finally destroy evil and resurrect the fallen Osiris.

It is when the natural religion of antiquity reaches this stage of philosophical interpretation that we see the birth of the mystery religions, which are at the root of the Western tradition of White Magic.

We shall return to this, but first we should follow the early history of the Jews, who came forth from this Egyptian religious background, under Moses, probably about 1250 B.C.

Prior to this, the Jews, having come forth from Chaldea as a group of nomadic tribes under Abraham, moved down into Egypt during a time of great famine. There are independent records of an invasion of Canaan (modern Palestine) by a group of Semitic peoples in about 1750 B.C. This could well have been the period of Abraham and the patriarchs.

The bible story of Joseph rising to power in Egypt would normally have been highly unlikely, for the Ancient Egyptians despised the nomadic Semitic cattle herders as gypsies or "sand-dwellers." But there was a time when such a rise to power could have been likely; during the period of "the Hyksos Kings," (1720-1550 B.C.). The Hyksos Kings were an interlude in the long history of ancient Egypt when a mixture of Semites, Hittites and Hurrians from the north and east, with their mastery of the newly invented horse-drawn chariot, struck at a time of Egyptian domestic and political weakness.

The settlement of the Jews in the eastern part of the Nile delta could have occurred during this time, as described in the bible, though there are plainly mythical and legendary elements within the bible story. The twelve sons of Jacob for instance, apart from being patriarchs of the twelve tribes, probably derive from the twelvefold division of the sky into the signs of the zodiac. The civilization from which the Jews sprang were observers of the night sky over a period of several thousand years and the founders of both astronomy, in the scientific record of stellar and planetary movements that they kept, and astrology in their interpretation of them.

Originally driven to Egypt by famine, it seems that the Jews were not unwelcome there, and were allotted a certain area of land. However, the last of the Hyksos pharaohs was overthrown in about 1550 B.C. when Ahmose I restored the native Egyptian line of rulership. Ahmose I would probably have been, in biblical terms, "the King who did not know Joseph." The subsequent decline in the standard of life and eventual period of bondage and brick-making could have lasted from Ahmose I to the time of Rameses II, the great pyramid builder (*c.*1290-1224).

The forty years in the wilderness, on their way to seek the Promised Land, would then fall during the period between the accession of Rameses II in 1290 B.C. to some time before 1220 B.C., when there are Egyptian military records of there being Israelites in Palestine.

The bible story is of major interest to us in that it shows the myth-making faculty of the imagination at work in a monotheistic fashion, as opposed to the polytheistic myth-making of the other nations of the ancient world. The biblical tradition plays a major formative part in the general culture of the West, and particularly so in the religious and philosophical ideas of the magical traditions.

Jewish myth-making is seen at its crudest level in the magical battle between Moses and Aaron and the magicians of the Pharaoh's court. And it is perhaps here that we should draw a distinction between two aspects of magical tradition. One is theurgy and the other thaumaturgy. They may also be called high magic and low magic respectively.

Theurgy, or high magic, is the raising of consciousness to the appreciation of the powers and forces behind the external material world in a pious intention of developing spiritual awareness and subsequently helping to bring to birth the divine plan of a restored Earth. Thaumaturgy, or low magic (sometimes called sorcery), is the production of wonders by the use of little known powers of the mind.

Another distinction is that thaumaturgy relies much on personal technical ability; theurgy, which can be equally spectacular on occasion, is more dependent upon the grace of God.

In the confrontation prior to the Exodus the Egyptian magicians are the thaumaturgists as opposed to the theurgic intentions of Moses and Aaron, even if some of the events of this particular battle of wills (somewhat embroidered by legend) more resemble sorcery. Similarly all the later miracles in the Old Testament are regarded as being theurgic—the supernatural acts of God through chosen appointed agents rather than a combination of hypnosis, conjuring and mediumship that is the staple mixture of man-motivated thaumaturgy.

In the biblical accounts there is plainly much that is due to the imaginative embroidery of myth and legend—particularly as the traditions were to be orally transmitted for at least another two or three hundred years before being written down. There is, however, a disconcerting tendency for myths to be based on solid fact as was shown by the nineteenth-century archaeologist Schlieman taking Greek legend and myth at face value and digging up Troy.

There is also, we should add, the *mythical* truth, in which the deep working of the secondary imagination produces a meaning and destiny for the group or nation that weaves these historical tapestries of vision on the warp and woof of historical events.

A similar kind of mechanism works at an individual level; and one of the techniques of brainwashing is to destroy an individual's personal mythos and to substitute an alternative one.

The mythical truth of the Jews was that they were the chosen of God and thus what may have been quite natural events, though possibly occurring at singularly opportune moments, have been incorporated into the general corpus of belief as evidence of miraculous divine intervention.

Examples of this are the parting of the waters of the Red Sea to allow their escape from the pursuing Egyptians. This cannot for geographic reasons have been the Red Sea, but is more probably the reedy swamps of the Nile delta, where a combination of climatic conditions can cause dry land to appear in the midst of water. Similarly the flight of quails and even the manna that sustained them in the wilderness are natural events in that part of the world to be seen to this day.

It would take us too long to speculate over the validity and origins of every miracle in the Old Testament. Some, such as the plague of frogs, are probably natural events read into a specific historical context. Others, such as the story of Joshua causing the Sun to stand still, appear to be physical impossibilities, though the apparent gyrations of the Sun before a huge crowd at Fatima in the twentieth century suggests that the event may not have been unique, whatever explanation one wishes to put upon it, from divine intervention in the natural order to mass hysteria.

On other occasions, superior geological knowledge may have been at work. Moses striking water from the rock shows a desert herdsman's knowledge of survival. He had moreover been in exile from Egypt as a herdsman with the opportunity to learn such lore. More patently deceptive was the miraculous burning of water by Elijah in a successful attempt to impress the priests of Baal. This suggests less the divine intervention that it was supposed to be, but rather a knowledge of the properties of liquid naphtha, which is natural to that area.

As M. J. Field has pointed out in his book *Angels and Ministers of Grace,* primitive man (and not so primitive man) tends to prefer a supernatural explanation to a natural one. He cites the case of a colonial official in Africa walking to a certain village along the seashore in preference to an arrival by road in his official car. To the local natives, astounded at seeing him on the beach, it seemed more natural to assume that he had risen from the sea (like Aphrodite or the fish-god Oannes) than that he, an important official with a car at his disposal, should have made the unthinkable choice of walking! Field felt that many instances of angels in the Old Testament are in fact similar government officials or land-agents.

Miraculous legends should not be written off as ignorant superstition. It is evidence of the secondary imagination at work, and has a transpersonal significance. Such beliefs should never be written off as *mere* mythology. Mythology, legend, religious belief or even deeply pondered scientific speculation are never "mere" and should not lightly be degraded to the level of fancy.

As we have seen, the probable period of the Hebraic tribes' sojourn in Egypt was c. 1650 to c. 1275 B.C., a period of some 400 years, which tends to be foreshortened in the bible narrative. It may be significant that this period coincides with the rule of that most untypical pharaoh Akhnaton, who tried to introduce a religious revolution in Egyptian thought and practice. During his reign he attempted to replace the traditional Egyptian gods by a monotheism based on the worship of the disc of the Sun. The monumental artwork characteristic of his reign shows a breaking free from the rigid formal lines of the Egyptian hieratic style of temple and funerary art to an engaging naturalism. The portraits of his Queen, Nefertiti, are to this day, famous; and a characteristic picture is of Akhnaton and his family sitting under the Sun from which myriad rays emanate with little hands to caress and protect them.

This religious revolution was put down immediately after the death of Akhnaton. His name was defaced from inscriptions in the immediate reaction and Egypt reverted to the old gods. It is interesting to speculate what interaction may have occurred between the Hebrews and the court. Was this Egyptian monotheistic experience a result of Jewish influence? As the story of Joseph implies, they had powerful influence at court, at least for part of the time. Or did Akhnaton's religion play a more positive role and bring monotheism to the Hebrews, which they subsequently wrote into their pre-Mosaic tradition? It is possible, in either case, that their fall from favor may have had a religious motivation if their beliefs seemed to align with those of the renegade pharaoh.

At any rate in their Exodus from Egypt under Moses, and their subsequent forty years in the wilderness and eventual conquest of Palestine (a period lasting from 1200–1020 B.C.) the Jews themselves experienced much conflict between the claims of the old gods based on natural phenomena, and the one God whose claims were based on supernatural revelation.

The spiritual and physical leadership of Moses seems, under the legendary miraculous gloss, probably to have been related to the symbol of God under the image of fire. There is the celebrated instance of his seeing God in the burning bush, where he learned the name of the One God EHEIEH ('I become", or "Becoming", or "I am that I am'). And the Israelites being led by a pillar of fire by night and a pillar of cloud by day, to a mountain that rumbled and shook and poured forth clouds, suggests very strongly a volcano.

The story of Moses returning from the mountain top with the Tables of the Law after communing with the One God, to discover the people below worshipping a golden calf, indicates the rival religious allegiances experienced—probably a reversion to Egyptian Apis worship.

This conflict continued through subsequent years although it became less a reversion to Egyptian animal forms than a merging with the local nature gods of the Canaanites whose land they infiltrated and conquered. This period of settlement ended with the foundation of the prophetic tradition in Samuel. The prophets subsequently interpreted Jewish history in terms of their faithfulness to the covenant with the One God in a series of rewards and punishments.

The focus for the worship of God by the Jews was no longer an idol or representative totem but a box containing the scrolls of the Law. This was called the Ark of the Covenant. It was carried about with the twelve wandering tribes and in periods of settlement deposited in a tent behind a veil.

With the territorial settlement of the Hebrew tribes, the rule of tribal elders gave place to judges, and the judges gave place to a king of the unified nation. The first king, Saul, was succeeded by David, who reigned in what was later to be regarded as a golden age in Jewish History, (1000–961 B.C.). David was succeeded by his son Solomon (from 961 to 922 B.C.). During Solomon's reign, for a combination of economic and political reasons, the Jews experienced great prosperity, free from the rigors of being a buffer state between rival empires, and with newfound mineral resources to exploit. Thus we have the tradition of the great riches of Solomon, and it was in his reign that the great Temple of Solomon was built, to replace the humble Tabernacle of the Ark of the Covenant.

The Temple is of great importance to later Western magical tradition. Its structure and furniture are described in detail in the bible and the symbolism that can be read into this detail formed a rich quarry for

Freemasonry. There is reason to have some doubts about Solomon's religious orthodoxy. His legendary thousand wives and entertainment of the Queen of Sheba do not seem to accord too well with the stern moral principles of Mosaic Law. And there were no doubt some conservative misgivings about breaking with the tradition of a tent-borne deity to enshrine the Ark of the Covenant in a static, if imposing, edifice.

The basic principles of design were similar to that of the earlier tent. The populace were allowed only into the forecourt. Only the priests could enter the temple, as with the tent, and within was an inner sanctum, corresponding to the veil in the tent, into which only the High Priest was allowed to go, and then but once a year. Within the holy of holies was the Ark of the Covenant—the Mercy Seat of God upon which the Invisible Glory sat.

It may well be that Solomon attempted a more syncretic approach to religious belief and worship. His reign certainly shows an international awareness. He would have needed to import foreign expertise for the construction of the Temple, just as he had to import "gold from Ophir, cedar from Lebanon" for its fabric. Again, some elements of the design, such as the dual pillars, have obvious connections with Egyptian architraves and even prehistoric dolmens.

Yet Solomon developed a reputation for wisdom and is credited with writing the Book of Proverbs as well as much of the other biblical "wisdom literature." The erotically phrased Song of Solomon, or Canticles, is attributed to him, and this is obviously an influence from local nature religions. It has become expedient to interpret it as a celebration of the mystical union between the soul and God but there is much that is reminiscent of the type of liturgy that might have come direct from a philosophically refined nature religion.

> Hark! My beloved! Here he comes,
> bounding over the mountains, leaping over the hills.
> My beloved is like a gazelle
> or a young wild goat:
> there he stands outside our wall,
> peeping in at the windows, glancing through the lattice.
>
> My beloved answered, he said to me:
> Rise up, my darling;
> my fairest, come away.
> For now the winter is past,
> the rains are over and gone;

the flowers appear in the countryside;
the time is coming when the birds will sing,
and the turtle-dove's cooing will be heard in our land;
when the green figs will ripen on the fig-trees
and the vines give forth their fragrance.
Rise up, my darling;
my fairest, come away.

And again, in similarity to the wandering mourning Egyptian Isis, or Greek Demeter, or Babylonian Ishtar:

Night after night on my bed
I have sought my true love:
I have sought him but not found him,
I have called him but he has not answered.
I said, "I will rise and go the rounds of the city,
through the streets and the squares,
seeking my true love."
I sought him but I did not find him,
I called him but he did not answer.
The watchmen going the rounds of the city, met me,
and I asked, "Have you seen my true love?"

A very similar type of tradition is to be found in the pagan Mysteries and the story of Cupid and Psyche as described in *The Golden Ass* of Apuleius some 1300 years later.

Solomon might even be seen as forerunner of what were to become the pagan mystery religions. These were paganism's way of approaching the direct monotheistic religious awareness of Israel. We come upon the traditional influence of Solomon time and again in the later history of unorthodox spirituality—whether it be in the secret rites of the Knights Templar at the time of the Crusades, or the rituals and legends of Freemasonry, or the spate of doubtfully edifying medieval magical recipe books—such as the Clavicle of Solomon.

The prophetic tradition in Israel led away from this line of development however. The kingdom itself split into two at Solomon's death in 922 B.C., and within two hundred years the Northern Kingdom of ten tribes had reverted to paganism and been assimilated into the local nations. The Southern Kingdom, which centered about that of David and Solomon, consisting of the two tribes of David and Benjamin, was eventually crushed by the might of Nebuchadnezzar, King of Babylon, and a mass deportation took place together with destruction of the Temple.

This exile lasted from 597 to 525 B.C., when a later generation, or a remnant of it, was allowed to return to Jerusalem to rebuild the Temple and city walls. From this time on they experienced, in turn, Greek, Egyptian, Syrian and Roman rule until New Testament times, when in A.D. 70 they were finally crushed and dispersed and the Temple and Jerusalem destroyed.

We have traced the development of Jewish religious awareness because it was unique in its day and it plays a fundamental role in later Western religious attitudes. We should also examine some of the religious traditions that surrounded them, which the Jews felt impelled to reject.

Ancient Egypt had a formative influence on the ancient world through its stability and links with the remote past. Its reputation for secret wisdom and magic may have been in part due to the peculiar geographical and climatic features of the country.

The agricultural livelihood of Egypt depended upon the River Nile which ran through it from an unknown source in the south, to the wide delta in the north. It was upon Nile water that irrigation and therefore life itself depended.

However, the Nile behaved in a strange way. Without any rains occurring to explain the phenomenon, it would suddenly burst its banks, between what was normally seedtime and harvest, and inundate the surrounding land. This annual event, although disastrous if unexpected, served to bring life to the land, not only by irrigation but through the deposition of rich alluvial soil. And if one could forecast when the inundation would occur then a very fruitful agricultural cycle could be worked.

At one level, the inundation helped the foundation of mathematics in that the land had to be resurveyed each time the waters receded and "geometry" literally means "land measurement". It also led to the practical application of astronomy, for it so happened that the annual inundation, regularly caused by tropical rainfall in the far south, coincided with a particular configuration of stars in the sky. In fact this was quite spectacular, for in those latitudes, in early August, the brightest star in the northern sky, Sirius, rises over the horizon.

To the ancient Egyptians this star was a warning of the sudden and unexplained inundation shortly to come, and they called it Sothis, the Dog Star, as it warned them like a good watchdog. And of course their god Anubis, the dog-headed, the Opener of Ways, became associated with it, and also Isis and Osiris.

The idea of a heralding star persists into Christian tradition. A star shone over Bethlehem and guided the "wise men" to the seat of the Divine Incarnation. A star also plays a part in later Masonic symbolism. Symbols of this kind became the psychic material of the ancient mystery religions which lie at the root of White Magic.

The mystery religions developed and flourished during the time of Alexander. They varied as to the gods they invoked but they had a unified basis, which depended upon the needs and aspirations of the human soul. There were particularly famous mystery centers such as those of Isis and Osiris in Egypt; Demeter and Persephone at Eleusis in Greece; Ishtar and Tammuz in Mesopotamia; and Mithra/Mithras at the outposts of the Roman army. Some of these we will examine, although the task is not easy for these rites were traditionally surrounded by secrecy—and the secrets were, on the whole, well kept.

A basic pattern can be discerned in the impressive papyrus of Ani, which appears, writ large, as a frieze in the Egyptian Galleries of the British Museum. It describes the after-death condition of the scribe, Ani. Insofar as initiation carried with it the symbolism of death, in order the better to impress the idea of being spiritually reborn, so Egyptian funerary rites provide a background for Mystery religious belief and practice. It is significant of this dual purpose that the collection of papyrus scrolls which treat of this matter are generally referred to as *The Book of the Dead,* but in the original Egyptian they are called the *Book of Coming Forth By Day.*

The Egyptian *Book of the Dead* is in fact a collection of scrolls of varying origin and date. The conservative Egyptian mind hated to throw anything away and new ideas from whatever source, if adopted, were incorporated into the tradition along with the old. In course of time this led to some complication and parts of the human psyche that they analyzed bear some evidence of duplication and over-subtlety. They saw man as consisting of nine parts:

(1) the physical body;
(2) the "double," which was an ethereal counterpart of the body, capable under certain circumstances of being separated from the body and being seen;
(3) the heart-soul, a similar concept though perhaps less associated with the physical body as a whole;
(4) the heart itself for which they had great reverence and which was the seat of the heart-soul;
(5) the shadow, which was closely associated with the heart-soul but which, like the "double," was capable of independent travel from the body;

(6)   the immortal spiritual soul which had its seat in:

(7)   the spiritual body;

(8)   the "power," which was a personified form of the vital force of man as associated with the higher elements or soul and spirit;

(9)   the name, which, like the heart, was held to be of singular importance, for power over the name meant control over the man or even the God. Gods therefore tended to have secret names as well as their more public ones, and extinction of the name meant extinction of the person.

We would simplify this into a more manageable threefold division of man on the lines of Spirit, Soul and Body, which accord with later magical theorization and even with the New Testament views of St. Paul.

Thus the body (*khat*) and its double (*ka*) constitute the phenomenal, physical part of man and its electromagnetic or psycho-physical matrix.

The mind and feelings are composed of the soul (*ba*), which has its seat in the heart (*ab*) and an imaginatively formed vehicle of its own called the shadow (*khaibit*).

The spirit or divine/immortal part of man (*khu*) which has its seat in the name (*ren*), and besides a conceptual body of its own (*sahu*), derives its manifest existence from the power (*sekhem*), which likewise provides vitality for the lower vehicles.

The *Ka* hovering over the mummy.

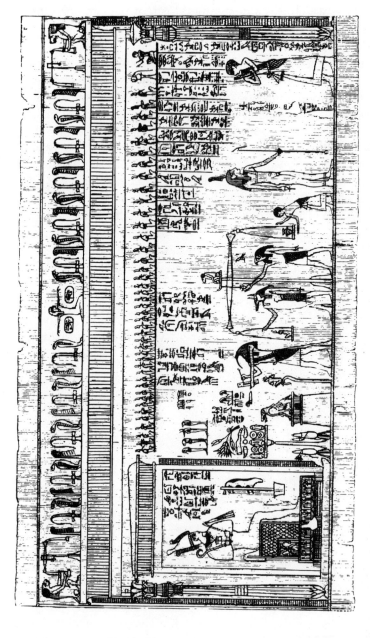

Weighing the Soul in the Judgment Hall of Osiris. The heart of the candidate who stands at the portal is weighed in the balance by the dog-headed Anubis, Opener of the Ways, and the hawk-headed Horus, divine son of Osiris and Isis, Ancient Egyptian Lord of the Underworld and his consort. The ibis-headed Thoth, Lord of Magic, Books and Learning, records the result, and Maat, goddess of Law, Order and Regularity, confronts the soul whose heart is being weighed against a feather provided by her. Before the throne of Osiris is a banquet laid for the worthy, and the bestial Devourer of Souls, who consumes the unworthy. These funerary rites are also applicable to the rites of initiation.

The purpose of Egyptian funerary rites was to help preserve the lower vehicle of man to ensure an easier transition between birth and death. The god who presided over these Mysteries was Osiris, who appears crowned, and wrapped in bandages of mummification, holding the scourge and crook, signifying that he has attained mastery over death.

In the papyrus of Ani we find the general process summarized in convenient form. The scribe Ani is welcomed to the Underworld by Anubis, the dog-headed, the Opener of the Ways. From here he enters the Judgment Hall of Osiris where he is weighed in the balance. Sometimes this is depicted as his heart being weighed against the feather of truth. On his heart being weighed and not found wanting he is declared to be *"maa kheru,"* which means one whose word is right and true, or "having the right word". It was a misunderstanding of this that led opponents of the Mystery Religions to consider them to be offerers of salvation in return for the purchase of secret passwords—possibly deriving also from the Egyptian reverence for secret or "true" names which can give power if indiscreetly admitted. It may be that in times of decadence some Mystery temples did sink to this level but it is a far cry from the original high concept.

If the test of the balance was failed then the unfortunate soul was devoured by a crocodile-like beast called the Eater of Souls and went ignominiously to extinction. The results of the weighing were recorded by the ibis-headed god, Thoth, the Lord of Books and of Learning, and the whole procedure was witnessed by a company of gods (usually depicted as twelve in number).

From here the justified soul was taken by the hand by the hawk-headed Horus, son of Isis and Osiris, and led to the throne of Osiris behind which stood his divine consorts Isis and Nephthys. Here he was welcomed and took part in a mystical feast and was admitted to the Elysian fields of the Egyptian heavenly life, the *Sekhet-hetepet*. From contemporary accounts the Egyptians saw these as being very similar, though in a trouble and pain free fashion, to the life and topography of Earth.

Alongside this system of practice and belief which formed the early corpus of high magic was a lower side, incorporating perhaps misunderstood fragments of it couched in terms of expediency. Thus it is from the Egyptian reverence for names that we find the forerunner of a low magical obsession with incantations and "words of power" and the profession of itinerant priest to perform such magical rites. This is in direct line from the primitive medicine man or witch doctor, and indeed in times of little understanding of medical science as we know it, was a perfectly understandable utilization of current scientific knowledge in a religious context. It is to the Egyptians that we also owe the tradition of wax models or dummies as a focus of power or attention in magical rites, which has come down as one of the main characteristics of witchcraft, at least in modern popular imagination.

One of the best sources for the philosophy and practice of the Mystery Religions is the *Metamorphoses* or *Golden Ass* of Lucius Apuleius of Madaura. He was an initiate of the Mysteries of Isis and probably of some other Mystery cults too. In a tradition that was later followed by the seventeenth-century Rosicrucians and others, he wrote of high wisdom in a jocular vein. What at one level is a collection of funny, and sometimes vulgar or ribald stories, is in fact a treatise on initiation into high spiritual Mysteries.

At the same time it is very revealing of the types of religious and magical belief that were prevalent in those times. He writes in about A.D. 250 but his general picture is valid for several hundred years previous to this. He takes little note of Christianity in his writings and writes from the point of view of an intelligent pagan.

The general thread of the story is of his being transformed into an ass, and his adventures until such time as he can regain his human form. His original transformation came about partly through concupiscence and partly through curiosity. He forms a sexual liaison with a servant-girl who reveals that her mistress is adept at witchcraft. Secretly they watch her smear herself with a strange ointment late one night and turn into an owl. Lucius immediately tries the ointment as well but, by a mishap, takes the wrong jar and turns into an ass instead. The counter-charm to restore his human form is to eat some roses but before he can do so thieves break in and steal him in his asinine form in order to help carry away their booty. After many trials and tribulations in which he is often frustrated from eating roses because there are others watching, with the consequent risk that he will be accused of witchcraft if he changes back before their eyes, he prays to Isis and in a vision is directed to a source of roses where he may regain his proper form. This is in a religious procession at a festival of Isis wherein a sacrifical boat laden with votive offerings is to be launched onto the sea. One of the high priests carries a garland of roses and Lucius is enabled to eat them. Subsequently in gratitude he devotes his life to the Mysteries and becomes a member of the Isiac priesthood.

He says, of his initiation, that he is forbidden to reveal that which occurred to him in the holy of holies.

Thou wouldest peradventure demand, thou studious reader,

what was said and done there: verily I would tell thee if it were lawful for me to tell, thou wouldest know if it were convenient for thee to hear: but both thy ears and thy tongue should incur the like pain of rash curiosity. Howbeit I will not long torment thy mind, which peradventure is somewhat religious and given to some devotion; listen therefore, and believe it to be true. Thou shalt understand that I approached near unto hell, even to the gates of Proserpine, and after that I was ravished throughout all the elements, I returned to my proper place: about midnight I saw the sun brightly shine, I saw likewise the gods celestial and the gods infernal, before whom I presented myself and I worshipped them.

Of course Lucius, having made this avocation of secrecy, is, true to the double and even multiple meanings that occur in such writings, making serious fun. He has in fact told us all, in the guise of the ludicrous stories of the book where he apologizes for using Egyptian paper written on with a pen of Nile reeds. This is no apology to sophisticated city Greeks and Romans for using ancient and rustic materials. Rather it is an indication to the wise to look for truths about the ancient Mysteries, which owe much to the accumulated knowledge and traditions of Ancient Egypt.

The Mysteries aimed to take man out of his semi-animal condition to a rebirth as one with the gods, with direct realization of his spiritual being and integrity. Lucius makes himself an ass by his own intemperate curiosity and sensuality but is redeemed by dedication to the goddess and participation, after many trials, in her Mysteries. He later goes on to be an initiate of the Mysteries of Osiris "which is the more powerful god of the great gods, the highest of the greater, the greatest of the highest, and the ruler of the greatest . . ."—in other words the "thrice greatest."

It is interesting to note the role that roses play in the Lucian story, as a vehicle for his redemption. The rose is a symbol that occurs again and again in our history. It is the rosa mystica of Dante's *Divine Comedy* where it is a pattern of heaven itself. It has central place in the Mysteries of the Rose Cross in seventeenth-century Rosicrucianism, representing the spirit that rules the four elements. It reappears as a symbol for the whole psyche in a psychotherapeutic technique in modern times.

Another way of expressing the spiritual teaching of the Mystery cults is given by Apuleius in a lengthy anecdote within the main body of his story: the love of Psyche and Cupid. Psyche is a young maiden who represents the human soul destined for a loving union with the God of Love. She falls away from the trust and faith of that love through listening to the envious wiles of her sisters. She allows curiosity and suspicion to arise within her breast to the point of the betrayal of Cupid her divine lover. This results in her meeting with many trials and vicissitudes. The trials consist of sorting into order thousands of seeds in a night; the quest of a golden fleece; fetching some of the waters that feed the rivers of the Underworld; and seeking some of the beauty of Proserpine, for which she has to descend into Hades itself. She achieves these tasks as much by the exemplary love and service of others as by her own merit—and in the end is restored to her divine marriage.

This allegory shows the heights of spiritual sublimity of which the pagan world was capable.

The pagan world was also capable of considerable debasement of spiritual values, which Apuleius also describes. In certain parts of Greece bodies had to be closely guarded to prevent their being mutilated by witches seeking ingredients for their spells. Part of the rationale of the lowest forms of magic is to achieve an expansion of consciousness of sorts by shock and disgust, or by overcoming natural revulsions. There were also bands of vagrants, alleging themselves to be devotees of various Eastern gods and goddesses, carrying their idols on the backs of slaves or donkeys, and performing self-flagellating dances whilst they collected money from the audiences who gathered to watch the spectacle. This way of earning a living frequently went along with group indulgence in unnatural vice.

As Christianity became the official religion of the later Roman Empire, and the bearer of the torch of learning through the Dark Ages, we fail to get a full record and appreciation of the higher side of pagan spirituality. This is particularly so with the cult of Mithra, which had a tremendous following in the Roman army, rising to its apogee in about A.D. 250, and running Christianity a very close race as to which should become the official religion of the Empire. It thus attracted considerable Christian hostility which erupted into systematic persecution when Christianity became the official religion.

In certain respects Mithraism was very similar to Christian teaching. Its god was a savior of humanity, born on December 25th, and celebrated with a mystic feast of bread and wine. These similarities were so striking as to lead St.Augustine to regard the Mithraic cult as a deliberate counterfeit inspired by the Devil.

In spite of the similarities of external observance the interior theology was, however, very different. Mithra, like the other pagan gods, was a mythical being whereas the Christians revered an historical person. To the Christian, God had actually incarnated in human form in the body of Jesus Christ. This led to a very different theology and to a belief that God's concern was for *all* men. Even the Jews were spiritually elitist in their beliefs, in spite of accepting Gentile converts from time to time. And the grading system of the Mithraic Mysteries, for example, was foreign to Christian belief. The Christian belief was in a once-for-all conversion or act of faith, confirmed in simple baptism, as opposed to a ladder of grades and tests.

In spite of later hierarchical institutionalization, Christianity was at root a refreshingly down to earth and egalitarian religion—which led to the jibe of its being a cult for slaves. It was also by implication revolutionary and highly subversive. The many later reforms in Christian history, from those of the monastic orders to the Reformation itself and since then the diversiveness of the Protestant denomination, have been largely conceived with attempts to return to the purity and simplicity of early Christianity.

The Mithraic Mysteries had a system of initiatory grades, which corresponded to the planets. These were the Raven (corresponding to Mercury); the Mystic Bride (Venus); the Soldier (Mars); the Lion (Jupiter); the Persian (the Moon); the Heliodromus (the Sun); and the Father (Saturn). These led upward from the world of the Elements to Paradise. Honor was given to Mithra as god of light, or more specifically (like the ancient Egyptian Akhnaton) of the sun-disk, who by a mystical sacrifice of a bull gave new life and fertility to the world. The higher grades of Heliodromus and Father were considered representatives of the divine Sun and of Mithra himself respectively.

One drawback to the celebration of the Mysteries was that of limited entry; the cult of Mithra was, for the most part, confined to men. It also, in common with other Mystery celebrations, had symbolism and rites that, though spiritually significant to the participants, could appear bizarre and even repugnant to outsiders. Christians had similar difficulty over their supposedly eating the flesh and blood of Christ.

Religious human sacrifices in the pagan religions are reckoned to have ceased during the reign of Hadrian (A.D. 117-138) but rites such as the taurobolium, where a bull was sacrificed over a pit in which the initiate stood to be drenched in the falling blood, have an element of the barbarous about them. There was probably also an element of crude horseplay in some of the army branches of the cult with cult members roaring like lions, flapping their arms and cawing like ravens and so on, a kind of rugby club horseplay usurping the place of spiritual values. At the other end of the scale there were ascetic branches that had as many as eighty initiations, attended with tests and trials of very great rigor—even to the point of endangering life.

Human nature being as it is, such deviations attended all types of religious belief and observance. The Christians had similar problems as St. Paul's letters, particularly to the Corinthians, indicate. But if we compare their beliefs in terms of the evolution of consciousness the Christian vision represents a certain advance. God is seen as so loving that he is willing to sacrifice himself by constricting Himself into human form and undergoing all that follows. This is rather as if a human lover of cats were to consent to incarnate as a cat in order to communicate a means of individual salvation to them, in full knowledge of the limitations of power and consciousness this would entail, and in the full foreknowledge of being cruelly rejected and booted to death in an alley by hooligans.

Whether one chooses to believe in this God or not, it is a sublime conception, and one of a universal personal decision.

There was however much of great value in the pagan spiritual traditions that the early Fathers rejected. In forging their new truth they understandably, if regrettably, felt that rival theories were not so much complementary as antagonistic.

There were those however who were able to forge a synthesis between the old and the new. The result of their labors was to have profound effect on Western culture. These were the founders of the Hermetic tradition.

Note: Old Testament sources and chronology are matters of continuing debate among scholars. I have used as a guide in this chapter *The Bible as History* by Dr. Werner Keller and *The Living World of the Old Testament* by Prof. B. W. Anderson.

Chapter 3
The Hermetic Tradition

With the development of Christianity as the dominant religion of Western civilization four strands emerge that not only play a vital part in the tradition of Magic but carry the seeds within them of what was later to become the scientific method. The four strands are Gnosticism, the Hermetic literature, Neo-Platonic philosophy, and the Jewish Qabalah.

Gnosticism, in broad terms, was an amalgam of Christian belief with the Mystery Religions. The Hermetic literature reflected the impact of Christian belief on Greek philosophy and Egyptian magic. Neo-Platonism was a resurgence of the ancient traditions of Greek philosophy, which had gone through a barren and sceptical period; and the Jewish Qabalah was a mystical tradition of the Jews which produced its first written literature at this time.

It is difficult to piece together an adequate picture of Gnostic belief and practice. As with Mithraism, its close association with Christianity caused it to be ranked as a heresy. It was thus duly stamped out and obliterated more effectively than most alien traditions.

Most of the recently discovered Dead Sea Scrolls represent Gnostic beliefs however, and there is also extant an important manuscript entitled the *Pistis Sophia*. We may however also include the writings of pseudo-Dionysius. He is so-called because we do not know his true identity, but only that he wrote under the pseudonym of Dionysius the Areopagite. There is nothing reprehensible about this as this was common literary practice in those days. It caused, however, his writings to be accepted as important early source material by the Christians of the Middle Ages, because Dionysius the Areopagite is recorded in the New Testament as being one of the close companions of St. Paul. In fact pseudo-Dionysius wrote his four principal works about the year A.D. 500 although recent scholarship is tending to put them rather earlier. The tenor of some of his writings at any rate probably reflect Gnostic categories of thought. His most important work, which earned him the respect of the Fathers of the Eastern Church, was *The Mystical Theology*. But in another, shorter work, *The Celestial Hierarchies*, he gives a detailed description of the orders of angels that mediate between God and man.

The Gnostic world view was one of various grades of existence between God in the realm of light and man immersed in dense matter. The world of matter came under the control and influence of various Archons or intermediary beings, who might be represented by astrological symbolism. The Gnosis was the knowledge of how the soul could progress through these spheres to return to its true origin, becoming once more at one with God.

This was combined, in the neo-Christian Jews of Gnosticism, with a very fervent and mystical religious belief that transcended the limitations of the flesh and concentrated more on the Risen and Ascended Jesus than on the Incarnation and crucified Christ. While St. Paul, with his Pharisaic preoccupation with guilt, emphasizes "Christ crucified" in his Letters, it should also be borne in mind that no representations of the crucifixion occur in the first three centuries A.D.

The *Pistis Sophia* is a dialogue between Jesus, referred to as the Savior or the First Mystery, and the disciples, who have assembled with Mary Magdalene, eleven years after the crucifixion, on the Mount of Olives. The twelfth year of the ministry of Jesus in the Resurrected body marks the end of His ministry on Earth and he is enfolded in a triple robe of glory which contains all the powers of the universe, and he ascends into heaven in a great light. Thirty hours later he returns, in compassion, withdrawing his dazzling splendor from the eyes of the disciples, in order to give a final teaching.

This teaching presupposes an inner world of aeons and powers of considerable complexity but this is not emphasized. Central to the whole is the tragic story of *Pistis Sophia*, the World Soul, an allegory which has parallels with Apuleius" story of Cupid and Psyche. The emphasis is on salvation and redemption of *Pistis Sophia* by repentance, and faith in the Savior, which also serves as an example for the individual soul.

Pistis Sophia had originally belonged to the heavenly powers, like the Twelve Great Aeons, elsewhere identified as rulers of the signs of the Zodiac; but by a combination of ambition and betrayal she had fallen into an abyss half-way between Light and Matter. Thus we have the human condition of being partly angel and partly beast. The object of the Incarnation of the Savior was to enable the separation of this commingling of Light and Matter.

Half the text of *Pistis Sophia* is taken up with her ascent through the Twelve Aeons aided by the Savior, at each stage of which she sings a psalm of confession in celebration of her deliverance from chaos. Jesus asks a disciple for an elucidation of each confession, though most of the wisdom in this regard is shown forth by Mary Magdalene, somewhat to the indignation of St. Peter! However, just as the Mount of Olives as a starting point signifies a teaching of wisdom (olives were in pagan times sacred to Pallas Athene—the virgin wisdom) so is the teaching from the mouth of Mary Magdalene particularly appropriate. As the fallen and redeemed woman she is a human counterpart of the soul of the world, *Pistis Sophia.*

In the course of the discourse Jesus gives a description of the soul of man in response to a question by Mary Magdalene on the cause of sin. This sees man as a fourfold being. In essence he is a divine spark entangled in the threefold envelope of matter formed by the rebellious Rulers of the Zodiac, and unable to escape from subjection to their passions.

A Dungeon of Outward Darkness contains places of torment for various sins of mankind and provides a kind of purgatory before the divine spark is allocated another set of bodies for a further life on Earth. The most wicked however may be destroyed; and the judge of souls is a Virgin of Light attended by seven handmaidens.

In all this there are strands from many traditions. The general structure is similar to the pagan Mysteries, with the same tendency for a belief in the efficacy of words of power and secret names. The Mystery transcending all Mysteries is, however, seen as Jesus the Savior. The Zodiacal symbolism of astrology, which stems from Babylonia, is also in evidence although the predictive element of astrology is discountenanced by the belief that the Savior has, by his intervention, overcome the powers of the Zodiac.

Another notable feature, which may come from the East, is the strong belief in reincarnation, which is at odds with the more general Christian belief of the times, of an imminent Second Coming and End of the World. Along with the high magic of the Soul's cure and regeneration there are also accretions of low magic and superstition but this is common

The Holy Mountain of Initiation. An engraving from *Cabala, Spiegel der Kunst und Natur,* by the physician Steffan Michaelspacher, of the Tiro, published in Augsburg in 1616. The steps show the alchemical process within the Mount of Initiation, about which are the Four Elements, the Seven traditional Planets and the Zodiacal Signs. The candidate for initiation is traditionally blindfolded, representing man's spiritual blindness in the material world. Note the hint that the way to go is into the Earth.

to most apocryphal Christian literature. The general tenor of the manuscript is not, however, that of a decadent and corrupt sect, as the contemporary Christian descriptions of them would have us believe. They were obviously confident in the reality of a continuous revelation that should be a help in the work of Christian evangelism; though as part of the Mystery tradition some teachings were reserved for those felt capable of understanding them—a body of initiates.

A similar mixture of sources is found in the Hermetic literature. And although some commentators deny a Christian influence within it, the writings of Hermes were so similar in tone to Christian presupposition that for nearly 1500 years they were acceptable to the church in one form or another, and play an important part in Western culture.

Although it came from a variety of sources the Hermetic literature was loosely bound together through being credited to the pen of an ancient Egyptian priest called Hermes. In order to distinguish him from the Greek god of the same name he was often referred to as Hermes Trismagistus—Hermes the Thrice-Greatest.

There are two varieties of Hermetic literature, a higher sort and a lower. The higher is a teaching of the inner make-up of the soul of man and the means of spiritual rebirth; the lower is a debasement and misunderstanding of these principles in a series of spells and charms.

The higher branch is referred to as the Divine Pymander from the subject matter of the first fragment—the Pymander being the great Shepherd of Souls.

As in the Gnostic *Pistis Sophia* man is seen as partaking, in his inmost essence, of the nature of God. He is a brother of the Word, or Logos, who as the Second Person of the Christian Trinity, the Cosmic Christ, created the universe.

The Hermetic texts describe the creation of the world, which is seen in the Aristotelian form of a fixed Earth, surrounded by whirling crystalline spheres upon each of which is affixed a planet, and beyond them the crystalline spheres of the Zodiac and the Primum Mobile or that which gives motion to the rest. We shall come upon this world picture later, in the great metaphysical system of Dante, for although it was later disproved as a true model of the *physical* universe, its validity remains as a model of the psychic structure of man.

The similarity of the Hermetic creation story to that of Genesis also caused great respect to be paid it. It describes the creation of man by the Father of All, and because of this fact unfallen man is later referred to as brother of the Logos, the Second Person of the Trinity, who was also created by the Father. Man is even given, by the Father, the ability to be creative. But there follows a catastrophe, rather after the lines of both Psyche and *Pistis Sophia*. Man, leaning down through the crystalline spheres, became too closely involved with Nature. Man, who is made in the image of God, appeared as beautiful as God to Nature, and Nature, acting as a mirror to him, involved him in a Narcissus-like fall.

> And Nature, seeing the beauty of the form of God, smiled with insatiate love of Man, showing the reflection of that most beautiful form in the water, and its shadow on the earth. And he, seeing this form, a form like to his own in earth and water, loved it, and willed to dwell there. And the deed followed close on the design; and he took up his abode in matter devoid of reason. And Nature, when she had got him with whom she was in love, wrapped him in her clasp, and they were mingled in one; for they were in love with one another.
>
> And that is why man, unlike all other living creatures upon earth is twofold. He is mortal by reason of his body; he is immortal by reason of the Man of eternal substance. He is immortal and has all things in his power; yet he suffers the lot of a mortal, being subject to Destiny. He is exalted above the structure of the heavens; yet he is born a slave of Destiny.

The way out of this condition of spiritual oblivion and enmeshment in matter, according to the first script of the *Corpus Hermeticum* is a recognition and love of God in filial affection. In other words, as a self love of his own God-like image reflected in Nature caused Man's fall into matter, the way back is by recognizing the actual godhead within and the real unreflected image of God beyond the created heavens.

In the Hermetic scripts the way back to God through the heavens is through a series of "planetary" initiations in a pattern similar to the Mithraic mysteries and the Gnosis. Upon dissolution of the bodily senses at physical death:

> Man mounts upward through the structure of the heavens. And in the first zone of heaven (i.e. the Moon) he gives up the force which works increase and that which works decrease; to the second zone (i.e. Mercury) the machinations of evil cunning; to the third zone, (i.e. Venus) the lust whereby men are deceived; to the fourth zone, (i.e. the Sun) domineering arrogance; to the fifth zone, (i.e. Mars) unholy daring and rash audacity; to the sixth zone, (i.e. Jupiter) evil strivings after

wealth; and to the seventh zone, (i.e. Saturn) the falsehood which lies in wait to work harm. And thereupon, having been stripped of all that was wrought upon him by the structure of the heavens, he ascends to the substance of the eighth sphere (i.e. the Fixed Stars) being now possessed of his own proper power; and he sings, together with those who dwell there, hymning the Father; and they that are there rejoice with him at his coming. And being made like to those with whom he dwells, he hears the powers, who are above the substance of the eighth sphere, singing praise to God with a voice that is theirs alone. And thereafter, each in his turn, they mount upward to the Father; they give themselves up to the Powers, and becoming Powers themselves, they enter into God. This is the Good; this is the consummation, for those who have got *gnosis*.

The theology of the writings under the name of Dionysius the Areopagite complement the Hermetic scripts, although they are couched entirely in Christian terms rather than the Egyptian names and references that are a feature of the Hermetica.

Dionysius gives details in *The Celestial Hierarchies,* of the angelic intelligences that minister between God and his creation, and who help the aspiring soul.

They are divided into three sets of three choirs which comprise in descending order—the Seraphim, Cherubim and Thrones; the Dominions, Virtues and Powers; and the Principalities, Archangels and Angels. In their relation to the soul of man, the lowest triad have a purgative and purifying function; the middle triad are illuminators; and the triad nearest to God give perfection. All these various choirs are generally known to man as angels, this order of the celestial hierarchy being closest to him and the mundane world.

The Angels work with individual souls, according to their receptivity, and pass forth the divine revelations and wishes that they receive from the mediating Archangels who interpret the illuminations from on high into terms comprehensible to those below. The Principalities are the highest rank of this lowest triad and reflect forth in their being the ruling and orderly governing principle of the Prince of All, God Himself.

The Powers signify an orderly and unconfined regulation of intellectual and supernatural power that is never tyrannical but which is irresistible in its innate principle of due order. The Virtues show an unshakable virility and power in welling forth the energies of God; and the Dominions demonstrate an unbounded elevation free from all discord, aspiring to the One perfect divine pattern of lordship and leading those below them to the likeness of this true lordship themselves.

The Thrones show forth glory, exaltation and immovable and perfect establishment. The Cherubim are bounteous channels of Divine Wisdom, receiving this direct from the All-Highest and pouring it forth to all below them. And the Seraphim are like consuming fires, unhidden, unquenchable, changeless, radiant, enlightening in intense, perpetual, tireless activity in Divine Principles.

It may be discerned that there is a similar chain of correspondence to the planetary principles that we have met before. The Angels relate to the Moon, the Archangels to Mercury, the Principalities to Venus, the Powers to the Sun, the Virtues to Mars, the Dominions to Jupiter, the Thrones to Saturn, the Cherubim to the Fixed Stars, and the Seraphim to the Primum Mobile, beyond which is God.

Dionysius also gives explanations of the forms in which the angelic hierarchies have appeared to man, particularly recorded in the Old and New Testaments. Of particular importance are the fourfold forms of Man, Lion, Ox and Eagle—a complex of symbols that appears first in the Vision of Ezekiel and is also to be found in the Revelation of St. John the Divine. These play a recurring part in the magical and mystical symbolism of the West, and appear in Christian iconography as representing the four gospels: Matthew the Man, Mark the Lion, Luke the Bull and John the Eagle. The origin of the symbolism is probably zodiacal, in the signs of Aquarius, Leo, Taurus and Scorpio.

Both Hermetic and Dionysiac literature show an impact of traditional Greek philosophy and speculation allied to theocentric preoccupations of Jewish religious revelation. The ancient Greek conception of philosophy was not so much a specialist academic discipline as it has become today, but rather a pursuit which engaged the whole man and his attitude to the world. The modern philosopher would probably consider such a pursuit to be the seeking for an ideology rather than the discipline of academic philosophy.

Greek philosophy had its classic age in the time of Plato and Aristotle in the third century B.C., though it owes a considerable debt to the more ancient mathematical mystical speculations of Pythagoras and his school. In the centuries during and after the time of Alexander, Greek philosophy tended to founder on its own rationality, and it became sceptical and fragmented like our own today. This trend changed at about the commencement of the Christian era. In the first century B.C. when the Roman Cicero was looking back into the heritage of Greek philosophy

The Emerald Tablet of Hermes. Included in *The Secret Symbols of the Rosicrucians* published in Germany in 1710. The initial letters of the motto around the edge spell out VITRIOL, signifying the Universal Solvent, which is to seek and rectify the hidden stone within the interior of the Earth. In various forms this is an ever persistent theme in the annals of magico-spiritual attainment from ancient to modern times. Within the emblem are to be found the Eagle, Lion and Star, Celestial and Terrestrial Spheres, and Sun, Moon and planets. The Sun and Moon unite their forces within a cup supported by Mercury.

and translating what he thought would be interesting to the polite Roman society of his times, two important philosophical traditions were experiencing a resurgence. These were Stoicism and Platonism, both of which had a profound influence on later European thought.

The traditional Stoic view was of a universe that is at the same time God. Everything is divine and we ourselves are part of this divinity. This is very close to pantheist religion, the worship of nature, even though it conceives nature in its broadest possible sense. Stoicism could provide the philosophy for the pagan type religion that the Jews were, for instance, opposed to. The Jews, with their theist position, saw nature as the creation of a God whose being was *beyond* nature.

Traditional Stoicism was however transformed by an injection of Platonism, largely through the influence of the geographer, historian and philosopher Poseidonius of Apamea. This added a cosmic element to the somewhat static and materialist traditional Stoicism. The divinity which was part and parcel of the physical world in traditional Stoic eyes was, as it were, centrifuged out. This led to the divinity being seen as in and of the stars, with the physical world, in a rather inferior and corrupt condition, at the center. It was therefore man's destiny to purify himself of his corrupt material nature and return to his true home in the starry heavens.

This worldview, in which religion and science are inextricably combined, lies close to some quasi-religious speculations expressed in terms of science fiction today, with theories about coming from higher civilizations in intergalactic space. The new Stoicism developed a further element however in the belief in a God beyond and transcending the heavens.

The world view of a central earth with surrounding heavenly spheres became incorporated in the natural philosophy of Aristotle, and eventually, by the efforts of St. Thomas Aquinas and Albertus Magnus, into the structure of Christian theology, whence it finds its supreme literary and philosophical expression in *The Divine Comedy* of Dante.

At the same time that Stoicism was being Platonized, Platonism itself was undergoing change, following the increasing development of ideas that occurred as a result of Alexander's empire.

This had led to the many local nature gods becoming amalgamated. It also led, in philosophy, to an increase in scepticism. As one world view was compared with another many were seen to be in opposition, though not easily refutable in their own terms. This led to a Neo-Platonic view of God as being in essence unknowable. In this view, by whatever terms we try to describe God, He is beyond the world of our limited conceptions and perception. Thus whatever we say about Him is untrue.

This led to an important Christian tradition of negative theology—which attempted to describe God only in terms of what he is *not*. He is not this, not that, not the other thing and so on through the whole gamut of possible comparisons. This in turn develops into an important type of meditation leading to deep interior mystical experience. An example of this type of negative mysticism in medieval Christian literature is *The Cloud of Unknowing* by an anonymous English mystic.

In terms of interior religious experience this is the *via negativa,* or "Negative Way." The alternative "Positive Way," or *via positiva,* approaches interior religious experience by way of symbolic images. This is also very much the province of White Magic.

In positive terms the new emphasis in Platonism developed a greater awareness of the importance of God—sometimes called the One and the Good. The archetypal ideas, that were thought to form the basis of eternal reality in original Platonism, are now seen as ideas within the Mind of God. It is not too great a step from this for God's ideas to be correlated with the angelic hierarchies envisaged by Pseudo-Dionysius.

An important influence in the first century A.D. was Philo of Alexandria. He was an orthodox Jew who had received a Greek philosophical training and he proceeded to interpret the Old Testament in allegorical terms. This had little effect on orthodox Judaism but was a deep and lasting influence on Christian thinking and philosophy. Many scholars have seen, in the Fourth Gospel, a deliberate bringing of Greek philosophical thought to bear in communicating the Christian message to a Greek-thinking world.

We find too the roots of later Christian Trinitarian theology in Greek philosophical speculation of this time. Numenius, for example, distinguished between a Supreme God, a Second Mind or Logos responsible for the creation of the universe, and a deified World Soul. This is not the exact equivalent of the Christian Father, Son and Holy Spirit but is certainly of a similar pattern.

In the course of time the various strands of Greek philosophy gave way in importance to the work of Plotinus (A.D. 204–270), whose thought, until the end of Greek philosophical teaching in the sixth century A.D., was dominant, and had great influence on later European thinking.

Plotinus is particularly interesting in that he obviously writes from the basis of personal religious experience and his philosophy is an attempt to account for this experience, rather than to satisfy a taste for intellectual speculation.

He calls God the One or the Good, who creates from himself without diminution, just as a candle flame can create more candle flames without lessening its own light. The prime creation of the One and the Good is the Intellect, which is not a dry philosophical abstraction but a teeming, joyous state of perfect life. Intellect has two modes. One is to return to the One and the Good, there to remain in a loving face-to-face relationship with God. The other is to seek similar Oneness and Goodness on its own account, for which purpose it divides into many individual lives or centers of creative energy.

This level of Intellect corresponds to the archetypal forms and ideas of original Platonism, and to the upper celestial hierarchies of Dionysius. God is not an abstraction but a being; not so much a Father, as a Divine Lover. Another important point in Plotinus" inner-world view is his distinction between the religious experience that is possible between contemplation of the One, and the realization of at-one-ment with the Universal Intellect.

This is a distinction that tends to be overlooked, although it is plainly indicated in works such as Ruysbroek's *Spiritual Espousals* and Dante's *Divine Comedy,* and Professor R. C. Zaehner in his book *Mysticism Sacred and Profane* has analyzed it in relation to Aldous Huxley's account of drug experience.

In the philosophy of Plotinus there is a lower creative level called Soul, and this realm sees an imaginative attempt to embody forth the ideas and forms of the world of Intellect. It results in discursive rather than unified use of the mental powers, and by this means space, time, and the world of Nature are brought into being. The natural world itself is formed by a collective entity, the World Soul, to which human beings, having their roots in Intellect, are as younger brothers and sisters, rather than creations of it. Thus man is *in* the natural creation but *not* of it.

The psychological makeup of man, according to Plotinus, corresponds to the larger world. Man has his own physical body corresponding to the physical world; he has his own soul (the level of everyday consciousness) corresponding to the World Soul; and his own higher intuitive faculties corresponding to the Intellect. In most men these higher faculties are dormant and it is our task to reawaken them.

The awakening process is generally achieved by continuing experience in the natural world through a series of incarnations. There is no conscious memory of previous incarnations because the permanent unit of consciousness is the Higher Self. The Higher Self is on the plane of Intellect, and the mundane personality, or Lower Self, is its projection. The wordly experience of the Lower Self is absorbed by the Higher Self after physical death prior to projecting forth into incarnation another Lower Self.

This doctrine of reincarnation is similar to Eastern Hindu belief which explains the trials and tribulations of life as the just results of sins performed in a previous life. This is the doctrine of *Karma.* It has the attraction of a certain logic in accounting for the apparent inequalities and injustices of wordly life, but has less sublimity than the teaching of Jesus, which prevailed over it.

Jesus taught the Divine forgiveness of sins and of the ways of God not being readily subject to the understanding of men. This is epitomized in the parable of the workers in the vineyard where those who worked a short time received as much as those who worked long. This view emphasizes the selfless love of the ideal family rather than a "balance sheet" approach to human and divine relations. The *karmic* view might consider the forgiveness of sin to be the condoning of evil. However, the theory of reincarnation disappeared from the traditional religious consciousness of the West, and also, with certain minor exceptions, from the magical traditions until an influx of oriental ideas, through Theosophy, in the nineteenth century.

Plotinus did not advocate either religious or magical practices. He believed that it was not so much by ritual observances in the world that one achieved enlightenment and freedom as by philosophical reflection and aspiration

Theurgic and religious practices were later introduced to the system however by such writers as Iamblichus, who also had an intense interest in the revival of the ancient Egyptian Mysteries.

This movement, very much a part of the prevailing cultural milieu, can possibly be seen reflected, in Christian terms, in some of the speculations of Origen, and in the Cappodocian Fathers. In the West, the ex-Manichaean Augustine, and possibly Ambrose, might be seen as reflecting the same milieu; it is certainly discernible in the writings of Pseudo-Dionysius.

A final strand in the network of religious, mystical and philosophical speculation which accompanied the slow breakup of the Roman civilization was that of Jewish mysticism, and in particular the Qabalah or "received teaching."

There was little of the Greek type of mystical speculation in orthodox Jewry, which tended to concentrate upon observance of the Law, the moral, social and ritual code of the Old Testament. An exception was certain enclosed communities, such as the Essenes, of whom we know little, although more is coming to light from archaeological finds such as the Dead Sea Scrolls.

The full flowering of the teachings of the Qabalah did not take place in Western consciousness until the Renaissance, but an early document shows that a type of Qabalism was extant in the second or third century A.D. though the date is uncertain. This is the *Sepher Yetzirah* or *Book of Formation.*

The letters of the Hebrew alphabet also serve as numbers and the *Sepher Yetzirah* is an account of the formation of the world in terms of the forces of letters and numbers. There are first of all three Mother letters, that provide the primal elements from which the universe can be built by God. There then follow seven Double letters (so-called because they have alternative pronunciations). Each of these double letters presides over a different direction of space, so that a six-sided cube is formed, representing the universe, with the seventh letter as its center. The remaining twelve letters of the Hebrew alphabet are allocated to the twelve edges of the Cube of Space.

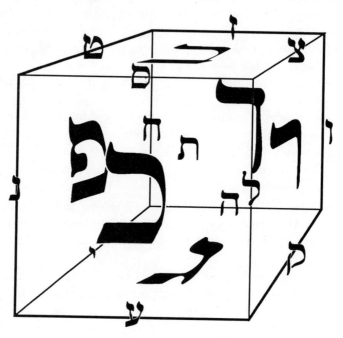

Qabalistic Cube of Space

This plainly does not afford a very convincing model of the physical universe, though with its sevenfold and twelvefold symbolism it is as effective a model of the interior universe as the concentric spheres of the Aristotelian world picture. Onto the faces of the Cube, represented at first by the bare bones of letter and number, may go a host of attributions and correspondence so that the whole content of human experience, represented by planetary, zodiacal and other signs, can be categorized and related.

As an example, the seven traditional planets have their allocation in the *Sepher Yetzirah* as follows: Venus to the East, the Sun to the South, Jupiter to the West, Mars to the North, Mercury Above, the Moon Below,

Saturn in the Center.

To these planets are associated a whole host of traditional attributions. Thus all things to do with mental activity, trade, books and learning are attributed to Mercury; all things to do with love and close relationships to Venus; of restriction and limitations to Saturn; of rulership and order to Jupiter; of radiation, light and inspiration to the Sun; of flux, reflux, cyclic events, tidal flows, to the Moon; martial and combative or active things to Mars, and so on. Similar categories of experience pertain to the twelve signs of the Zodiac in a detailed astrological tradition that goes back to remote antiquity and the stargazers of ancient Babylonia.

The cubical structure has an unexpected advantage in that it is plainly ridiculous to confuse it with the actual physical structure of the universe.

The Aristotelian model of central earth with concentric crystalline spheres about it became confused with physical astronomy, and resulted in embarrassing consequences when Copernicus, Galileo and others demonstrated that the physical world of astronomy just was not like that.

The Aristotelian model is correct enough when seen as a projection of man. It has the Earth at its center because man's consciousness is centered within his physical body. Man's consciousness has four functions, as categorized by Jungian psychology—intuition, ratiocination, feeling, and sensation, corresponding to the four earthly elements of the ancients— air, fire, water and earth.

There are then various ways in which these elements of consciousness may be experienced or expressed, and this is symbolically expressed in terms of the seven traditional planets (including the Sun and Moon) and the twelve constellations of the Zodiac.

The crystalline spheres around the Earth may be seen as a kind of ladder by which man's consciousness can ascend step by step to its true home in the stars and eventual at-one-ment with God the Creator beyond the stars. This conception reached its full flowering in the High Middle Ages in Dante's *Divine Comedy*.

The Hebrew Cube of Space does not have this ladder of conscious spiritual growth or evolution so readily apparent. This is largely because of the different Jewish slant on things which at the same time was more materialistic and more spiritual. Instead of a gradual gradation of being from spirit to matter of Greek thought the Jews saw a firm divide between God and the Creation.

The Cube of Space represents the Creation and its relation to God is found in Jewish "Throne" Mysticism, which in its more dynamic symbolism is "Chariot" Mysticism. A full expression of this type of mysticism is to be found in the *Book of Enoch*, a fairly late text that probably typifies Essene mystical belief, but it is also apparent in the earlier Vision of Ezekiel in the Old Testament.

In the Vision of Ezekiel the created universe is like a cube, a sea of hot coals within the compass of four pillars upholding a starry ceiling, and all moving through space on strange angelic wheels. Above the heavenly canopy is a throne, which is the throne of God, of the Creator.

Just as the pious Jews forebore to mention the holy Name of God when reading the bible, so did they show reverence by preferring not to depict God in terms of images (an early form of *via negativa*). Thus it is the Throne, or the Chariot of God, which receives symbolic depiction and reverence—a parallel to the Seat of Mercy associated with the Ark of the Covenant.

And we find this same tradition being repeated in Dante, the archapostle of the *via positiva*, when having ascended to the highest heaven after all the experiences of a veritable encyclopedia of human symbolism, God is described on his throne entirely in abstract geometrical terms.

In the Greek and Dantean system one could climb to God by the various rungs of creation. In the Hebrew system it tended to be a more dramatic and sudden translation. Enoch and Elijah were suddenly caught up into heaven, the ascent of the latter in a chariot. And even when Jacob dreams of a ladder between heaven and earth it is only angels who are ascending and descending it.

The Jews were always anxious to make a distinction between the Creator and the Creation to avoid the worship of Nature followed by their pagan neighbors. This distinction is made in Dante in the gap between the Actuality of God in the heaven of the Rosa Mystica, and the system of crystalline spheres of the creation; but in symbol systems of this kind it is easy for them to be blurred into a system where there is no qualitative gap between Creator and Created. Then matter is seen as condensed divinity and God as attenuated matter, a pantheist philosophical position as opposed to a theist one.

The theist position can be regarded as a stage in the evolution of consciousness wherein man separates himself as an individual entity from the great womb of collectivity. It is therefore an important distinction. By a recognition of an Uncreate God man establishes his own spiritual position independent from nature.

The belief in the All being identical to the One, however philosophically expressed, denotes a stage in consciousness prior to cutting the umbilical cord between group and individualized consciousness.

In the evolution of consciousness in Western civilization this step seems generally to have been taken at the beginning of the Christian era. In the dawning of the Christian belief in God-made-Man taking Manhood up into God-head there are parallel movements, of a somewhat abortive nature, in the deification of Roman emperors.

At the same time the ending of human sacrifices and the gradual decline of slavery indicate a general dawning realization of the sanctity of individual human life, and of its importance beyond the interests of the collective group. This is a movement in consciousness that is only coming to fruition gradually, over the 2,000 years of subsequent civilization, and with many relapses and deviations on the way.

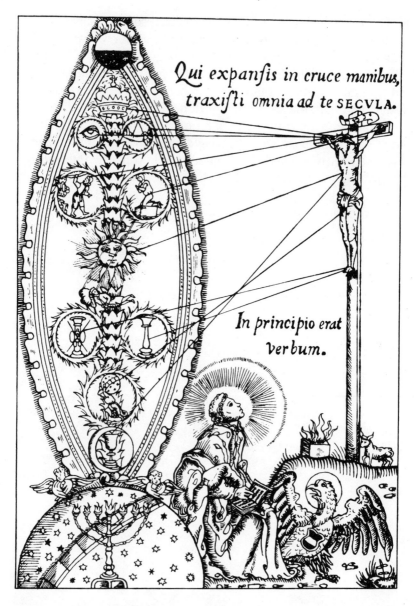

Qui expanſis in cruce manibus, traxiſti omnia ad te SECVLA.

In principio erat verbum.

Tree of Life. Qabalistic Tree of Life featured in the frontispiece of a sixteenth-century Gospel of St. John, with lines of attribution running to a figure of the Incarnate Logos. The Tree of Life rises above the starry universe and contains within its spheres the Grail Cup in a Lunar Crescent, Atlas up-holding the universe, the Pillars Jachin and Boaz, Jacob's Ladder going through the Sun, Abraham prepared to sacrifice his innocent son Isaac, the All-seeing Eye, the Horn of Plenty and Heavenly Crown.

Chapter 4
Visions of the Quest

Roman civilization collapsed into barbarism in the West, and in the slow recovery from the Dark Ages to the High Middle Ages the history of magic is fragmented and obscure. We can discern however a fascinating mosaic of brilliant conceptions, which we have to link together with a certain amount of conjecture. Taken together we have a considerable body of knowledge and belief which falls into Legends of the Quest on the one hand, and Spiritual Alchemy on the other.

Legends of the Quest represent a search for the spiritual in man, usually expressed in terms of seeking a great treasure, or the rescue of a maiden from danger.

The spiritual may be represented as a divine object or a divine place or even a divine person. This type of story has its pattern in classical antiquity. The Quest of the Golden Fleece or the Labors of Hercules (which were, significantly, twelve in number) are examples. They now appear as the Holy Grail legends, and in course of time are combined with the cycle of King Arthur and his Knights of the Round Table.

Other strands of the same psychological complex appear as the legends of paradisiacal lands, such as Hy Brasil, or the Isles of the Blessed, or the strange Eastern empire of Prester John (John the Priest). Some of these had such impelling force that they stimulated actual physical exploration, and in his search for the Isles of the Blessed, St. Brendan the Navigator may have discovered the Americas long before Columbus.

When the story is one of rescue of the soul, the soul invariably appears as a maiden in distress, after the manner of Cupid and Psyche, or Persephone in the ancient Mysteries, or the legend of Perseus and Andromeda. Similar episodes appear in the Grail and Arthurian cycles.

A particularly important variant is that of St. George and the Dragon. He is the pattern for the red cross knight, whose emblem became the badge of the Crusaders, who were themselves physically seeking a holy place—Jerusalem—to rescue it from evil domination. St. George, in origin an obscure Cappodocian Christian saint of the second or third century, became in this role patron saint of England, and of the noble order of chivalry, the Order of the Garter.

Allied to this stress on the rescue and cherishing of a maiden, there was a profound social and cultural reorientation. This was the raising of the status of women to a higher level than being simply goods and chattels. With it came the institution of codes of honor in war. It was the birth of the code of chivalry.

This influence was spread by a strange body of men, traveling players or musicians, called *troubadours, trouvères* or *jongleurs* in France, or *minnesingers* or *meistersingers* in the German states. It is probably significant that they center about areas where Christian heresies flourished. Provence was particularly important in this respect, where the church eventually mounted a Crusade of incredible ferocity against the heretical Albigensian church.

The Albigensian, or Catharist, churches derived, via probably the Bogomiles of the Byzantine Empire, from the teachings of Manes (d. *c.* 275). A principal feature of a teaching, Manicheeism, which took a number of forms over the centuries that followed, was world-rejection. The universe was seen as a battleground between equal contending forces of Good and Evil, and this philosophical dualism almost certainly owes its origins to Zoroastrianism.

This curious amalgam of Zoroastrianism and Christianity tended to regard the physical world as intrinsically evil, and in its Albigensian form taught that Christ was an angel with a phantom body who neither suffered and died, nor rose again.

The violence of the Church's reaction stemmed from the theological falsehood that these doctrines implied. Evil as strong as good, and unconquered; the Incarnation denied. And following upon this the redemption of man denied. The Church saw evil only as a localized absence of God, and only existing because of the willful error of created man. God permitted evil to exist, in accordance with his covenant with Noah, so that fallen man could win his way back to paradise by a renewal of faith and belief, and a turning of the individual selfish Will back into alignment with the Will of God. Hence the Church's belief in obedience—which could nonetheless have unfortunate organizational consequences.

The Church also believed in the sanctity of the physical creation, that it was redeemable as the New Jerusalem, and not to be shunned in violent asceticism.

It is true that some ascetic saints of the early church seem to have fallen into this trap without incurring official censure, and an earth denying hyper-ascetic tradition existed, particularly in the enclosed orders, for many centuries. The same tendency existed in Manicheeism, with full theological justification, but tending by its violently unnatural standards to fall into quasi-spiritual forms of unnatural vice.

The other strand of tradition that carried the theory and praxis of Magic was alchemy. The origins of alchemy are of uncertain date and have been variously traced to China and to Ancient Egypt. The word alchemy has an Arabic prefix indicating that it came, like algebra, from or through Islamic sources, and it can be derived from Al-Khymia—the name of Ancient Egypt.

Alchemy is usually looked upon in too narrow a sense, as primitive chemistry. In its fullness it was a theory of being, or process, embracing all creation. It saw all forms of existence, even the inanimate, as rooted in one basic ground of beingness and capable of growth, evolution and transformation.

This is exactly the same pattern that we observe in our theory of the evolution of human consciousness. Consciousness starts as an apparently confused elemental mass of group consciousness, it distills into individualized and eventually spiritualized separate parts, which then attain to a higher synthesis of unity-in-diversity instead of unity-in-mass. The spiritualized units can then act as a focus of transformation for less developed units about them.

This appears in the teachings of Jesus where he talks of the redeemed Christian acting as leaven or yeast in the solid dough of humanity. This is the *modus operandi* of the Philosopher's Stone—the object of the alchemical quest—the mysterious substance, the product of great art and distillation, which can transform base metal into gold. Variants are the Elixir of Life or the Perpetual Lamp.

Laboratory alchemy which acted as a forerunner to modern chemistry is but a specialized and limited application of the general theory—applying it to mineral substances. It is a similar type of misunderstanding of the subject as is to be found in projecting the inner realities of ancient astronomy onto the physical universe; or in Brendan's seeking the Isles of the Blessed by physical exploration; or in later attempts to create a New Jerusalem, or Utopia on earth, by political or military means.

The wider applications of alchemy were well realized in the High

Middle Ages and alchemical symbolism appears in cathedral construction during the sudden explosion of Gothic architecture. Chartres and Notre Dame are but two examples of alchemical and magical textbooks in stone, comprising examples of direct alchemical symbolism and the number mysticism of the Ancient World in the use of the Pythagorean "golden section."

So we have, in alchemical terms, starting from the obscure and confused crucible of the Dark Ages, a rich efflorescence of mystical lore that distills in the High Middle Ages, through romantic love and chivalry; the Holy Grail, the Holy City and Legend of the Quest; and alchemy and Gothic architecture.

This is also a period of great beauty in the human conception of White Magic, although not called by this name. Before this period initiatory magic tends in antiquity to be shrouded in portentous mystery, the candidate's soul moving amongst great obscure forces and mighty gods, dwarfed by their power and apparent capriciousness. It is a stage not unlike the consciousness of early childhood.

After the period of the High Middle Ages man becomes more the controller than the controlled, and his personal inquisitiveness built a body of personal knowledge and powers that express themselves in later science and technology, with magic itself as a part of that technology. The modern age is thus a period corresponding to the freeing of consciousness from the archetypal parental figure that corresponds to early adulthood.

The period of the High Middle Ages is akin to racial adolescence. It is a period of great wonder and naivete. Against a relatively stable background of a single Creator, with his church well established as a pillar in society, a place for everything and everything in its place in feudal hierarchical consciousness, there are the great dreams of wonder that express themselves in the Holy Grail legends and romantic love.

In their effects they become certainly more than dreams however. The dream of the Spiritual Quest was realized in what was perhaps the first international political movement, the Crusades. There were no doubt other factors, social, political and economic, that contributed to the Crusading movement, but above all this was the high fever of the religious quest.

The historical circumstances were that, in 1094, the Pope announced the formation of a Crusade to rescue Jerusalem from the hands of Islam. There is evidence of certain political self-interest here, for the Turks were encroaching upon Byzantium, the Christian religious center of the Eastern Mediterranean, and following the Great Schism between Christian East and West in 1054 there was much that must have appealed to the Papacy in the thought of sending troops to rescue its rival. The Papacy had become, by force of historical circumstances, an Italian feudal principality, and tended to think in terms of the power politics of the time.

In fact Jerusalem had been in the hands of Islam since 638, when it was captured by the Caliph Omar, and little concern had been expressed during the ensuing five hundred years. On the whole free access was allowed for Christian pilgrims.

What is astounding is the enthusiasm with which the Pope's call was taken up. There was some self-interest in certain of the Frankish knights who, through the feudal system of primogeniture, found themselves landless and impoverished younger sons. To them the chance to hew out lands for themselves in the East had a material attraction. But above all this was a very considerable genuine religious enthusiasm, and one which rapidly became out of control. Even the common people desired to go on the Crusade, and before a properly organized army could be formed a Peoples' Crusade set off, a great horde of men, women and children, that was met with amazed horror by the Emperor of Byzantium, who shipped them across the Bosphoros where they were massacred, and such few as survived taken into slavery. This was followed by even more bizarre and tragic events, such as the Children's Crusade, the origin of the legend of the Pied Piper of Hamelin.

The actual history does not make inspiring or pleasant reading. The main force of Crusaders fought its way to Jerusalem over a long and bitter campaign, captured the city with pious atrocity, and succeeded in forming a Christian kingdom in Palestine that lasted fitfully for some two hundred years (1099–1291), riddled with internecine bickering, until succumbing finally to Moorish recapture.

But the motivation behind it was one of great spiritual idealism. Again we see the familiar mechanism of inner psychological patterns and processes being projected onto the outer physical world. The Jerusalem which they fought to rescue was not a physical city under imperial domination. It was a divine city, fallen from grace, and persecuted by demons. In these terms it formed an analog of the soul of man.

In practical terms the Crusades led to certain cultural benefits. The Saracens were by no means the semi-barbarous hordes that had poured forth from the Arabian desert under Mohamed five hundred years before. In fact they were somewhat more civilized than the Norman

knights, who but a few generations back had been Norsemen. A considerable cultural interchange took place and this included mystical and religious ideas.

Mohamedanism in its institutionalized and orthodox form was as
stultifying as most religions when they achieve social establishment, and
had developed a semi-heretical movement known as Sufism. As a reaction to the orthodox Islamic view of God, or Allah, being a high and remote potentate whom it would be blasphemous to represent in any form
of pictorial art (hence the emphasis on calligraphy) Sufism developed an
intimate form of semi-erotic mysticism that saw God as the Divine Lover.
In effect we have the myth of Psyche and Cupid over again, or the Song of
Solomon, or the Gnostic conception of Jesus and Mary Magdalene.

It is this which probably lies at the root of the Courts of Love which
sprang up during the ensuing century. The first Troubadour we know
about, William of Poitiers, died in 1127. The Courts of Love show the
marks of a system of mystical initiation. The lady love is seen as being unattainable, married to another, and from this is formulated a complex
code of etiquette and expression of passion for the unattainable.

One may see a certain social pattern behind this in that it would have
been the actual situation in many a Norman castle, with the lady of the
castle and her retinue of damsels cloistered in the midst of a group of men
without women. However, the psychological pattern involved was one
that has had profound reverberations down the centuries. The pattern of
romantic love starts as a movement whereby a code of chivalry replaces
the Norman brutishness of rule by force, with women regarded as property or animals. It developed into a code of honor and convention that finally finds its natural expression in the romantic novel and the "eternal
triangle." The mechanisms are, it would seem, more profound than a sublimated desire for adultery. In one way of regarding it, the beloved is the
image of the Divine; and in another the beloved is the soul fallen and held
captive by alien and evil forces.

The tradition of Courtly Love achieved high patronage in that
Eleanor of Aquitaine was Queen of the Troubadour Minstrelsy. This remarkable woman, the mother of the English kings, Richard the Lionheart
and John Lackland, was first Queen of France, and subsequently, having
married the little known Henry Plantagenet, the Queen of Henry II of
England, whose family was ecclesiastically referred to as "The Devil's
Brood" for certain anti-clerical indiscretions.

The troubadour traditions continued into popular legend with
Richard I as their focus. He was in fact an absentee king in England; all

but a few months of his ten year reign being spent crusading or in other military adventures. This may have helped the legends in that, being absent, he attracted wishful thinking and "divine projections." When he was held captive for ransom in Europe (a common way of raising revenue in those days), legend has it that he was found by his minstrel servant Blondel. And more significant are the Robin Hood legends that arose about his reign, with a Maid Marian as the sole woman in a group of dedicated warriors who strove to bring succor to the kingdom which had been usurped while the true king was away. On one level this refers to the kingdom of England but it is also referable to the Universe and the Divine King.

An interesting feature of the legends is the frequency with which the name of the Virgin Mary is invoked in conversation, for whether as a counter to these semi-heretical movements or as a symptom of the same preoccupation with the feminine, the Cult of Mary begins to assume an important role in the beliefs of the Catholic Church.

Mary is seen as a pattern of perfected spiritual humanity. In the Christian mythos she was the one human being on whom the Incarnation of God depended. By her saying "I will" to the proposition of providing the womb for the Virgin Birth, the Divine Incarnation could take place.

Whether or not the Virgin Birth is historical fact is, in a sense, beside the point; it is a valid and meaningful mythical fact. In Coleridge's terms it is the reality of the secondary imagination, not mere fancy.

The acceptance of the belief that Jesus the Christ was Virgin-born implies a number of other beliefs that follow from it. A Virgin Birth of a Redeeming God means that the Virgin must have volunteered. It could hardly by its very theological context have been undertaken by force, overriding human spiritual free will. To volunteer for such a cosmic act, the medieval theologians felt, must entail a unique suitability. This implied that she was born free from the taint of Original Sin. This is the dogma of the Immaculate Conception (often confused with that of the Virgin Birth) and the belief that the Virgin Mary herself was also born of a virgin, St. Anne.

Also, having been the physical vessel of the Incarnate Christ, it follows that Mary must have been the first Christian, the foundation of the Church later to be built by the mission of Jesus and the disciples. This fundamental role was seen to link back to the strange prophecy in Genesis of Eve being destined to bruise the head of the serpent, the evil cause of man's Original Fall from Paradise. Accordingly Mary is later believed to have been taken up into Heaven in a uniquely physical sense in the dogma of the Assumption; and to have been crowned Queen of Heaven.

Much of this became accepted Roman Catholic dogma at a comparatively late date, but the cult of the Blessed Virgin Mary has ancient roots. Its flowering takes place during the medieval period but its origin can be traced far back into antiquity. Feasts such as the Purification of the Blessed Virgin Mary or Festival of Lights in February and the Physical Assumption of the Blessed Virgin Mary in August, go back to the Mysteries of Isis and coincide with major pagan festivals. The August one coincides with the Isiac festivals celebrating the rise of Sirius predicting the inundation of the Nile in Ancient Egypt, and the February one with Isis as Queen of Lights. These pagan parallels, and the development of a mythical body of dogma through "tradition" were later unacceptable to a large body of Christians. Puritans and Protestants, with a more individual approach to religion, saw salvation in terms of personal faith and works rather than in sacramental powers of a large group transcending individual conscience. This might be interpreted as another facet of the evolution of consciousness from group to personal dynamics.

The psychologist C. G. Jung spent much time and effort in analyzing the psychological significance of the Marian doctrines, which, with the advent of Mary to Heaven, make the Holy Trinity into a Quaternio, which is a figure of psychological balance. In the medieval period, however, such psychological speculations were not possible, at any rate in this form. The psychospiritual dynamics that were operating produced however, in the church and society, a great reverence and respect for the feminine.

This crystallized in a unique literary way into the Holy Grail legends. These appear quite suddenly in a period between A.D. 1180 and 1230. The precise nature of the Grail is curiously ill-defined, and it is variously described as a cup, a dish or a stone, borne by a Grail Maiden and a retinue of damsels.

It is plainly closely connected with the Mysteries of the Crucifixion as in the most popular versions it is in the form of a chalice, thought by some to be the Cup of the Last Supper, used to collect the blood of Christ at his deposition from the cross by Joseph of Arimathea. There is plainly a great deal of speculative mysticism involved in this part of the Christian story which is commonly glossed over or taken for granted. Joseph of Arimathea is a key figure in the Resurrection story for without his application to Pilate for custody of the body of Jesus, and his provision of a secure tomb, there would have been far different circumstances for the resurrection. Such an emphasis on Joseph of Arimathea is to be found in the

Apocryphal Gospel of Nicodemus or Acts of Pilate, probably of the fourth century A.D.

Joseph of Arimathea is, in the Grail legends, the custodian and bearer of the Holy Grail, which has miraculous qualities. He brings it, through many vicissitudes, to Europe via Spain and the North African coast. This journey is significantly the route of much mystical lore and we later come upon much the same kind of quasihistorical pattern in seventeenth-century Rosicrucianism. It is in fact the route of new culture to Europe from Moorish influence. The Moors absorbed a great diversity of cultural traditions from their international conquests, which extended to the Orient, and passed this on in diverse ways to a Europe emerging from barbarism.

There are various versions of the Grail legend, some transmitted through the French and others through the German traditions. The German tradition of Parsifal, the Grail hero, stems from Wolfram von Eschenbach. Wolfram writes later than the French authority Chretien de Troyes, but claims that his version, obtained from "a Jew of Toledo," is more accurate. It was this version that was subsequently made into an operatic sequence by Richard Wagner.

Other versions of the story, of Belgic origin, feature Lohengrin and the swan maidens. The swan maidens revert to very ancient mythology both in Ireland and in Ancient Greece where they are found depicted on vases associated with the Kabyric Mysteries, an underground cult of the Great Mother.

The most well known version today stems from the amalgamation of legends undertaken by Sir Thomas Malory, a knight at the time of the Wars of the Roses, whose book was one of the first printed by Caxton in 1485, an indication of its popularity.

Malory welded together the legends of King Arthur and his Knights of the Round Table, together with those of the magician Merlin, the tragic romances of Tristram and Isolde of Cornwall, Lancelot and Guinevere and others, and also the Holy Grail legends.

These stories provide a heritage of symbolism for the post-classical Western world. They are the collective imagination of the race, group daydreams shadowing forth great complexes and processes in the soul of Western man, individually and collectively. They thus provide the material for fairy stories and tales of adventure, and in a Magical context, for psycho-spiritual initiation.

The Round Table stories show forth a pattern of ideal democracy. All are united in equal rank in loyalty to the King, who is first among

Vision of the Holy Grail. Vision of the Holy Grail appearing to the Round Table of King Arthur and his knights, from a fifteenth-century French manuscript. Although often associated with the Cup of the Last Supper its form in the legends is rarely described and has an element of mystery about it, like the identity of the retort in which the alchemical process takes place. In fact both are functions of human consciousness duly prepared for revelation and transmutation.

equals. All are dedicated to service of the common good and to protection of the weak.

The great ideal of feudal chivalry was embodied historically in some notable knights of the time such as William the Marshal, but it had an altogether coarser reality. Errant knights in real life tended to be landless younger sons in search of booty by casual banditry. Jousting tournaments were frequently unseemly brawls between rival gangs with the object of capturing an adversary's horse and armor for resale. The chivalric ideal was an attempt to curb the more brutish side of this kind of warrior-dominated society, and was encouraged by the Church with endeavors to introduce some rules of conduct into war as a means of containing it.

According to legend, the Round Table was set up and initially maintained by wondrous means through the efforts of Merlin the magician. The magician is an important archetypal figure. He is one who sees the psychological and cultural dynamics involved, who consequently foresees the trends of future events, and endeavors to guide those entrusted with power to wise use of it. To a certain limited degree the modern scientist has taken over this role. Merlin's magic is simply science of a particular kind.

The Merlin involvement shows the antiquity of some of the legendary material. In the *Red Book of Hergest* (a late manuscript but plainly containing primitive material) certain well known knights of the Round Table appear with primitive magical attributes. Sir Kai for instance can make himself taller than a tree, and live for nine days and nights underwater.

Around the Round Table the pattern of Courtly Love is played out by the knights and their ladies, particularly in the great mutual infatuations of Lancelot and the Queen, Guinevere; and of the magical potion that determines the ill-fated love of Tristram and Isolde.

The Holy Grail legends are in a sense an interlude in the story of the Round Table Fellowship although they mystically transcend them. At the Round Table there is a seat which is left vacant, called the Siege Perilous, which is reserved for the one destined to be Grail Winner. It is also the destiny of the Grail Winner to become the king of a mystical city.

The Grail legends describe how Joseph of Arimathea brought the holy vessel from Palestine and after many miraculous adventures founded a lineage of Grail Kings. The duty of the Grail Kings was to maintain custody of the Cup and also of the Holy Lance, said to have been the spear with which the centurion Longinus pierced the side of the Christ.

So things continued until the event known as the Dolorous Stroke.

This occurred when one of two brothers, Balin and Balan, attending a feast at the Grail Castle, saw seated there an evil knight who had the power of invisibility by which means he struck down good knights in a deadly and cowardly fashion. Balin straightaway arose and killed the evil knight.

This, however, as a profound breach of chivalry and hospitality, scandalized all present and the Grail King, Pelles, rushed to attack Balin. Balin fled through the corridors of the castle. Hotly pursued, he came to a small chapel, and throwing the door open saw, over the altar, a lance with drops of blood dripping from it into a chalice. Unbeknown to him this was the Holy Lance and the Holy Grail. Thinking only of saving his own life he seized the Holy Lance and struck the pursuing King Pelles with it.

The wound was in the thigh, and immediately the whole land fell under an evil enchantment, and King Pelles was destined to lie in pain, unhealed, until such time as a knight should arrive worthy enough to win the Holy Grail. The eventual fate of Balin was similarly tragic, in that by combination of circumstances he and his brother fought each other, unaware of each other's identity, until they both fell mortally wounded.

There is much that can be read into the symbolism of this story. The evil invisible knight may be regarded as a figure of disease, pestilence and sin. Balin's action is a tragically human and well-intentioned one but overthrows the laws of chivalry, the laws of civilized human society and by extension the laws of the universe, which permit good and evil to flourish together. One is reminded of the parable of Jesus about the tares and the wheat being allowed to grow together until the final harvest. This is a traditional method of Palestinian agriculture, where the full grown wheat, standing higher than the tares, can easily be harvested, after which the remaining tares, and stubble left standing, are burned off.

Balin compounds his error by seizing sacramental vessels, or holy powers, to further his own ends, even though these ends are the preservation of his own life. This blasphemous action strikes at the creative powers of the world, as is indicated by the wound being in the Grail King's thigh, and the Land of Logres being laid to waste. The eventual fate of brother killing brother of Balin and Balan is a harsh, but not inappropriate consequence, of the original act. Even the evil knight was in a sense his brother, and all human conflict is a species of fratricide.

The stricken Land of Logres awaits the coming of a Redeemer. In a sense the Land of Logres stands for the whole world and also the human soul. The Grail Winner is Christ's representative helping to redeem the world, and in personal terms the awakening of a spiritual basis for consciousness.

The conditions for being a Grail Winner are twofold. One is a life unstained by sin or compromise of one's spiritual integrity. Thus Lancelot in spite of being the "best knight in the world" fails because of his adulterous relationship with the Queen. This causes him to be physically and spiritually blasted by the presence of the Grail—which withers up all imperfection or evil. This does not necessarily mean that all sinners are unworthy, but only that unrepentant sinners choose to keep themselves in a condition of unholiness. As in Dante, those in Hell actually prefer their self indulgence to the glories of Heaven. Their fate is self-imposed and would be ended by repentance.

The other Grail requirement involves asking an important question. What usually happens is that having located and entered the Grail castle, the seeker is invited to a banquet. Suddenly the lights go dim, and a maiden with a retinue of damsels appears, bearing the Holy Grail under a cloth of white samite. At the same time the favorite food of each one present appears miraculously on the table before them.

It is necessary that at this point the Grail seeker asks a certain question or series of questions. If he is too bemused by the marvel to speak, everything vanishes amid cries of lamentation, and he finds himself wandering lost in the wasted Land of Logres, conscious of his failure and lost opportunity.

The threefold question that needs to be asked is what is the Grail, what is the purpose of the Grail, and who is served by the Grail. These questions also relate to the manifestation and *raison-d'etre* of the human spirit, though they also apply to the whole doctrine of the Incarnation of Jesus as Christ.

The whole Arthurian and Grail literature is a rich tapestry of magical dynamics, in which many traditions are woven together. The Grail Cup has its antecedents, for instance, in the primitive Celtic Cauldron of Ceridwen, a miraculous vessel which was a cornucopia of plenty for the warriors and also a vessel of regeneration for the slain. The scholar Jessie Weston has also traced influences which go back to the ancient mysteries of Ishtar and Tammuz.

Certain episodes, such as those of Sir Gareth of Orkney, give indications of a system of mystery training grades, as he fights and defeats a succession of knights of different colored armor in order to rescue a damsel in distress. He later reappears at King Arthur's Court jousting anonymously in armor that keeps changing color. In this he becomes a version of Le Bel Inconnu, the Beautiful Unknown One, who is the hero of other Grail traditions.

The Christian elements surrounding the legends of Joseph of Arimathea originate in one of the apocryphal books of the New Testament, the Gospel of Nicodemus or Acts of Pilate. There is also the link with the legends of Glastonbury, which Joseph of Arimathea is believed to have visited and there founded the first Christian community in a little mud and wattle church. Legend has it that he struck his staff into the ground from which grew the holy thorn which still blossoms every Christmas. Allied to this are the traditions of the infant Jesus having visited this region, allegedly in company with his uncle, Joseph of Arimathea, presumably with the Phoenician merchants trading in tin.

Such stories are easily dismissed by the barren analytical mind, but they have a truth of their own which lights up the soul of man and the backdrop of the physical world, by the illumination of their higher truth.

The corpus of tradition had a profound effect upon the society of the times, in its twofold aspect as a code of laws enhancing human dignity, and as a tradition of higher truths or spiritual realities set forth in symbolic form. One aspect of this was the founding of Chivalric Orders such as the Order of the Garter, limited to 24 members, and with which the Round Table at Winchester is probably connected. The story of its originating to save a lady being compromised is a fiction or "ludibrium" of the type that is familiar in the magical tradition. Its motto in old French— *Honi Soit Qui Mal Y Pense*—carries a significance in epistemological terms far beyond the expediencies of court etiquette. Similarly, in the literary field, Rabelais' Abbey of Thelema with its motto *Do What Thou Wilt* was not so much a sanction for moral license as an emphasis on the importance and responsibility of the individual spiritual will. Again an example of spiritual truth in ribald or jesting guise.

In the Prologue to *Gargantua and Pantagruel* Rabelais advises the reader:

> . . . you must, by a sedulous lecture, and frequent meditation, break the bone, and suck out the marrow; that is, my allegorical sense, or the things I to myself propose to be signified by these Phythagorical symbols; with assured hope, that in so doing, you will at last attain to be both well-advised and valiant by the reading of them: for, in the perusal of this treatise, you shall find another kind of taste, and a doctrine of a more profound and abstruse consideration, which will disclose unto you the most glorious doctrines and dreadful mysteries, as well in what concerneth our religion, as matters of the public state, and life economical.

It will serve a useful purpose if we examine in some detail another major literary work which is a treasure-house of symbolism and a more systematic exposition of the principles involved. This is *The Divine Comedy* of Dante Allighieri.

The Divine Comedy is a great synthesis of High Medieval culture, in which the orthodox science and religious beliefs of the time are combined with an initiatory drama of the soul that is a Christianization of White Magic and the Ancient Mystery religions.

The backdrop of this drama is the Aristotelian astronomy, which Thomas Aquinas and his teacher Albertus Magnus introduced to the Christian Tradition. This pictures the Earth at the center of the universe, surrounded by the planetary crystalline spheres, the sphere of the fixed stars and that of the clear Primum Mobile, which keeps all the rest turning. Beyond this outermost heaven is the great Empyreum, the seat of God the Creator.

The Earthly Paradise, or Garden of Eden, from which man was banished by his Fall, is on the top of a high mountain in the Antipodes. Souls of the blessed are taken there by an angel in a boat. There they have the opportunity to regain the Earthly Paradise by climbing to the summit of the mountain upon which it stands. This mountain, which rises straight into the air like a huge spike, is called Mount Purgatory. It consists of a series of graded terraces, each of which corresponds to one of the Seven Deadly Sins, and upon each of which the souls of the aspiring and repentant can by penance atone for their sins on Earth. Thus we have another graded system of soul growth corresponding to the ancient mystery systems, and to the graded heavens beyond the Earth.

Within the Earth itself lies Hell. It is a gigantic cavern hollowed out, and graded into a kind of inverted mockery of the steps of Mount Purgatory and of the Heavenly Spheres. Whereas the steps of Mount Purgatory climb upwards though, the steps of hell climb down. And whereas the Crystalline Spheres of the Heavens expand further and further in even more spacious freedom to God, the Spheres of Hell are a funnel of ever constricting depravity and inhumanity finally centering in frozen darkness around the ravening Devil himself, locked in the ice and darkness of his own egocentricity, the complete negation of light, life and love.

Against this backdrop is enacted the Quest of the Soul portrayed by Dante himself, wandering in a dark forest (like the wasted Land of Logres) trying unsuccessfully to make his way to a far green hill which in fact is the Earthly Paradise. But every way that he tries he is stopped by thorns, barriers or labyrinthine diversions. This is a portrayal of the human condition, striving for salvation or visionary good but unable to realize it in terms of physical life.

To add to his dilemma he finds himself stalked by three wild beasts—a leopard, a lion and a wolf. These represent his own sinful nature. The three beasts represent sins of self-indulgence, of violence and of fraud and treachery respectively. In despair Dante is almost relieved to find a ghostly figure in the way. This figure turns out to be Virgil, the great classical savant and poet, who is Dante's ideal of what he himself would like to be.

Virgil says that he has been sent by heavenly powers to guide him but that the way is perilous and leads through Hell. Dante accepts this, and with his guide, descends into the mouth of Hell.

As they descend through the inverted grades of Hell so they see enacted the condition of the soul if it surrenders itself to any particular form of vice in preference to its ultimate heavenly home beyond the stars.

This commences with the simply aimless, neither good nor bad, who spend eternity in mobs vainly running behind colored banners rather in the manner of modern football crowds. Also in the ante-chamber of Hell is the limbo of intellectual philosophers who are too enwrapped in their own theories to respond to reality. Beyond the River Acheron are the regions of those who are victims of their own appetites in lust, gluttony, avarice or profligate waste, tossed in storm clouds of lust or wallowing like pigs in the mire, or bickering and fighting over treasure.

Within these circles are the walls of Dis, the City of Hell, which is a travesty of the Heavenly City, the New Jerusalem. Within Dis are to be found those whose rule of life is violence, whether against themselves, against God, against their fellow men, or against nature, immersed in blood, reduced to vegetable condition or wandering in a lifeless desert.

At the center of the City of Hell is a great pit within which are those whose rule of life is fraud and trickery, which leads logically to the disloyal, the betrayers of trust, and the traitors.

The depicted model of Hell is not so much a literal place of postmortem punishment as a picture of the human soul as it is. All have within them their areas of self-indulgence, of violence and of duplicity and betrayal. In modern terms it might be called the subconscious.

Having reached the center of the world Dante and Virgil climb from this freezing center of introverted pride through a passage which leads to Mount Purgatory. This they ascend and although the condition of those they meet may not seem much more enviable than those they met in Hell, there is a fundamental difference. Those in Hell revel in their iniquity, and thus imprison themselves beyond hope. Those in Purgatory have recognized a higher purpose, and though they may still be in the grip of sin they are gradually making themselves free of it. They also have the certain hope of ascending, having been purified, to the Earthly Paradise and thence to the Heavenly Spheres.

It is when they reach the Earthly Paradise, the Garden of Eden, that Dante loses his companion and guide Virgil. Virgil represents the highest in human nature, the natural man, but to ascend to the heavens one needs more than the heights of human reason and intuition, one needs Divine Grace and the guide is love, not knowledge. Therefore in place of Virgil, Dante finds Beatrice.

Whereas, in life, Virgil had represented, to Dante, the embodiment of all ambition, as a highly cultivated major poet; Beatrice was the great idealized love of his life. It was a love founded in early adolescence, and which was never in fact consummated. Beatrice is thus the embodiment of divine love; as Virgil is the embodiment of human virtue.

Beatrice proceeds to lead Dante up the heavenly ladder to the stars. There, in a way which parallels the old Mystery grades, they proceed from the Heaven of the Moon, through that of Mercury, Venus, the Sun, Mars, Jupiter and Saturn, at each stage in their journey outward from the body of the physical Earth meeting saints, or exemplary humans, appropriate to the nature of each planetary sphere.

The shadow of the Earth, in Aristotelian cosmology, was held to extend as far as Venus, and so the lower three Heavens are, in a sense, marred from their heavenly purity by this, in that the denizens of these heavens have a love for some earthly thing that counterbalances their love of God which, by itself would take them higher in the heavenly hierarchy.

In the case of those inhabiting the Moon's sphere this has resulted, like the inconstancy of the Moon, in an inconstancy of vows or divine dedication. In the spheres of Mercury and Venus respectively a great love for ideals, ambitions, or political ideals; or for individual people, come before a complete love for God.

In the heavenly spheres beyond the Earth's shadow, there are the great teachers (in the Sun's sphere), the soldiers of the church militant (in the sphere of Mars), the just (in Jupiter), and the contemplatives and martyrs (in the sphere of Saturn).

Then in the high heaven of the Fixed Stars, or the Zodiac, they meet the archetypal human patterns, of Adam, the primal man; Jesus, the god-man; the disciples Peter, John and James, who were closest to Jesus and witnessed his Transfiguration in life, and who together with the Virgin

Mary represent the four cornerstones of the Church of the Christ.

Beyond the stars, in the Heaven of the Primum Mobile, the clear sphere that sets and keeps all the others in motion, are the serried ranks of the angelic hierarchies, which have been delineated in the mystical and Gnostically influenced work of Pseudo-Dionysius, *The Celestial Hierarchies.*

Finally, in the great Empyreum of cosmic outer space is a huge white mystic rose. Dante then realizes that the persons he met in the lower heavens have been but projections of the essences of spirits clustered about God like the petals of a rose. St. Bernard of Clairvaux, the renowned monastic contemplative, finally takes over as guide from Beatrice, and brings Dante before God, who is seen as a vast throne upon which are to be discerned three colored circles combining one with another—the pure forms of mathematics being the only way that God can be represented in his essence to human speculation. But then finally a human figure is seen to coalesce with these spheres in a great ultimate synthesizing Mystery of human and divine identification.

Put into psychological terms the system of Dante is all-inclusive. It demonstrates the lowest and the highest of which the human being is capable, ranging from the most inhuman and callous rejection of love through to the most transcendent transfiguring love of all, of God and the whole Creation.

The whole spectrum of human consciousness is seen in terms of love, its out-turning or its in-turning, for the levels of Purgatory are shown as grades of distorted or misapplied love, and even the depths of hell are self-created through self-love that has festered upon itself.

Alchemy presents a similar all-inclusive system based upon a simple fundamental principle of "first matter." If we judge alchemists in the most vulgar light of looking for easy miracles or easy wealth we shall miss a great deal. Similarly if we view them with the fragmented vision of our own analytically and scientifically biased minds we shall also miss much. We shall lose sight of their magical universe, where all parts relate and cohere, and be left with a complex jigsaw of seemingly incoherent fragments.

Even so, the comprehension of alchemical texts is far from easy, for they are a combination of intentional blinds or codes exacerbated by the struggle to express physical and spiritual dynamics in terms of a nascent physical science. Underlying all however, we have a conception of process, or growth, leading to transformation.

Much depends on the correct identification of the *prima materia,*

Mutus Liber, or the Silent Book. An anonymous series of alchemical diagrams featuring a male and female alchemist, published in France in 1677. This final plate shows the final attainment of the work of transformation. Jacob's Ladder is no longer required, for the pair are drawn up via a god-like figure holding roses by two cherubim. From their mouths issue the words "Provided with eyes, thou departest." Beneath is the body of Hercules, with lion skin and club.

the first matter, with which one starts and upon which one works. It is frequently stated that this is everywhere to be found, and is overlooked or rejected by many. We suggest that the primary imagination of Coleridge, giving recognition and even existence to the world that we perceive, makes a reasonable modern definition for the *prima materia.*

The process itself commences with solution in a confused dark mass, the *massa confusa,* and then as gentle heat is applied to the womb-like retort so the solution clears. From the black stage of first solving (the *solutio,* or *nigredo,* commonly symbolized by a raven) there is at first a greening, indicating organic growth (*viriditas*), and then a whitening (*leukesis* or *albedo*) which is the stage of alchemical silver.

This is the state of normal human reflective consciousness that has progressed by the normal process of life from the infantile to individualization by the dual experiences of life, the active and negative, male and female, principles that are signified alchemically by sulphur and salt, acting upon the four elements (of which all is made) with the addition of the philosophical mercury, the principle of consciousness itself.

In alchemical writings it is an indication that something more than chemical material or processes are being described when the word "philosophical" or the phrase "of the wise" is used—as in "philosophical mercury" or "fire of the wise." No terms are used with universal consistency, and there is also use of a type of symbolism similar to heraldic bestiary.

The fish is often used as a symbol of first matter; the raven as an emblem of decomposition prior to growth; and the green lion and red lion are indications of organic forces in course of growth, proceeding possibly to the white eagle. Dragons fight with one another as do lions with unicorns. Similar symbolic use is often made of the stag.

Thus the vision of St. Eustace hunting a stag that leads him into a forest, there to confront him with a blazing cross between its antlers, has also an alchemical significance—as does the nursery rhyme of the lion and the unicorn who fought about the town.

The quest for alchemical gold is the further processing of consciousness by techniques of prayer, meditation or magic. In short, this is the manipulation of the imaginative faculty. It leads to a demonstration of all the colors of the rainbow (like Sir Gareth in the Arthurian legends), often called the *cauda pavonis* or peacock's tail. Finally there is the great experience of unification in the *mysterium conjunctionis.* At its individual level this is a manifestation of the divine spirit completely expressed in the personality. It is marked by what is called a yellowing (*xanthosis* or *citrinitatis*) which is the first foreshadowing of the distillation of the principle of bright, light, gold more precious than any found upon earth, and which is itself capable of making transformations. In religious terms this might be expressed as transfiguration.

In view of this close connection with the preserves of religion in a way that could, by the standards and conventions of the time, be condemned as blasphemous or heretical, it is small wonder that these mystical dynamics were expressed in the obscure technicalities of a new science rather than in theological terms. In so far as they are the basics of a mystical psychology, they partake in fact of both.

There was however a way of expressing the process in a religious way without the possibility of misunderstanding. This was that of the *via negativa*, expressed in a remarkable practical little book, *The Cloud of Unknowing*.

Although a religious manual written for the instruction of members of monastic orders and Christians called to contemplative prayer, it is interesting to note that its introduction contains caveats that very closely resemble the type of warnings that often preface alchemical writings. "In the Name of the Father and of the Son and of the Holy Ghost I charge and beg you, with all the strength and power that love can bring to bear, that whoever you may be who possess this book. you should neither read, write, or mention it to anyone, nor allow it to be read, written or mentioned by anyone unless that person is in your judgment really and wholly determined to follow Christ perfectly." And in more down to earth fashion, "I do not mind at all if the loud-mouthed, or flatterers, or the mock-modest, or fault-finders, gossips, tittle-tattlers, tale-bearers, or any sort of grumbler, never see this book. I have never meant to write it for them. So they can keep out of it. And so can all those learned men (and unlearned too) who are merely curious."

The technique that it teaches is one of raising consciousness to a direct awareness of God. This is not by an evocative use of religious symbols but by a complete lack of them. The mind is schooled to empty itself of all that is not God, by selecting a single word, perhaps the word "God" itself, or "Jesus," or simply "Help!", and repeating it continuously. This has to be accompanied by right intent and love of God, hence the author's formal warnings, otherwise it is liable to degenerate into a mechanical kind of self-hypnosis leading to hysteria or neurosis. The anonymous author puts down such abuses to the devil's wiles, for the intention is not to limit consciousness to a narrow constricting band but to widen it out in an expression of love of God unbounded by intellectual speculation or imaginative visions.

There are direct parallels between this practice of the *Cloud of Unknowing* and Eastern forms of mantra-yoga where a pious phrase or holy word may be the focus of attention for long periods. The Orthodox Church has a similar type of practice in the Jesus prayer: "Lord Jesus Christ, Son of God, have mercy on me, a sinner," which is prayed vocally or silently, sometimes in time to slow rhythmic breathing.

The process, for all its simplicity, is very similar in action to the complex symbolic structure of the alchemical process. The one-pointed emotional direction towards God is the heat applied to the hermetically sealed retort. The contents of ordinary consciousness are dissolved and vaporized by this steady heat and pressure. A purification sets in by this distillation of consciousness and the later stages are the contact of the soul with God and the transfiguration and transmutation of consciousness that this entails. This final gold-making process, based upon loving aspiration, is the *mysterium conjunctionem*.

The Jews of medieval Europe, who by their semi-ostracism formed a society within a society, became vehicles for new ideas and an international counterculture. It is significant that Wolfram von Eschenbach, on claiming his version of the Holy Grail legend to be the most accurate, traced his source via "a Jew of Toledo." Toledo was a great international trading center and also linked to Moorish influence—which was also a source of stimulus for new religious and scientific ideas.

The Jews had their own magical subculture which had already produced the *Sepher Yetzirah*, or *Book of Formation*. In the early fourteenth century a new and major work appeared that was to have a profound impact upon the magical theories of the Renaissance. This was the *Zohar*, or *Book of Splendor*, for the most part written in Aramaic and claimed to be of great antiquity. Scholarly opinion is of the view however that it cannot confidently be traced back further than Moses de Leon, a Sephardic Jew of Spain, in 1305, who is consequently credited with being its author, though he is more likely to be the editor of oral traditions.

It is a vast book of mystical exegesis on the Pentateuch, and as far as the Western Christian world is concerned, has had more influence through piecemeal interpretation by various Gentile enthusiasts, down to the present day, who have based their own theories upon it. In fact it forms but the tip of an iceberg of Jewish mystical writings, most of which are not available in translation.

The Zohar to a large degree incorporates within itself the known Jewish Qabalistic schools of the previous century or so—including the

School of Gerona of which Isaac the Blind was the most prominent member (active 1190–1210); the School of Segovia, of which Joseph Ha-Levi Abulafia (1234–l305) achieved prominence as physician and financier in the court of King Sancho IV of Castile; and the School of Abulafia— named after Abraham ben Samuel Abulafia (1240–*c.* 1292) who in 1281 narrowly escaped being burned at the stake after attempting, following a call from God, to convert Pope Martin IV to Judaism. He later received another revelation from God after which, in 1254, he announced himself as the Messiah, predicting the end of the world and the restoration of Israel in 1296. Thousands of Jews believed him and prepared to return to Palestine but many thousands more did not, and their hostility forced him to flee to the small island of Comino, near Malta, for many years.

He was not alone in his predictions of the end of the world, which was "in the air" in the whole Christian world not only prior to the year 1000 A.D. (superficially the obvious date for the millennium) but also as a result of the predictions and speculations of Joachim de Fiore, who by biblical analysis and some degree of assumed direct revelation, considered the world to be structured historically into three epochs—the Age of the Father, the Age of the Son, and the Age of the Holy Spirit. The Age of the Father was that of the Old Testament Times; that of the Son ran from the birth of Christ to 1260; and the New Age of the Holy Spirit was about to dawn. The doctrine was given credence by three Popes although in general millenarianism was often a focus for anti-clerical feeling. It is an important phase in the history of ideas as these mass movements anticipating the Millennium are an early manifestation of trends that came to fruition in Protestantism, and democratic and revolutionary ideas of the eighteenth and nineteenth centuries.

The Jewish Qabalists who taught in a millennial fashion were therefore not so much typical of Qabalism as typical of the times. It is true however that much millennial thought stemmed originally from Jewish Messianic aspirations.

The Qabalah derives from a Hebrew word meaning "to receive," implying that it is an oral tradition passed from mouth to ear. In the Zoharic tradition it consists of high flying speculative exegesis of biblical texts, principally from the first five books of the Old Testament.

This speculation is considerably expanded by the use of certain conventions whereby words can be transformed into other words. As Hebrew letters also serve as numbers, one convention is to add up the number values of words or phrases and to substitute any other word or phrase of the same numerical equivalent. Thus the words of Gen. 18.2, "Lo, three men stood by him" is equivalent numerically to "these are Michael, Gabriel and Raphael"—three principal archangels.

Another convention is to regard each letter of a word as the initial of the words of a sentence. In this fashion the first word of Genesis, "In the beginning" (BERAShITh), can be expanded to "In the beginning God saw that Israel would accept the Law."

Other conventions are the use of initial and final letters of words to make other words; the joining together of words; and the arrangement of certain passages into squares and then reading their possible meaning in different directions.

Sentences of similar length may also be juxtaposed and used as the basis for forming other words, and meanings to words or sentences may also be used as the basis for anagrams.

This devious manipulation of biblical texts in a literal and arbitrary fashion sounds to modern ears to be a completely worthless occupation. However it was done for the most part with impressive sincerity—for the text is seen as the actual word of God and therefore capable of infinite expansion if approached in a reverent and aspiring state of mind.

It may well be thought that by such means one could prove anything, yet this indeed is perhaps the strength of the method. It can act rather after the fashion of a Rorschach psychological test, or a Jungian word association, bypassing the rational faculty of the mind to get to that which lies beyond. But instead of contemplating inkblots in a consulting room where personal introspection is the expressed or implied aim, it is a contemplation of holy writings in a reverent and pious fashion. There is therefore a possibility that what will be revealed may well be, not arbitrary nonsense (though this is not entirely to be excluded), but the lineaments of the structure of the psyche. From this vast mass of free textual interpretation will emerge patterns that derive from the imaginative faculty divorced from external perceptions. Being free, through this method, from interpreting external sense impressions, it selects and arranges concepts that reflect its own structure.

In this exegetical work the Qabalistic rabbis felt they were describing the lineaments of God and his mode of manifestation. Be this as it may, it seems evident from modern comparisons with other religions and mythologies that they were in fact describing the lineaments of the human spirit and its expression in psychological terms. Of course it can be argued that the human soul is a reflection of God, made in God's image, so one is not necessarily reducing or "explaining away" Qabalistic mystical intuitions as "mere psychology." Truth may perhaps exist in similar forms on various levels.

The principal structure emerging from Qabalistic exegesis is a diagram known as the Tree of Life, which was to form the backbone for most later magical theory and practice.

The Tree of Life is, in essence, a description of how God manifests himself to the world. It was later to be extended, principally by Gentile interpreters, to a description of the inner structure of the world itself. This is quite an important sea-change, the implications of which become far-reaching. If the Tree of Life is a description of God then it pertains to mystical theology; if it is a description of the Creation then it is science, albeit of a metaphysical nature. It is the fusion and even confusion of these two approaches that characterizes much of the Gentile approach to magic, from the Renaissance to the present day. Blurring these distinctions can result in considerable misunderstandings.

The Qabalistic idea of God is as a series of Emanations or Rays (called Sephiroth). The Source of these Emanations is a Great Sea of Non-being, the Un-Create, called variously the AIN (Nothingness), the AIN SOPH (the Limitless), and AIN SOPH AUR (the Limitless Light), the closer that it gets to actual creation.

The first manifestation of God is observable to the subsequent created beings as a fount of ineffable light, called the Crown of Creation. The presence of God within his own Creation takes place by means of self reflection. There being nothing else in existence but God he makes a projection of himself, so introducing the principle of reflection and duality. This principle by its very existence brings into being the archetype of form, which is based upon three. If there is two, subject and object, then there is also the possibility of the relationship between them which is a third factor.

It was this principle which was seized upon by later Christian enthusiasts, such as Pico della Mirandola, who saw in it a description of the Christian Trinity—God the Father giving birth to God the Son with the Holy Spirit being created from their love for each other. Needless to say the Jews did not take kindly to such interpretations, and neither was the Papacy encouraging towards amateur theologians speculating on other creeds.

From this fundamental threefold establishment of God in a Creation of his own making, more personal attributes of God follow—again reflecting the threefold system. His further emanations are therefore of Magnificence as a Merciful Just King, balanced by Awesomeness as a Just and Stern Punisher of transgression, resolved by the concept of a Messianic Beautiful Savior. This latest emanation is called Beauty and, as it is the central one in the completed Tree of Life, it signifies the innate beauty and harmonizing principle of God behind the Creation.

From thence there is a further triad of Divine Emanations in which God is seen principally in terms of Victory and Successful Endeavor, then of Glory, and finally as the firm Foundation of the whole Universe that he later creates. These concepts are resumed at the end of the Lord's Prayer as "the Kingdom, the Power and the Glory."

The Tree of Life thus appears, in its diagrammatic depiction of God, as three oval-shaped veils which surround three triads of Emanations. A tenth Emanation completes the diagram, at the base of the three triads, called the Kingdom, and this represents God's presence on Earth to his creatures. The Jews called it "the Shekinah"—the "presence of God" that could be sensed within the Temple or the Tabernacle of the Ark of the Covenant.

Upon this simple structure, based on a triune configuration three times repeated, a complex range of mystical symbolism can be built. As illustration we can take two that appear in original Jewish Qabalistic writings. One is the Lightning Flash, which shows the descent of power from the all-Highest to the presence-of-God-in-the-World. Another arrangement that can be superimposed upon the Tree is that of the Three Pillars. These have a correspondence with the Pillars of Solomon's Temple and their symbolism is considerably elaborated in the rites of Freemasonry. In simple general terms the right-hand Pillar (called Jachin) symbolizes the active, male aspects of God; the left-hand Pillar (called Boaz) symbolizes the passive, female attributes. The Pillars are usually represented in dark and light colors respectively, though not in a sense of good and evil, for God must be, by his very nature, all-Good. The central pillar is provided by whomever stands between these two Pillars and represents a line of growth in consciousness from lowest to highest. The awareness of the physical appearance of God is the lowest point, and the ultimate union with God, outside and beyond creation itself, is the highest point.

It is the Qabalistic system, at any rate as interpreted by Gentiles, that forms the blueprint of Western magical theory and practice since the Renaissance, through the considerable impetus and publicity given to it by Pico della Mirandola. There were Gentiles who knew of it and worked with it before Pico however. Of such was Raymond Lully (1236-1315), of Majorca. He was the first Christian Qabalist, who after a youth devoted to the arts of war and erotic poetry experienced a conversion and became a man of great piety and learning. He learned Hebrew and Arabic to aid his

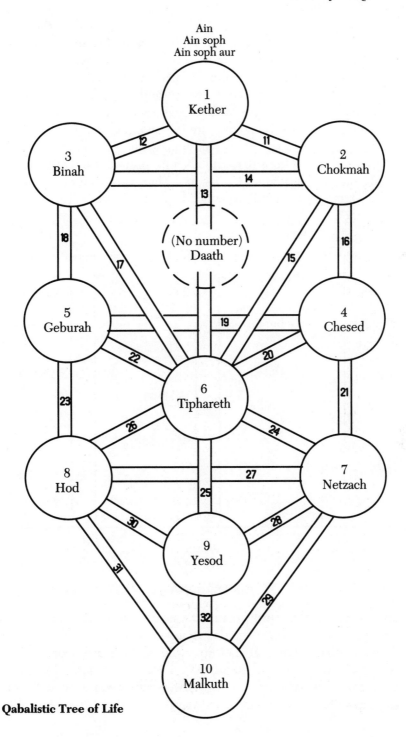

Qabalistic Tree of Life

researches, and lost his life by martyrdom in trying to convert the Moors of North Africa to Christianity. His reputation as "Doctor Illuminatus" and his unorthodox pursuits were however not such as to encourage the church to confer sanctity upon him, his martyrdom notwithstanding. It is difficult to judge just how much alchemical and magical lore interpolated the Christian orthodoxy of the Middle Ages. Fulcanelli has demonstrated that a series of alchemical statues are incorporated into Chartres cathedral, and Gothic architecture has inherent within it mathematical measurements and proportions that could be interpreted in a mysticalfashion after the ancient tradition of Pythagoras. There has been some speculation about the sudden efflorescence of Gothic architecture, with its

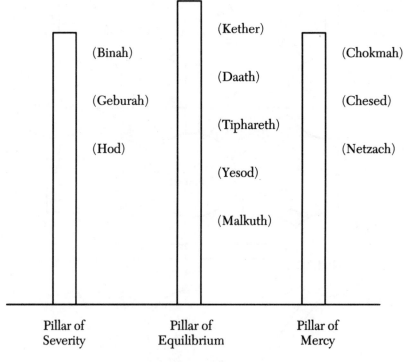

The Three Pillars

soaring aspiring otherwordly nature. Some even feel that some physical alchemical manufacturing of gold must have been achieved to pay for the great mass of buildings that shot up, often in otherwise poor andbackward communities. Farfetched though this may seem there is certainly a mystical tradition in the old building trade, which is expressed in the symbolism and rites of Freemasonry.Interwoven with all this high philosophic speculation is also a "lower" side, evidence of which is the expression of similar ideas by the common people. This can also be seen in the old cathedrals in the form of "green men," faces whose hair is formed of leaves, much of which may cover the face. This is evidence of the "Old Religion" which continued in various forms, in folklore customs such as the Maypole dance and other nature festivals. The Church was generallywise enough to try to sanctify rather than to suppress them—although Puritans later took a sterner, less tolerant view.

Along with this subculture are the various herbal remedies, charms and potions of the local wise man or wise woman. We should remember that these might be the only means of assistance to those in trouble in times when doctors and veterinary surgeons, where they existed, were not readily available to the poor, or possessed of a science much in advance of the country cures anyway. Official doctors put their faith in academic authorities such as Aristotle and Galen rather than in contemporary traditional indigenous beliefs. There was little to choose between them in effectiveness and possibly the balance of evidence is in favor of the indigenous country cure. These were neither good nor evil in themselves. Just as drugs can be used as medicines or poisons, so it was possible to have charms and spells of goodwill or ill will performed or commissioned at the behest of those who were either benevolently or malevolently inclined. The root of the morality is in the motive rather than the technique.

Some of the old remedies eventually found their way into early medical science. There were various books of magic and spells circulating in manuscript form, the most well-known of which was called the *Picatrix*. Most country lore was however orally transmitted through families by tradition, as might be expected in a populace which had little book-learning or skill in reading, even if they had the opportunity to consult manuscripts, which in the days before printing were the prerogative of the wealthy, and mostly produced by monks.

The Temple of Pansophia. An eighteenth-century symbolic drawing from an anonymous work, "Compass of the Wise" published in Berlin, 1779. The masonic influence is shown in the Squared Pavement, the two Pillars Jachin and Boaz, and the Royal Arch of the heavens above. Again, the usual principles of dual polarity apply with celestial influences from the Superior World working down to the seven pillared House of Wisdom. Signs of the Four Elements also appear at the base and capitals of the pillars.

The Temple of the Rosicrucian Brotherhood. This plate, from Theophilus Schweighardt's *Speculum Sophicum Rhodo-Stauroticum* (Constantz, 1618) is by no means as ludicrous as it might at first appear. In the spirit of a Mystery *ludibrium* high serious matters are presented in jest, and the diagram is full of Rosicrucian symbolism. This includes sinners being saved from an underground dungeon, the new stars that appeared in the constellations of the Swan and the Serpent in 1604, all being under the shadow of Jehovah's wings, the winged messages. etc.

Chapter 5
Renaissance Magi

A key figure in the development of magic in the Renaissance was Marsilio Ficino, a scholar, physician and priest, who was employed by the Prince Cosimo de Medici as a translator of ancient works from the Greek. In 1453 he was commissioned to translate the works of Plato, but this task was postponed in favor of one which was considered even more important—the translation of the *Corpus Hermeticum*.

This was a collection of manuscripts that resulted from the confluence of spiritual pagan ideas and early Christianity in the first to third centuries A.D. To the men of the medieval and Renaissance period, however, the *Corpus Hermeticum* was thought to date from remote antiquity. There was a general belief in a primeval Golden Age in which Moses, the author of the *Pentateuch*, and the Egyptian priest Hermes were contemporaries.

The fact that part of the Hermetic literature made reference to a new religion, obviously Christianity, was held to be evidence for the divine inspiration and accurate prophecy of the supposed ancient Egyptian. Hermes was accorded the distinction of being a divinely inspired pagan, and his figure appears in ecclesiastical art of the period, as for example in the mosaics at the Cathedral in Siena.

The fact that there were also magical elements in the *Hermetica* intrigued Marsilio Ficino and caused him to experiment along these lines. The work that he did we should regard today as the beginnings of simple psychotherapy and quite harmless. But Ficino realized that his researches could possibly be misunderstood and condemned as the conjuration of spirits. He was thus particularly careful to state that he was concerned simply with *natural* magic rather than *angelic* or *daimonic* magic.

The general idea of the Universe of those times followed the world view of Aristotle which received its supreme spiritual exegesis in the *Divine Comedy* of Dante. In simple terms it could be resolved into a three-tier structure, with the earth at the center, the celestial crystalline spheres between, and the angels, heavenly powers and God beyond that. There could thus be two levels of influence from higher levels of the universe to the lower. There was the influence of the heavenly angelic powers upon the planetary bodies, which caused their motion, and there was the influence of these planetary bodies upon the earth beneath.

The powers of heaven were definitely the exclusive prerogative of the church and jealously guarded. However, the powers of the planetary spheres upon the things of earth was another matter, partaking entirely of the natural world. Hence Ficino's emphasis on *natural* magic.

It was held that the seven visible planetary bodies that moved erratically against the stable backdrop of the fixed stars were representative of seven types of influence. It was therefore possible to regard things as under Solar, Lunar, Mercurial, Venusian, Martian, Jovian, or Saturnian influence—or a mixture of all or any. The words still retain a meaning of sorts in current language.

Great lists could be compiled of the various correspondences between these powers and terrestrial objects; one of the most famous of these was that of Cornelius Agrippa, *De Occulta Philosophia* published in 1531.

Thus the profession of scholar tended to fall under Mercurial and Saturnian influences, the one tending to books and learning, the other to serious philosophical deliberation. It could thus happen that scholars might become unwell or depressed by too much Mercurial and Saturnian influence. Ficino felt that this could be remedied by concentration of compensating influences, in this instance those of Venus and the Sun, which could be most simply done by walking the fields on bright and sunny days.

As an elaboration of this, however, he took note of the actual positions of the planetary bodies in relation to his native Florence and plotted their future angular configurations. This is the science of astrology, which is of immense antiquity, and still pursued today though with less universal recognition, and subject to considerable popular journalistic debasement. It is a highly mathematical computation of the angles of incidence of the Sun, Moon and planets to particular points on the Earth's surface over a specific period of time, and their subsequent interpretation.

Whether the heavens are regarded as a kind of symbolic clock, or whether actual subtle influences are transmitted across interplanetary space is a matter for theoretical debate among astrologers.

Ficino went further than the analysis of character, and prediction of future trends, that are the staple basis of astrological investigation. He, as a doctor, wished to use the astrological influences in a remedial or preventive fashion.

Thus if study of a personal astrological chart indicated that a certain configuration of planets was likely to produce unfortunate effects then he thought it should be possible to counteract this tendency by concentration on counter-influences.

To this end Ficino composed hymns or songs devoted to each of the various planets, based on a symbolic harmonic structure of his own devising, and aided with representations of the various planetary bodies in the form of lights and appropriate symbolic objects. It is possible that certain famous paintings, such as Botticelli's "Primavera" or "Venus," may have been intended as symbolic figures with this intention. These he grouped about him in carefully calculated ways and so aimed to counterbalance any unfortunate influences. This was Ficino's natural magic, and although it included the production of talismans—parchment or metallic discs with a particular planetary influence—he was careful to emphasize that it simply utilized and channeled natural forces and had nothing to do with conjuring spirits.

By his caution Ficino escaped censure by the church but his tentative beginnings were seized upon and extended by the brilliantly gifted Pico della Mirandola, who knew Hebrew as well as Latin and Greek, and introduced the Jewish Qabalah to the system. This was very dangerous because the Qabalah dealt with angels and archangels and the emanations of God himself and so another layer was added to the magical technology. No longer was it simply a case of utilizing natural forces as Ficino had attempted, but now angels and archangels could be appropriately conjured to operate through the various planetary bodies and thus produce effects upon Earth.

Pico, at the tender age of twenty-four, arrived in Rome with 900 theses of universal philosophy which he offered to defend against all comers. And his advocacy of the Qabalah was forthrightly proclaimed as a means of converting the Jews to Christianity through their own mystical teachings.

Some of Pico's theses were adjudged to be heretical however. He was later imprisoned by the Inquisition and knew many vicissitudes as alternate popes condemned or proclaimed his work.

It is from Pico that we have the start of the tradition of Gentile interpretations of the Qabalah which are somewhat at variance from the original Jewish mystical conceptions. In the Gentile systems the tenfold Tree
of Life is used as a cataloging system for objects in the created world as
well as an outline of the lineaments of God.

In the original Qabalistic system God may be worshipped under all
or any of his ten aspects or emanations. Later embellishment provides
archangels corresponding to each of these divine emanations. From each
of the archangels there then depends a choir of angels. And then—a most
significant and far-reaching step—each is allocated one of the planetary
bodies.

We now have a situation where tables of correspondences can be
drawn up giving appropriate divine names for invocation, and archangels
and angelic powers for conjuration in any of the various provinces of life.

Thus whereas Marsilio Ficino might be content to open himself to
Solar and Venusian influences by culling appropriate flowers or contemplating symbolic pictures, the *spiritual* magic of Pico would add the invocation of spirits. It is not surprising that the church took alarm at this new
development, which did not stop at utilizing the powers of God and his
angels by knowledge and utilization of appropriate formulae. Their fears
were not allayed by claims from Pico that it was by Qabalistic magic that
Jesus performed his miracles. The consequences were enormous. On the
one hand Jesus was seen to be admitted as simply an operator of techniques; or on the other hand anyone by studying the art of magic could
produce miracles like Jesus.

In its dilemma the church had hardly helped itself by its general attitude towards miracles and divine intervention. Whatever the fine theological distinctions, to a largely illiterate and superstitious populace the
church seemed to be a custodian of magical powers. This is so to this day
among certain backward communities. In Italy and Spain saints' images
are popularly accorded miraculous powers that go far beyond informed
theological opinion. Images have even been physically assaulted when
the required magical effect (for instance, rain in a period of drought) has
not been forthcoming.

The doctrine that the Mass is effective no matter what the spiritual
condition of the priest, and irrespective of the cooperation of the congregation, led to a similar state of affairs. The service was carried out by
priests in a language unintelligible to the congregation, and where there
was very little interest required of them. This, together with the rever-

ence paid to the Host, and the dogma of physical transubstantiation, easily encouraged a superstitious attitude.

Thus magic, holding common ground between infant science and established religion, found itself in the center of very far reaching and bitter controversies. The Renaissance meant a disturbing of traditional medieval values, and magic was a part of this urge for speculative inquiry that threatened to overthrow the pious Christian medieval world view. The new Renaissance man wanted to manipulate the creation to his own advantage, not simply be a humble observer of it.

Similarly magic was at the center of the trauma of the Reformation. It had common ground with both Catholic and Protestant sides and by that very fact tended to be condemned by both.

From a psychological point of view, in the sense of regarding magic as the technology of the imagination, the old liturgical customs of the church did have a place. Although capable of providing a hotbed of superstition, the awe-inspiring mystery engendered in the pious believer was such as to lift consciousness beyond that of daily common perception. And though this begets a credulousness that makes all evidence of miraculous or unusual phenomena suspect, there is a hard core of fact that cannot easily be explained away; of healings and conversions and visions that do not appear in a more religiously prosaic Protestant society. The burning of votive candles at the shrines of the various saints is not so very far distant in practical terms from the mystical planetary lamps of Marsilio Ficino and the images of the powers of planetary bodies such as Botticelli's Venus—which might well be compared with a contemporary Madonna. It is true that the theological ideas behind the cult of the Blessed Virgin Mary and the natural magic of Marsilio Ficino might differ substantially but they follow very similar outward practices.

It may be that the church realized this, which caused a hostility towards magical theory and practice on parallel lines to the opposition engendered to the Mithraic religion, which in its outward forms had much in common with Christian worship and liturgical practice.

The common people were little affected by the writings of Ficino or Pico della Mirandola and others however, which were for the most part inaccessible to them. The popular magic of the herbal, love philter and charm had survived intact from antiquity, little affected by theories of the intelligentsia, though the atmosphere of mystery engendered about the ceremonial of the church meant that a considerable degree of popular magical belief centered about the Eucharist.

From popular ideas of the theological subtleties of physical transubstantiation of the bread and wine sprang beliefs such as the bread turning into the actual lamb, and parallels with ideas of alchemical transmutation. Fragments of communion wafers, particularly if blessed, became important ingredients in magical formulae at a popular level.

In the first prayer book of Edward VI was the instruction that the bread should be placed directly by the priest into the communicant's mouth so as to prevent its theft. Nonetheless some still managed to secrete it and take it home as, for example, James Device, one of the Lancashire witches, in 1612.

Similar beliefs attached to various other religious practices, and just as attendance at Mass, besides bringing spiritual blessings, also was held to have physical beneficial side effects, such as safe journeys, inducing fertility in barren women, helping childbirth, curing fevers and toothache, protecting livestock and recovering lost property, so baptism, confirmation, the churching of women after childbirth, marriage, and the rite of supreme unction all developed a magical reputation. The belief that children "came on better" after baptism, still held to in some rural areas in our own times, can be traced back to the medieval belief that it was essential for the child's physical survival. Also the baptism of livestock in the sixteenth and seventeenth centuries to preserve them from harm. Thus holy water became a coveted magical commodity and it became necessary to lock this up as well as the bread and wine.

There was of course also the Catholic reverence for relics and medallions which in the popular mind were indistinguishable in purpose from the talismans or lucky charms of the wonderworker. This ranged from the belief in the efficacy of holy bells as a remedy for thunder, to the throwing of an *agnus dei* onto a conflagration as a means of helping to put it out (*cf.* Keith Thomas: *Religion and the Decline of Magic*).

Here again there is a narrow dividing line between the consecrated object and the talismanic object of Ficino. To aid his concentration of planetary forces Ficino would use plates of the appropriate metal (copper in the case of Venus, iron for Mars, silver for the Moon, etc.) as a kind of physical focus. With the angelic magic of Pico della Mirandola superimposed on this we have the natural transition to magical talismans inscribed with divine and angelic names and consecrated with due elaborate ceremony. What, it could be asked, is the difference between one of these talismans and say a consecrated medallion or an *agnus dei*?

Thus we find a Puritan reaction to Roman Catholic religious practice on the grounds that it was superstitious and magical; yet at the same time magic comes in by the back door in the Puritan's attitude to the bible and his conceptions of Providence.

Just as the prophetic tradition in Israel sought to explain major calamities as a divine judgment, so the Protestant regarded natural calamities as having been engineered from a higher level. Thus an incidence of fire at Tiverton was ascribed to allowing preparations for market day to profane the Sabbath. And the Elizabethan prayer book emphasizes that sickness is a visitation from God. Some Puritans compiled books describing judgments that had befallen different types of sinner, from murderers and adulterers to blasphemers and Sabbath-breakers. With this went the corollary belief that the pious man could influence events by his good living and petitionary prayer.

While some taught that it was immoral to pray for material benefit, even the relief of sickness, there were others who prayed prior to sitting at the gaming tables or even prior to committing highway robbery! The middle way of belief was that one's petitionary requests should be of a seemly nature; not likely to result in another's personal disadvantage; and should preferably relate to the general public good.

The same criteria have always exercised reasonable practioners of magic—and they also apply to those who administer the utilization of physical technology and science.

There is also a very narrow dividing line between those who attempt to improve the human condition by prayer and those who would use quasi-magical formulae. In moral terms there is little, if any, difference between the aims of science and the aims of prayer or magic. It is simply that the *modus operandi* differs:

(1) in prayer one requests manipulation of the created universe by God or his agents;

(2) in science one manipulates parts of the created universe oneself;

(3) in magic one does the same though with the utilization or cooperation of non-physical agencies.

All three modes of action can be abused, or used for trivial ends. To the medieval mind both (2) and (3) would seem impious. To the modern materialist scientific mind (1) and (3) would seem impractical. The magical or neo-Platonic mind would, however, see (3) as the link and reconciler of the other two, without condemning either.

The polarity between science and religion was by no means clear cut. Galileo was a pious Catholic, so was Copernicus. Calvin did not object to the Copernican theory on theological grounds. He opposed it because a moving Earth seemed ridiculous!

We thus have a long period of confusion between the due preserves of religion (knowledge of God) and those of science (knowledge of the mechanics of creation)—with magic holding a confused ground in between. This difficulty lasted from the beginnings of the scientific method with say Roger Bacon in the thirteenth century until the great geological and evolutionary controversies of the nineteenth century.

Intermingled with all this were theories of society and consequent political experiment and complications. One of the latest Renaissance magi was the Dominican Thomasso Campanella. Born in 1568 he was imprisoned in 1599 in Naples for his involvement in the Calabrian revolt against the Spanish, in which he had hoped politically to express his utopian ideas of a City of the Sun—a combination of the two important concepts:

(1)   the central importance physically and philosophically of the Sun;

(2)   the fourfold pattern of a city that is a representation of the cosmos.

Contemporaneously, his fellow Dominican, Giordano Bruno, was burned at the stake in 1600 for heresy. And although Bruno has been hailed as a martyr for science, recent scholarship has revealed that he was in fact advocating a new religious system wherein the solar system was of the pattern of many other suns and systems created by God. This is close to the physical pattern of the universe revealed by modern science but Bruno's motives were principally religious. He saw man as capable of expanding his consciousness by his own efforts until be became as God. In another sense this was a system of magical initiation.

Campanella was sentenced, after considerable torture, to perpetual imprisonment in 1603, having escaped death by feigning insanity. He spent his time writing, with the intention of interesting the pope in his religious ideas, which still centered about the importance of the sun, and the need to build a great City of the Sun which, if sponsored by the pope, he felt could usher in a new millenium under a reformed, universal religion.

In this he was eventually relatively successful. He was consulted frequently by Pope Urban VIII during 1628 and released from imprisonment in 1629. The following year he received permission to found a college in Rome for training missionaries in accordance with his religious beliefs.

There is good evidence to suggest that he actually practiced magic with the pope in 1628, as a means of neutralizing the possible maleficent effects of the eclipses of the Moon and of the Sun that year. An unauthorized publication of this fact by rivals caused his temporary loss of favor, though his books on the type of magic they used (which was similar to that of Ficino) were officially examined and cleared of heresy or superstition.

Campanella's idea of the ideal city is worth examination and comparison with similar ideas before and since. The City as an archetype of ideal heavenly and earthly society is fundamental to Dante's *Divine Comedy*, and is also to be found biblically in the Book of Revelations, where the Heavenly City, the New Jerusalem, descends from on high at the end of the world.

In the New English Bible this is described in the following terms:

Then I saw a new heaven and a new earth, for the first heaven and the first earth had vanished, and there was no longer any sea. I saw the holy city, new Jerusalem, Coming down out of heaven from God, made ready like a bride adorned for her husband. I heard a loud voice proclaiming from the throne: "Now at last God has his dwelling among men! He will dwell among them and they shall be his people, and God himself will be with them. He will wipe every tear from their eyes; there shall be an end to death, and to mourning and crying and pain; for the old order has passed away."

The holy city of Jerusalem is then described as being four-square, with the number twelve playing an important part in the design. There are three gates at each side of the four sides of the city, and the city is twelve thousand furlongs high, wide and long; with a wall 144 cubits high.

There is no temple in the city for it contains God himself and thus has no need of one. All the light there stems from the glory of God, which makes Sun and Moon unnecessary too. In the center is the throne of God and of the Lamb, from which flows a river of the water of life, sparkling like crystal, with a tree on either side (similar to the Garden of Eden), yielding twelve crops of fruit and with leaves for the healing of nations.

Thomasso Campanella's city, which he hoped to establish on earth as herald of a new age, was constructed on similar principles, with the added refinement that like Aristotle's and Dante's view of the structure of things, it had seven concentric circular walls called after the seven traditional planets. The fourfold theme was again dominant. Four main roads led to the center where there was a circular domed temple. Within the dome were representations of all the stars, with two great maps on the altar, a juxtaposition of the heavens and of the earth.

The walls of the city were to be like a practical encyclopedia with representations of all forms of life, art, science, culture and mathematics. A Sun Priest would rule the City, assisted by three others, each responsible for a department of Power, Love and Wisdom. All property would be held in common and life regulated harmoniously by consultation of astrological influences.

This is worth comparing with a passage from the *Picatrix*, to most intents a magical recipe book that circulated during the fourteenth and fifteenth centuries. This also gives plans for a magical city "in the East of Egypt," twelve miles long, within which is a castle with four gates, the symbolism being an interesting combination of biblical (from the Vision of Ezekiel) and Egyptian.

> On the Eastern gate he placed the form of an Eagle; on the Western gate, the form of a Bull; on the Southern gate the form of a Lion; and on the Northern gate he constructed the form of a Dog. Into these images he introduced spirits who spoke with voices, nor could anyone enter the gates of the City except by their permission. There he planted trees in the midst of which was a great tree which bore the fruit of all generations. On the summit of the castle he caused to be raised a lighthouse (rotunda) the color of which changed every day until the seventh day after which it returned to the first color, and so the City was illuminated with these colors. Near the City there was abundance of waters in which dwelt many kinds of fish. Around the circumference of the City he placed engraved images and ordered them in such manner that by their virtue the inhabitants were made virtuous and withdrawn from all wickedness and harm. The name of the City was Adocentyn.

The cities so conceived are symbolic models of the universe and in the light of modern knowledge, and particularly the Jungian psychology, we can see that they are unifying symbol systems that give a sense and direction to psychological integration. They are in fact patterns of the ideal structure of the psyche, projected onto the screen of the speculative and the unknown. Thus they appear as cosmologies in the world view of Aristotle or Dante or John of Patmos, or as utopian social structures in the case of the backward-looking *Picatrix* (allegedly describing ancient Egyptian practice) or the forward-looking visionary, Campanella.

The Sun as the great life-giving luminary of the sky had received special veneration in pagan times. The Christianized Aristotelianism that placed the earth in the center of the universe had obscured this high regard for the sun. The new scientific theories that the sun was the center about which the earth and other planets revolved, revived the sense of mystical exaltation that the sun naturally attracted to itself. It was for try

Geocentric System of the Universe. The Aristotelian view of the universe, showing the four Elements of Earth, Water, Air and Fire in the center, surrounded by the crystalline spheres bearing the planets and beyond that those of the Fixed Stars and the Primum Mobile. This version, from a sixteenth-century Dutch manuscript, shows an extra sphere between the latter. Note that all is contained within God as emphasized by the legend around the edge: "Heavenly empyreum inhabited by God and all the Elect."

with the new science that Giordano Bruno was burned at the stake. Similar ideas can also be seen in the thinking of others.

Copernicus had described the sun as "ruler of the universe" and central "throne" of the universe and Kepler and Galileo found such arguments attractive enough to cause them to try to prove the thesis scientifically. For Kepler, light and power radiating from the center of the universe was convincingly representative of God the Father; and Galileo used the following description of the Sun as center of the universe, rotating upon its own axis:

> If we consider the mobility of the Sun, and the fact that it is the fount of light which (as I shall conclusively prove) illuminates not only the Moon and the Earth but all the other planets, which are inherently dark, then I believe that it will not be entirely unphilosophical to say that the Sun, as chief minister of Nature and in a certain sense the heart and soul of the universe, infuses by its own rotation not only light but also motion into other bodies which surround it. And just as if the motion of the heart should cease in an animal, all other motions of its members would also cease, so if the rotation of the Sun were to stop, the rotations of all the planets would stop too.

Although there is no evidence to suggest that Galileo was anything but a devout and orthodox Roman Catholic, the correspondence of the sun with the heart in the physical body is in accordance with astrological and Qabalistic symbolical correspondences, which suggests that science and magic were closely interrelated. It is interesting to note that with Galileo the central sun has become the provider of motion for the universe, rather than the peripheral Primum Mobile of Aristotle.

The separation of magical ideas from physical science did not occur until the movement in the seventeenth century that sees the great divide between the age-old conception of the universe as an organism and a new conception of the universe as a mechanism. During this period contemporary writers held very different attitudes and even changed their ideas in the course of a few years.

William Gilbert (1544–1603) was a scientist of the old school. In his investigations into magnetism, he combined a very modern experimental approach with what might now seem quaint and antiquated occult ideas. This was because he assumed the whole universe to be alive. As the living universe includes the planetary bodies this also meant he believed in a Soul of the World. To his mind this explained the properties of attraction,

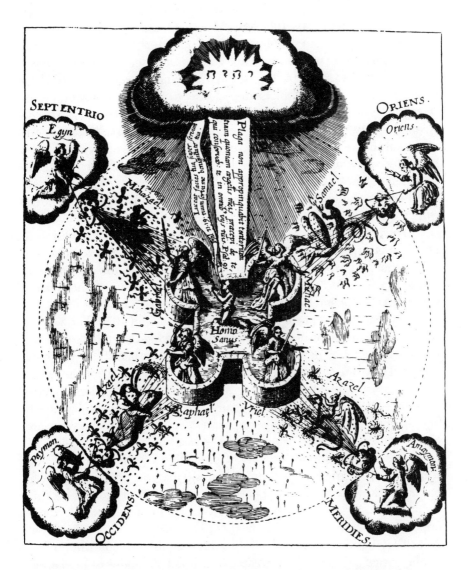

The Art of Preserving Health. From the physician Robert Fludd's *Integrum Morborum Mysterium* (1631). It is interesting by virtue of its fourfold schema which has parallels with Blake's Zoas and Jung's psychology and the fourfold magical symbolism. Archangelic figures repulse evil coming from the various four quarters, while the influence of God comes from another plane. The "sound man" (*homo sanus*) kneels within his magical fortress and addresses God with words from Psalm 19 "How great is thy goodness . . ." to which God replies, in the words of Psalm 91 "No evil shall befall thee, neither shall any plague come nigh thy dwelling; his angels shall have charge over thee . . ."

repulsion and discrimination that were expressed in the magnetic properties of the earth. His theories influenced the famous astronomer Kepler to try to explain all planetary motion in terms of magnetic flux.

Robert Fludd was perhaps one of the last of scientists and philosophers of nature to stand by the old standards and viewpoints. In 1631 for instance he wrote pamphlets in defense of the cure of wounds by "weapon salve." This cure worked on the principle that there is an occult sympathy between the body and the blood drawn from it; therefore one may treat the weapon to cure the wound. This doctrine of "sympathetical harmony" or "vital spirits" has now been rejected by medical science, although it still pertains in modified form in some aspects of "fringe medicine," such as radionics, dowsing or even homeopathy, which sometimes work where conventional drugs and surgery fail.

The concept had previously been advocated by one of the forerunners of modern science, Paracelsus (1493–1541), who pioneered an observational and experimental approach, as opposed to the authoritarian medieval medicine which simply repeated the ideas of the ancient Greeks, Aristotle and Galen.

A great gulf occurs in scientific thought in about 1650. This was the advent of the mechanical philosophy of nature, which after three hundred years of acceptance now makes all previous writers and thinkers appear quaint. There are grounds to believe, however, that this appearance of quaintness may be due in large measure to a certain superficial modern arrogance. We are sometimes too ready to assume human intelligence to have been steadily increasing in step with the advance of technology, and to look back through the "squint-eyed" glasses of our own conceit.

This has distorted a popular appreciation of Dr. John Dee, the Elizabethan geographer, mathematician and magical experimenter, who has come down to us as an eccentric dupe who spent most of his time trying to converse with angels through the mediumship of a dishonest opportunist named Edward Kelley. Yet Dee was one of the greatest intellects of his day. He made lasting and significant contributions to mathematics and assisted Mercator in the development of his famous projection for depicting the spheroidal shape of the earth on navigational charts. Dee had one of the greatest libraries of his time, collected at his own expense, which formed a center not only for scholars and the nobility, but for the great navigators of the time, Drake, Raleigh, and others, who consulted Dee before embarking on their practical ventures. In his magical and mediumistic experiments he may in fact even have been ahead of his time!

It is likely that Dee was engaged on diplomatic activity at a high and responsible level in his extensive European travels. And allied to this is the distinct possibility that he is a major influence to be found behind that strange seventeenth century phenomenon, the Rosicrucian Brotherhood from whom most modern beliefs and theories of White Magic depend.

The Rosicrucians caught the imagination of Europe when three pamphlets were anonymously published in the three successive years, 1614, 1615, and 1617. The first of these was the *Fama Fraternitatis*, subtitled "A Discovery of the Fraternity of the Most Noble Order of the Rosy Cross." The second was the *Confessio Fraternitatis* or "The Confession of the Laudable Fraternity of the Most Honorable Order of the Rosy Cross, Written to all the Learned of Europe," while the third was *The Chemical Wedding of Christian Rosencreutz.*

The *Fama* gives the biography of "the most godly and highly illuminated father, our brother C. R., a German, the chief and original of our Fraternity" of noble descent who, having spent his early years in cloistered poverty, learning Latin and Greek, at the age of 16 went on a journey to the Holy Land. He was attended by his brother who in fact died on the way, in Cyprus, but he continued alone on his way to Jerusalem. On arriving at Damascus he won great favor with the Turks because of his knowledge of medicine and in return their wise men showed him many wondrous secrets. He therefore stayed at Damascus, learned Arabic, and made translations of their work in medicine and mathematics. Three years later he traveled to Egypt and thence to Fez in Morocco, where the Arabians had directed him. Here, it is recorded, "Of these in Fez he often did confess that their Magia was not altogether pure, and also that their Cabala was defiled with their religion; but notwithstanding he knew how to make good use of the same, and found still more better grounds for his faith, altogether agreeable with the harmony of the whole world . . ." After two years he proceeded to Spain intending to reveal to the learned of Europe the great things he had learned:

> . . . showing unto them the errors of our arts, and how they might be corrected, and from whence they should gather the true *Indica* of the times to come, and wherein they ought to agree with those things that are past; also how the faults of the Church and the whole *Philosophia Moralis* was to be amended. He showed them new growths, new fruits, and beasts, which did concord with old philosophy, and prescribed them new *Axiomata*, whereby all things might be fully restored. But it was to them a laughing matter; and being a new

thing unto them, they feared that their great name should be lessened, if they should now again begin to learn and acknowledge their many years errors, to which they were accustomed, and wherewith they had gained them enough. Who-so loveth unquietness, let him be reformed.

The story so far is almost an allegory of the spread of new learning from the Islamic world which, as the Crusaders discovered, was in many respects ahead of Western Christian civilization. The general tone of the Rosicrucian writings is against the traditional scholasticism of Aristotle and Galen and also against the authority of the pope.

Finding no better reception in other nations of Western Europe the story continues with the return of Christian Rosencreutz to Germany to preserve his knowledge and to sow the seeds for a general reformation. There he founded a small brotherhood. The rules of this brotherhood were as follows:

(1) That none should profess any other vocation than to cure the sick, and that free.

(2) That they would have no special kind of distinctive habit or clothing, but would follow the custom of the country.

(3) That they would meet every year at their headquarters (called the House of the Holy Spirit) or write the cause of their absence.

(4) That they would each find a worthy person to succeed them in the fraternity upon their death.

(5) That the word C. R. would be their seal, mark and character.

(6) That the Fraternity would remain secret for one hundred years.

The *Fama* sketches in the lives of some of the early brethren, identified only by initials, and their residence in different countries. It then proceeds to a highly symbolic account of the subsequent discovery of the hidden tomb of Christian Rosencreutz.

It was found by one of the later members of the order, when he sought to make some alterations to a building and discovered a brass memorial tablet giving the names of all the brethren. In trying to remove this, a door behind a wall was revealed, on which was written *Post 120 annos Patebo.*

The symbolic nature of all this description is pointed up by the following remark in the *Fama* that "like as our door was after so many years wonderfully discovered, also there shall be opened a door to Europe (when the wall is removed) which already doth begin to appear, and with great desire is expected of many."

The following morning the door was opened, there to reveal a seven-sided vault, each side of forty square feet (8 x 5) and lit by a perpetual lamp which shone from the center of the ceiling like the Sun.

In the center of the vault was not a tombstone but an altar on which was inscribed on a brass plate an inscription, in Latin, reading "This compendium of the universe I made in my lifetime to be my tomb," and round a circle "Jesus, all things to me" (*Jesus mihi omnia*), and within four central circles "A vacuum exists nowhere"; "The Yoke of the Law"; "The Liberty of the Gospel" and "The Whole Glory of God" (*Nequaquam vacuum; Legis Jugum; Libertas Evangelii; Dei gloria intacta*).

We have here, once again, a symbolic model of the universe, after the fashion of the various holy cities, pictures of the starry firmament and so on, and serving once again to project an image of the psyche.

There follows a detailed description of the ceiling, walls and floor of the heptagonal room. The ceiling was bright and divided into seven triangles by lines proceeding from the central light to each angle of the walls. The walls themselves were divided into ten parts each, containing symbolic figures. And the floor, like the ceiling, divided into seven triangles each representative of one of the traditional planets (Sun, Moon, Mercury, Venus, Mars, Jupiter, Saturn), or "inferior governors." At each wall there stood a chest containing books of instruction and symbolic appurtenances such as magic mirrors or crystal balls, bells, lamps, incense burners, and symbolic songs—no doubt in the tradition of Ficino's planetary hymns.

The altar was then moved to one side, and beneath another plate of brass was found the body of Christian Rosencreutz himself in a perfect state of preservation, "whole and unconsumed," and holding a book "which next to the Bible is our greatest treasure." At the end of this book there was found the following expository passage, in Latin:

A grain buried in the breast of Jesus C., Ros. C. sprung from the noble and renowned German family of C.R., a man admitted into the mysteries and secrets of heaven and earth through the divine revelations, subtle cogitations and unwearied toil of his life. In his journeys through Arabia and Africa he collected a treasure surpassing that of Kings and Emperors; but finding it not suitable for his times, he kept it guarded for posterity to uncover, and appointed loyal and faithful heirs of his arts and also of his name. He constructed a microcosm corresponding in all motions to the macrocosm and finally drew up this compendium of things past, present and to come. Then, having

now passed the century of years, though oppressed by no disease, which he had neither felt in his own body nor allowed to
attack others, but summoned by the Spirit of God, amid the
last embraces of his brethren he rendered up his illuminated
soul to God his Creator. A beloved Father, an affectionate
Brother, a faithful Teacher, a loyal Friend, he was hidden here
by his disciples for 120 years.

Beneath this is a roll of the eight brothers and finally the mystical
motto: *Ex Deo nascimur, in Jesu morimur, per spiritum sanctum revivis-
cimus* (Of God we are born; in Jesus we die; through the Holy Spirit we
live again).

This gives some idea of the general pious and symbolical tone of the
Rosicrucian manifestos. The first one, the *Fama*, concludes with a general peroration, stating the belief that there will shortly be a reformation
"both of divine and human things"; and condemning "the ungodly and
accursed goldmaking" which many "renegades and roguish" people use
to dupe or cozen others in a travesty of the true meaning of the transmutation of metals, which is the highest point in Rosicrucian philosophy.

It invites like-minded people to join their society but gives no way of
enrolling, save that the Brothers will be aware of anyone who evinces a
true desire.

The *Confessio*, which appeared the following year, adds little to
what was contained in the *Fama*, and it again demonstrates a Christian
Protestant persuasion: "We do condemn the East and West (meaning the
Pope and Mahomet) blasphemers against our Lord Jesus Christ" and
mentioning the appearance of new stars in the constellations of Cygnus
and Serpentarius as heralds of the reformation to come. These new stars
in fact appeared in 1604, which, if the chronology of the story is calculated, give the same date at which the tomb of Christian Rosencreutz is
said to have been discovered. (He was born in 1378, lived to an age of 106,
and lay undiscovered for 120 years. 1378 + 106 + 120 = 1604.)

The third Rosicrucian document, however, differs markedly from
the others in presentation, and it is almost certainly by a different hand,
thought by most scholars to be John Valentine Andreae. Instead of being
a general proclamation it is in the form of symbolic fiction and tells the
story of the journey of Christian Rosencreutz one Easter Day to a marvel-
ous castle, wherein by dreams, pageants, chivalric initiations, and various
strange events he witnesses the marriage of a king and queen, their subsequent mutual death, and their resurrection by alchemical processes;
hence the title *The Chemical Wedding of Christian Rosencreutz.*

The conclusion of the story is that those who have been found worthy to proceed through the whole sequence are proclaimed Knights of the Golden Stone and presented with a white ensign bearing a red cross. Many of the symbolic images described correlate with diagrams from contemporary alchemical treatises and also with the pack of symbolic cards known as the Tarot.

The speculation considering the authorship and meaning of the *Chemical Marriage*, as with the *Fama* and *Confessio*, has been considerable. The French scholar Paul Arnold in his *Historie des Rose-Croix* has drawn parallels with Spenser's Red Cross Knight in the *Faerie Queen*, but the most interesting scholarship has been Frances Yates' *The Rosicrucian Enlightenment* where the Rosicrucian society is suggested as the nucleus for a third force of intellectuals attempting to construct an ideal state and buffer between the conflicting might of Catholic and Protestant Europe. The strange Rosicrucian castle of the *Chemical Marriage* has similarities with Heidelberg Castle and its many magic-mechanical marvels, the home of the Elector Palatine and his Queen, Elizabeth Stuart, the daughter of James I of England. The buffer state envisaged was the Kingdom of Bohemia—whose capital Prague is traditionally the home of alchemical research and scholarship.

In the historical event the King and Queen of Bohemia lasted but one winter, that of 1620, before being crushed by the Hapsburg forces. The experiment thus came to an ignominious political end.

The researches of Dr. Yates suggest most interesting lines of influence and learning, and demonstrate that spiritual magical theories were a strong undercurrent in the cultural and political life of sixteenth and seventeenth-century England and Europe. This is amplified in more general terms in her *Giordano Bruno and the Hermetic Tradition*.

There is, for instance, an intellectual Platonic and Hermetic strand that commences in England with John Colet's absorption of the ideas of Marsilio Ficino and Pico della Mirandola. Colet wrote a treatise on the Dionysian angelic hierarchies, and was in the circle of Sir Thomas More, who translated the biography of Pico into English (in 1505–1510), and in 1516 published his own *Utopia*. It is of considerable interest that More, who by his stand on principle has been canonized as a Catholic martyr, should have described an Hermetic type of natural religion, subsequently adapted to Christian belief, in his *Utopia*.

It is also significant that, although some of the less wise Utopians continued to worship the Sun and the Moon, the principle of toleration was held sacrosanct over all religious beliefs. The king "made a decree,

Title page of Dr. John Dee's 'Hieroglyphic Monad.' This book, written in thirteen days in 1564 by Dr. John Dee explains his discovery of the *monas* or unity underlying the universe as expressed in a symbol, which here appears in the center. It later appears in 'The Chymical Marriage of Christian Rozenkreutz' in 1616 as an important device on the invitation to the symbolic Royal Wedding, suggesting a ling between the Elizabethian *magus* and the Rosicrucian Brotherhood.

that it should be lawful for every man to favor and follow what religion he would, and that he might do the best he could to bring others to his opinion, so that he did it peaceably, gently, quietly and soberly, without haste and contentious rebuking and inveighing against others."

Such Utopian tolerance fell on deaf ears, as the subsequent history of the Tudors and Stuarts demonstrates. During this violent period More's ideals and principles were not to be found in either of the main religious parties but in private intellectual circles such as those of Sir Philip Sidney.

Giordano Bruno, the Renaissance magus, records that he received a more sympathetic reception from Sir Philip Sidney and his friends than from the pedants of Oxford University when he visited England in 1583. Sidney was much influenced by the Protestant theologian Philippe Du Plessis Mornay who, in common with many of the intelligentsia of the times, was striving to find a middle way between the fanatical religious and political controversies of Catholic and Protestant Europe. A synthesis of religion based on Hermetic principles seemed a valid way, and was also approached from the Catholic side in works such as the six-volume commentary on the Hermetic literature in 1585–1590 by Hannibal Rosseli, a Capucin monk. Another Catholic, Francesco Patrizi, was called to Rome by the Pope to teach Platonic philosophy at the university— though he soon fell foul of the Inquisition. Patrizi translated many Hermetic works and criticized the monopoly that Aristotle's philosophy had on religious and academic thought. He advocated the study of Plato, Plotinus, Proclus and the early Christian Fathers, and saw this as a way of winning intelligent men and "even the German Protestants" to a return to the Catholic faith. "It is much easier to win them back in this way," he writes, "than to compel them by ecclesiastical censures or by secular arms."

We therefore find an advocacy of the Hermetic philosophy as a means of finding middle ground between Protestant and Catholic, and it was this Hermetic philosophy that gave the theoretical basis for magic, alchemy, and indeed all science of a pre-mechanistic kind that saw nature as an organism rather than as a machine.

Naturally all who advocated the Hermetic philosophy as a means of religious reconciliation did not necessarily agree with the practical magical, alchemical or scientific applications that might be put upon it. Giordano Bruno, on the other hand, took the actual philosophy beyond that of a Christian Hermeticism, almost to a full-blooded return to Egyptian magic. We have already seen that the Hermetic literature stemmed from a fusion of pagan and early Christian belief. It was therefore open to interpretation how much of the pagan spiritual tradition and how much of the early Christian should be incorporated.

This of course had been a problem in the early centuries of the Christian era. Now the confrontation was in terms of the Catholic tradition (analogous to the old pagan side, with its established power, its hierarchies, rites and traditions), and the Protestants (analogous to the early Christians, with their emphasis on equality, the priesthood of all believers, justification by faith, and evangelistic preaching). In the third century, Hermeticism had provided a meeting ground between the two, at least for a number of believers. It was not too absurd to reason that the same accommodation might occur thirteen or fourteen centuries later. Rosicrucianism represents an attempt to do so.

The membership, authenticity, and even existence of the Rosicrucian brotherhood was never revealed or substantiated. Two writers spent much effort championing the Rosicrucian principles, however. These were Michael Maier in Germany and Robert Fludd in England.

Michael Maier was a Lutheran and yet had been physician to the Catholic Rudolph II in Bohemia, who, unlike his successors, encouraged the study of magic and science. Robert Fludd was a London physician, and an Anglican.

Maier was author of almost a dozen books published between 1614 and 1622, the most well known of which is *Atalanta Fugiens*, a series of symbolic pictures with musical analogies and philosophical commentaries. Like the symbolic pictures of another contemporary Hermeticist, Heinrich Khunrath of Hamburg, they have a very similar flavor to the symbolism described in *The Chemical Marriage* and *Fama*.

Neither Fludd nor Maier ever claimed to be a member of the Rosicrucian brotherhood, though their writings were highly sympathetic to it. Fludd's first two works were in fact *A Compendious Apology for the Fraternity of the Rosy Cross, washing away as in a Flood the spots of suspicion and infamy with which it has been aspersed* (Leiden 1616) and *The Apologetic Tractactus for the Society of the Rosy Cross* (Leiden 1617).

In his *Apology* Fludd praises the Hermetic tradition and claims that the Rosicrucians are true Christians, neither seditious nor wicked magicians. Like Luther and Calvin they are protestant against the pope but are not therefore heretical. He goes on to distinguish between good magic and bad magic, and in his definition of magic includes the mechanical contrivances or marvels that were fashionable at that time. Good magic, such as is used by the Rosicrucian brotherhood, is based on mathematics, mechanics, the Qabalah and astrology, pursued in a scientific and holy spirit. He emphasizes that the purpose of the Rosicrucians is a general improvement and reformation of the arts and sciences. In this he follows in the tradition of Dr. John Dee, who urged the same thing in his preface to the works of Euclid, and indeed Francis Bacon whose *Advancement of Learning* (1605) was likewise a general call to a new approach to natural philosophy with the aim of improving the lot of mankind. Bacon was not wedded to a specific return of Platonic as opposed to Aristotelian traditions, but as a high official of James I, it should be said that he would not have found it politic to be too specific in such terms. The highly superstitious James took a defensive attitude to such matters and considered himself an expert on demonology and witchcraft.

That there was much more to the Hermetic tradition than the folklore and superstitions of country magic was amply demonstrated by Fludd in his subsequent books. *The History of the Macrocosm* was an immense work of several volumes, giving an exposition of Hermetic philosophy in the tradition of John Dee; and *Utriusque Cosmi Historia* or *History of Two Worlds—the Great World of the Macrocosm and the Little World of Man, the Microcosm* showed the harmonious design of the cosmos at large, and of man, and the correspondence between them. This is clearly in the line of early Renaissance magic as developed by Paracelsus and Dee. It is full of quotations from Ficino and in general terms shows the familiar picture of Jehovah (the Glorious Name of God) reigning over concentric circles of angelic hierarchies, stars and planets with the elements and man at the center, and with astral linkages running through all. The Divine Name Jehovah, in glory and equipped with wings, figures often in Rosicrucian documents, along with the legend "Under the Shadow of Thy Wings, Jehovah" from Psalms 17 and 57.

With regard to Francis Bacon's involvement in this general movement there have been a number of exaggerated and imaginative claims that have not helped a balanced approach to the subject. Nevertheless there are some interesting parallels. Like Sir Thomas More, he felt impelled to project an ideal society in the Platonic mold, in his *New Atlantis*, which was found in his papers after his death. This was a vision of an evangelical Christian society in an advanced state of scientific knowledge. Its great college was called "Solomon's House," manned by scientist-priests who researched arts and sciences for the benefit of man. Frances Yates in her chapter "Francis Bacon 'Under the Shadow of Jehova's Wings'" in her book *The Rosicrucian Enlightenment* describes some of the evidences of Rosicrucian influence in Bacon's work and gives her

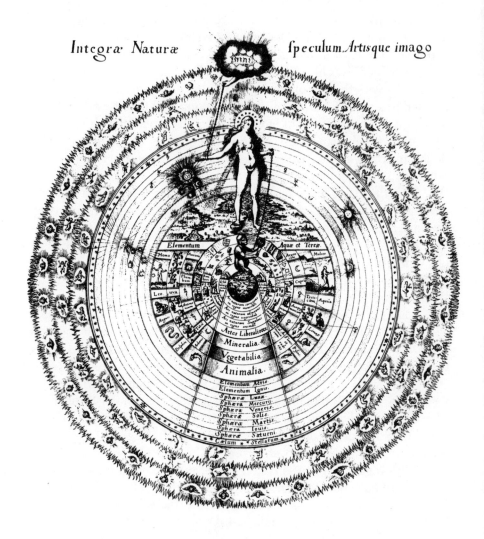

The Soul of the World as link between God and Nature. This magnificent engraving by de Bry is from *Utriusque Cosmi . . . Historia* by the Anglican physician, scientist and Rosicrucian apologist, Robert Fludd, published at Oppenheim in 1617. It shows the "inner" universe of elements, planets, stars and the Soul of the World subservient to God and the force behind external nature.

considered view of Bacon as follows:

> Recent scholarship has made it abundantly clear that the old
> view of Bacon as a modern scientific observer and experimen-
> talist emerging out of a superstitious past is no longer valid. In
> his book on Bacon, Paolo Rossi has shown that it was out of the
> Hermetic tradition that Bacon emerged, out of the Magia and
> Cabala of the Renaissance as it had reached him via the natural
> magicians. Bacon's view of the future of science was not that of
> progress in a straight line. His "great instauration" of science
> was directed towards a return to the state of Adam before the
> Fall, a state of pure and sinless contact with nature and knowl-
> edge of her powers. This was the view of scientific progress, a
> progress back towards Adam, held by Cornelius Agrippa, the
> author of the influential Renaissance textbook on occult phi-
> losophy. And Bacon's science is still, in part, occult science.
> Amongst the subjects which he reviews in his survey of learn-
> ing are natural magic, astrology, of which he seeks a reformed
> version, alchemy, by which he was profoundly influenced, fas-
> cination, the tool of the magician, and other themes which
> those interested in drawing out the modern side of Bacon have
> set aside as unimportant.

We shall find this a common fault in biographical historians, particularly in regard to the later major figure Sir Isaac Newton, and the scientists who formed the Royal Society in 1660 under the patronage of
Charles II. Through what has been identified by the historian Professor
Butterfield as a "Whig approach" to history, the ideas and concepts of the
past have been viewed through entirely modern prejudices, playing down
or even ignoring that which seemed out of key with modern ideas of
physical science, and emphasizing only that which accords with latter day
assumptions. Thus for a true appreciation of the role of magical theory
and practice in the fifteenth to seventeenth centuries much history needs
to be reconsidered and rewritten.

The general trend of the seventeenth century, in the realm of ideas,
is a gradual split between the world seen as a mechanism and the world
seen as an organism.

The reasons for this trend are very complex and still subject to historical debate. The impetus towards the mechanistic view came largely
from the French philosopher René Descartes who attempted to formulate an explanation of the world based entirely on reason. He attempted
to forget all received assumptions and to reason out things from basic in-

controvertible facts, of which the first, he concluded, was "I think, therefore I am." Needless to say, his brave attempt failed because it placed too great a demand on human reason, which is not necessarily capable of fathoming the Laws of the Universe, particularly without recourse to much scientific observation. Allied to this was his great fear of exciting condemnation from the Church. As a devout and rather timid Catholic he had been horrified by the treatment meted out to Galileo. There was thus an emotive drift in Descartes' thought which sought to avoid religious difficulties. It may have been this that led him to formulate a philosophical dualism that divorced matter from mind. He saw them as parallel and quite distinct.

This led him to construct a speculative theory of how the universe works in entirely material and mechanical terms. As the possessor of a very able intelligence this had a coherence and plausibility that caused many to believe its validity. Its faults lay in that it was not based on sufficient observation of natural phenomena and the system crumbled before the work of Isaac Newton, whose *Principia* (1687) provided mathematical proof of the way the solar system holds together. This completely discredited Descartes' plausible notions of stars being centers of swirling vortices of subtle matter, with comets being parts of other stars working their way between the boundaries of stellar vortices.

Newton's work was the culmination of the drift of scientific thought and endeavor towards mechanism. A mathematician of staggering brilliance, Newton actually worked out the complex interactions of the planets, and invented a new branch of mathematics (differential calculus) in order to do so. The principles of physics that he laid down have lasted, with a few minor modifications by Einstein, to the present day.

But the effect of the general drift in the seventeenth century was an "externalization" of science. There developed a split between an "inner" and "outer" view of the universe. The outer view commenced as mechanical speculation along the lines initiated by Descartes and was carried on by observational scientists such as Robert Boyle, John Ray, and Johannes Kepler until the great synthesizing triumph of Newton, which gave a triumphant flourish to this analytical way of examining the physical elements of the world in isolation.

This is not to say that this was a complete break with old tradition, but Descartes' early method had the seeds of atheism within it, as his early critics pointed out. As a pious Roman Catholic this worried Descartes not a little but he felt the risk not unduly great, and that it would be unlikely that anyone would take up such an extreme view. He was wrong in this because the trend of his thought did lead to a formal atheistic position, although it took several decades after his death to do so.

All of the scientists we have mentioned had a profound religious belief and attempted to reconcile this new way of looking at the world with religious belief, That they may have felt uneasy about the process may be evidenced by Robert Boyle making provision in his will for an annual lecture to prove the existence of God from nature.

What in fact was developing was a new emphasis on "natural theology" with attempts to demonstrate that God exists by virtue of the intelligent design manifest in nature. One of Robert Boyle's favorite instances was the eye of a fly, the design of which must have been made by an intelligent purposeful being with a knowledge of optics. His other favorite analogy was of the world like the great clock at Strasbourg, a complex machine of moving dials and figures. However the difficulty of such an analogy was that it tended to demonstrate a "clockmaker" God who, once having designed it, made and wound up the universe, then had no further part in it. God was squeezed out of the new concept of the universe.

This led naturally to deism, a movement which flourished in the eighteenth century, of which a principal exponent was Voltaire. This acknowledged the existence of God but put him beyond actual immanence in the world. This formed a rallying point for those who had lost patience with the shortcomings of organized religion, although it retained a religious arm of its own, emerging eventually as Unitarianism, a rejection of the orthodox Christian Trinity. Before this stage, however, the tendency toward it can be seen in the Arianism of major seventeenth-century Christian thinkers such as Milton or Newton, whose religious allegiance and belief tended to center upon the transcendent God the Creator, rather than upon an immanent God the Son or Holy Spirit.

The old premechanical tradition did not pass without a struggle. It was faithfully defended by Robert Fludd, who had a long running public debate with Johannes Kepler. Thomas Vaughan, brother of the poet Henry Vaughan, also championed the Rosicrucian cause, and published an English translation of the *Fama* and *Confessio*. Meanwhile, the Jesuits continued to use Hermetic philosophy as a means of making common ground with Protestants in order to restore them to the Catholic faith. It is thus that we have works such as *Ars Magna Lucis et Umbrae* (1646) or *Oedipus Aegypticus* (1652) by the Jesuit Athanasius Kircher.

There was also a group known as the Cambridge Platonists, led by Ralph Cudworth, Professor of Hebrew at Cambridge, who attempted to maintain an "internal" view of nature. Their influence was considerable

The Great Art of Light and Shadows. Title page of the Jesuit Athanasius Kircher's *Ars Magna Lucis of Umbrae* published at Rome in 1646. He is representative of a Roman Catholic school of thought which tried, like the Protestant Rosicrucians, to seek a "middle way" between the religious conflict that was enflaming Europe by use of the Hermetic philosophy and symbolism.

on leading scientists of the day and they also encouraged the great Bohemian reformer and educationalist Comenius to come to England in 1641. Comenius came in the expectation that "nothing seemed more certain than that the scheme of the great Verulam (i.e. Lord Bacon), of opening in some part of the world a universal college, whose one subject should be the advancement of the sciences, would be carried into effect." This expectation was frustrated by the disturbances of the Civil War, though a similar invitation was then made to Comenius to found a college in America, by John Winthrop of Massachusetts, who was later a member of the Royal Society.

This did not come to pass, though the President of Harvard College from 1684 to 1701, Increase Mather, did form a "Philosophical Society" in Boston. This was a parallel to the formation of the Royal Society in England under royal patronage in 1660. The roots of the Royal Society go back to 1645 and the meeting of like minds under the auspices of Gresham College, London—a center of the new scientific and technological learning. There is a definite link between Puritanism and the interest in science and technology, which at this time was still an amalgam of "inner" and "outer" sciences.

Of members of the Royal Society Kepler, despite his long debate with Fludd, was himself steeped in astrology and had tried to explain planetary orbits in terms of Platonic solids. Elias Ashmole, founder of the Ashmolean museum at Oxford, was quite at home in astrology, alchemy and magic. And Isaac Newton, the greatest scientist of his age and possibly all time, was preoccupied with alchemy and theology even more than with physics, mathematics and astronomy. It was Newton who proposed the Cambridge Platonist Henry More, author of *Conjectura Cabbalistica* (1653), for membership of the Royal Society.

It may have been the potential discord about speculative theology, allied to the religious troubles of the time, that decided the Royal Society to exclude religious matters from their meetings, despite the fact that many of its leading members were divines or eminently religious men. This had a profoundly unfortunate effect, for it encouraged the divorce between a science of the "inner" and a science of the "outer." This led to the study of science divorced from any religious or moral consideration. The effects of which, for better and for worse, we inherit today.

The Royal Society in this respect falls far short of the old Rosicrucian ideal of an "invisible college," although in another sense it embodied the ideal described by its historian Thomas Sprat (in 1667), "that it is to be noted, that they have freely admitted Men of different Religions, Countries, and Professions of Life . . . they openly profess, not to lay the Foundation of an English, Scottish, Irish, Popish or Protestant Philosophy; but a Philosophy of Mankind."

The implications of this are well summarized by Dr. Frances Yates in *The Rosicrucian Enlightment.*

> The rule that religious matters were not to be discussed at the meetings, only scientific problems, must have seemed a wise precaution, and in the earlier years, the Baconian insistence on experiment, and on the collecting and testing of scientific data, guided the Society's efforts. A permanent Society for the advancement of natural science had arrived, a real and visible, not an imaginary and invisible, institution but it was very restricted in its aims compared with earlier movements. It did not envisage the advancement of science within a reformed society, within a universal reformation of the whole world. The Fellows of the Royal Society were not concerned with healing the sick, and that gratis, nor with schemes for the reform of education. These men could have had no idea of what lay before the movement they were encouraging. To them its weakness would be more apparent than its strength, the danger of extinction which still beset it. They had arrived, they had made an Invisible College visible and real and in order to preserve its delicate existence great caution was required. It all seemed, and was, very sensible. And although Baconian experiment was not itself the infallible high road to scientific advance, yet the Royal Society, so respectable, so well organized, was a statement clear to all that science had arrived. Nothing could stop it now.

This represents the scientific side of the growing dichotomy. There is also a more directly religious side which has as its main representative Jacob Boehme, a poor shoemaker of Gorlitz near the borders of Bohemia, who was the recipient of a series of divine visions and revelations that excited the ire of the orthodox Lutheran church of the day. Boehme's visions are marked by a pious Christianity with strong correspondences with Roscicrucian symbolism. The first of his books, *Aurora,* was written in 1612, though it was not published until some years later.

Boehme's writings are by no means easy to understand as he had little learning, and in order to express his visions took recourse to an idiosyncratic terminology. He is a major representative of a distinct line of visionaries, often of little intellectual learning, who yet are overwhelmed by an awareness of the inner side of things. This is complementary to the type of intuitional rationalism that builds up an ordered universal pattern on the lines of a Robert Fludd, or a Michael Maier.

Where such visionary patterns purport to be theological they tend to excite the opposition of the religious establishment. Where they purport to be explanations of the universe they excite the opposition of the scientific establishment. Therefore they suffer from the same difficulties as the Hermetic philosophy and magic; indeed they deal with the same ground.

On a less visionary level the *Imitation of Christ* by Thomas Kempis was held by one important Rosicrucian commentator, Theophilus Schweighardt, to represent the true "magnalia," or what he called the final explanation of the macro-microcosmical mystery. This is summed up in the motto *Jesus Nobis Omnia* which appears in the *Fama* and which is also featured on a representation of "The Temple of the Rosy Cross" depicted in Schweighardt's *Speculum sophicum Rhodo-Stauroticum* (1618). The fifteenth century *Imitation of Christ,* a major work within a tradition of mystical Christianity, has much in common with the dissenting Puritan sects of the seventeenth century. Thomas á Kempis was, for an important part of his life, a member of the Brethren of the Common Life, a lay association of pious men and women typical of that time. Some of these mystics, such as John Tauler, remained in communion and favor with the church; others, such as Meister Eckhardt or Nicholas of Basle, were condemned as heretics.

In a technical sense a more magical approach to religious experience was to be found in the *Spiritual Exercises* of St. Ignatius, founder of the Jesuit Order, which was officially constituted in 1539. These exercises are a deliberate and controlled use of powerful symbols upon the imagination—though using events from the life of Christ rather than the celestial and angelic schemata of the tradition of Dante, Ficino, Pico or the Rosicrucians.

The typical procedure is first to take a sequence of events and to formulate the story. This might be highly metaphysical, such as the Holy Trinity looking down upon the earth and decreeing that the Second Person shall become man to save mankind. Or it might be some very human episode such as the Virgin Mary, nine months pregnant, setting off for Nazareth on a donkey, accompanied by Joseph and a servant leading an ox. This is pictured not only visually but also using all the sensory imaginative faculties. Then, as a third preliminary, the formulation of one's intention in experiencing this scene is made. This might be to attain a greater

Rose cross with the figure of Christ in the center, from the *Secret Symbols*.

knowledge of God, or for grace to make right choice of a path in life, or for the influence of God upon one's will.

These preliminaries are not ends in themselves. They are intended to lead to a period of colloquy with God. Colloquy is defined by St. Ignatius as "really the kind of talk friends have with one another, or perhaps like the way a servant talks to his master, asking for some kindness or apologizing for some failure, or telling him about some matter of business and asking for his advice."

It is unlikely that any Jesuit would lay claim to working magic, yet the techniques here used are plainly those of the magician, the deliberate use of imagined images to effect changes in consciousness. In the Jesuit case it is to raise consciousness to colloquy with God. In the case of the Renaissance magician or alchemist it is to equilibrate or transmute consciousness so that it becomes aware of its origins. In this there is no fundamental difference from the pagan mystery systems of old which, using mythological symbols, likewise sought self-knowledge and colloquy with the One and the Good.

Chapter 6
Secret Brotherhoods

The eighteenth century saw a reaction to all the religious "enthusiasm" and strife of the preceeding centuries. Although it is a period that is commonly called the Enlightenment, the enlightenment is that of the light of reason rather than of any Spiritual Sun. Religion tended to become "deism," with God well out of the way, as the original fabricator of the universe but taking little subsequent part in its running. Science became increasingly the investigation of the mechanics of the material world without recourse to any "inner" forces or correspondences, nor with any religious overtones.

To the leading scientists of the seventeenth century religion had been a motivating force in their pursuit of science; it was a means of demonstrating the power and wisdom of God through the wonders of His creation. In the eighteenth century this developed into the modern search for knowledge for its own sake, or for the technological benefits that the investigation of observational and experimental science could bring.

In so far that religion retained an interest in science it tended to be a reactionary and handicapping influence, attempting to harness the findings of science to the historical assumptions of the Old Testament. As the century progressed and passed into the nineteenth century this meant an increasing confrontation between a literal reading of the bible and the new science of geology. The discovery and classification of fossils, often high up the strata of mountains, imposed an immense time scale to history that far exceeded the four thousand or so years assumed by bible chronology.

This brought about the drawing up of entrenched positions which reflected badly on the religious party when, by the mid-nineteenth century, German textual criticism had eroded much of the validity from a literal interpretation of the bible. Darwin's *Origin of Species* and theory of evolution put the question to the biblically based belief in set particular species that had been divinely created and maintained since time immemorial.

In this intellectual climate there was a decline of interest in the old "organic" approach to the nature of the universe, and organized religion itself became formalized and stultified. This in time led to the reaction of the Methodist revival, for a whole sector of human experience and inner needs cannot simply be ignored; it will seek some manner of expression.

In the eighteenth century the eventual reaction against "blind reason" displayed itself in a number of new ways. The symbolic side of the Rosicrucian writings re-appear in the secret ceremonies of Freemasonry. The legendary belief in a previous "golden age" in remote antiquity becomes a speculative interest in the old stone circles and megalithic remains of Western Europe, and also an intense popular enthusiasm for Greek and Egyptian archaeology. The mystical experiences of the various sectaries of the previous century reappear in a scientific guise in the investigation and exploitation of "animal magnetism" and "mesmerism." And in the literary field the reaction expresses itself in the "Gothic" novel in a line that eventually enters modern popular culture with Mary Wollestonecraft Shelley's *Frankenstein,* and the subsequent genre of "horror" books and films.

All the ingredients are much as before, with the difference that, deprived of a proper and reverent attitude, the usurping reason causes the high symbolism of the past to be degraded. This resulted in the ill-understood charades of frivolous secret societies, while experience of the psychic dynamics of man became commercially exploited as stage entertainments or miracle cures, and an interest in the "unseen" side of the universe degenerated into a preoccupation with flesh-creeping horrors.

Freemasonry is however, an important development of this time. Its origins are obscure and it cherishes legends which ascribe its origins to remote antiquity. Insofar that its symbolism embodies ancient pagan mystery elements this has more than a grain of truth within it. However, confining ourselves to proven historical fact, the earliest record we have is in the seventeenth century. This is in the diary entries of one of the founders of the Royal Society, the famous antiquarian Elias Ashmole. His diary for October 16th, 1646 reads: "4.H.30P.M. I was made a Free

Mason at Warrington in Lancashire..." and later for 10th and 11th March, 1682: "10. About 5H.P.M. I rec'd a summons to appear at a Lodge to be held the next day, at Masons Hall London. 11. Accordingly I went, and about Noone were admitted into the Fellowship of Free Masons. .... [there follows a list of six names] ... I was the Senior Fellow among them (it being 35 years since I was admitted)..."

The probability is that Free Masonry started as one of the medieval Guilds of Free Journeymen of various trades, but that at some time it was taken over and transformed by some persons unknown who were concerned with using it as a vehicle for an initiatory system based on Hermetic philosophy. The stock in trade of the mason's trade is aptly suited for the symbolism of the building of a universe, or a structure in the psyche. We can thus make a distinction between the old operative masonry (a guild of tradesmen) and symbolic Masonry (a magic-religious society).

It should be said that most Freemasons today appear to have little knowledge or mystical interest in the inner meaning of their symbolism—although there are exceptions. Thus we can make a further distinction between the general run of Masonry, which is a friendly and charitable society with some quaint old customs, and a Masonry which is aware of the mystical heritage that it contains. (The latter includes branches called Blue Masons or Dormer Masons—the dormer in the sense of a high window, thus "seeing through" the symbolism to the heavens above).

Masonic symbolism is based firmly on the Old Testament and the description of the building of Solomon's Temple. It is possible that some of this ritual drama might have stemmed from mystery plays of the medieval trade guild. The building of Solomon's Temple would certainly have been an appropriate subject for the masons.

The circumstances of the building of the Temple of Solomon appear in the Old Testament Book of Kings, with a parallel account in the Book of Chronicles. Solomon's reign is summarized in 2 Chron. 9:22 in the following terms: "Thus King Solomon outdid all the kings of the earth in wealth and wisdom, and all the kings of the earth courted him, to hear the wisdom which God had put in his heart."

Solomon has come down to us as an archetype of power and wisdom, the ruler of an ancient Utopian society, with all that this implies. His temple is a symbolic pattern of an ideal universe along the lines of the other various holy cities, gardens and buildings.

The pattern of Solomon's temple is rooted in remote antiquity and

Masonic Symbolism of the 1st Degree. The Universe is shown supported by three Greek pillars, representing Wisdom, Strength and Beauty, while Jacob's Ladder show the way to the heights via the blazing Star of Glory of the Sun behind the Sun. Three of its rungs represent Faith, Hope and Charity, with their emblems of a cross, an anchor and a cup. At its foot is an altar with the volume of the sacred law upon it. The symbolic furniture of the Lodge includes three movable items—the square, the compasses and the book; and three immovable ones—the tracing board, and the rough and the perfect ashlar. These latter represent the plan of work, and the soul of the candidate before and after the work of attainment through initiation into the craft of the great work. The checkered paving on the floor of the Lodge, like the Sun and Moon above, indicates the polarity that rules the universe. The four tassels at each corner represent the cardinal virtues, Temperance, Strength, Prudence and Justice.

Masonic Symbolism of the 2nd Degree. A version of Solomon's Temple of Wisdom as conceived in the Scottish Rite of Masonry. The candidate, upon being admitted by the guardian of the threshold, through the pillars——each surmounted by a celestial and a terrestrial sphere—ascends a winding stair to a middle chamber and further portals beyond with Egyptian lotus head columns, and the dove of the Holy Spirit descends from the four letters of the Hebrew holy name of God.

follows the outlines of the tabernacle that housed the Ark of the Covenant, described in Exodus 25:27. This was based on a threefold principle—an inner holy of holies in which none might enter save the High Priest; a sanctuary or place of worship which enclosed this holy of holies; and a forecourt where the populace might come to worship and make sacrifices. Here we have, once again, an image of the three-tier universe. This consists of spirit, soul and body in man (the microcosm); and of God, planetary spheres, and sub-lunary world in the world (or macrocosm). Despite Jewish claims to exclusiveness of divine revelation their basic philosophical structure has much in common with pagan speculation. This is perhaps only to be expected if all are based on the projected pattern of the human psyche.

Solomon's Temple was located on a ridge north of the old city of Jerusalem on a site that David had purchased for an altar (1 Sam. 24, 18:25) and which may be the spot marked by a sacred rock enclosed in the present Mosque of Omar, or Dome of the Rock.

The most striking feature on approaching the temple would have been the two great bronze pillars at the top of ten steps, on either side of the high doors of painted cypress wood. These pillars play an important part in the symbolism of Freemasonry and of the Qabalah. There they represent the positive and negative, the masculine and feminine, light and dark, active and passive principles upon which the whole fabric of creation is woven. The ten steps similarly repeat the tenfold symbolism of the Sephiroth or Emanations of God in the Tree of Life, which, in Aristotelian terms, is comprised of the earth and the seven traditional planets, plus the zodiac of fixed stars and the primum mobile.

Through another set of doors was the sanctuary containing various symbolic furniture such as the seven-branched candlestick and table of shew bread. From thence a further flight of ten steps led to a cedar-lined, cubical, darkened room containing the Ark of the Covenant, the Mercy Seat of Jehovah—the innermost shrine.

Upon this basic structure the Masonic Lodge is developed. Reflecting the same dual principles as the pillars there is a Chequered Paving on the floor, and above, joining the tops of the pillars, is an arch. The Royal Arch, as it is called, signifies, amongst other things, the heavens; and is usually represented by six curved blocks locked in place by a central keystone.

In the associated lodge symbolism a Sun and Moon also refer to the dual principles (radiant and reflective) represented by the pillars; and the royal arch and chequered paving, representing heaven and earth, are also resumed in the Square and Compasses. The Compasses trace out circular dimensions, the Square rectilinear dimensions—all in accord with the Aristotelian principles that heavenly motions are circular and earthly motions rectilinear (i.e., the stars and planets wheel in apparent circles while on earth things tend to drop downward in a straight line toward the center of the earth).

There is also the symbolism of the rough ashlar and the perfect ashlar, a token of the spiritual evolution of man, rough hewn from nature to begin with, and then polished and lewised, to be raised in perfection to his proper place in the temple designed by the Grand Architect of the Universe.

Much of this symbolism is further amplified in masonic ritual and legend. An example is the legend of Hiram Abiff, a character who stems from the biblical account of I Kings and II Chron. although the earliest reference to the masonic Hiramic legend is in 1738 in the second edition of Anderson's *Constitutions,* an important Masonic history.

Briefly, Hiram Abiff was the architect in charge of the building of Solomon's Temple, and he divided the workmen into three grades, the Entered Apprentices, the Fellow Craftsmen and the Master Masons, each grade having its own password and secret signs of membership; means whereby interlopers could be excluded and the secrets of the craft protected.

Three particular fellow craftsmen aspired to a higher grade than they deserved and conspired to force Hiram to reveal the secret word of the master masons' degree. These three, named Jubila, Jubilo and Jubilum lay in wait for Hiram, one at each of the three gateways to the temple, after he had been praying at noon in the unfinished Holy of Holies, as was his custom.

Jubila confronted Hiram at the Southern gate armed with a rule and on Hiram's refusal to reveal the word struck him in the throat. The wounded Hiram rushed to the Western gate only to find Jubilo armed with a square who, on Hiram's refusal, struck him at the heart. Hiram staggered to the Eastern gate to be met by Jubilum armed with a mallet whom when Hiram for the third time refused to reveal the master's word, struck him between the eyes and killed him. The murderers buried Hiram's body on Mount Moriah, marking his grave with a sprig of acacia, an evergreen tree, which subsequently revealed the spot after the murderers had been brought to justice. Hiram was subsequently mysteriously raised from death by the Master Mason by means of "the strong grip of a Lion's Paw."

Without going into intricate details of symbolism it is plain that we have a modem form of an ancient mystery ritual, with the theme of death and resurrection. Hiram can be considered as a prototype, or Platonic ideal, of man. As Adam after the Fall signifies human degeneration, so Hiram in his steadfastness and resurrection signifies human regeneration. When he is raised from his grave Hiram whispers the word that was lost.

This in fact is but one, albeit one of the most important, of a whole range of masonic rituals that arose in the eighteenth century. It has been estimated that some 800 various degrees and rituals were developed during this time. There was also a tremendous vogue for secret societies of all kinds. The majority of these were quite superficial. In some circles it seemed impossible to meet for regular discussions of religious, scientific or literary matters without the rites and paraphernalia of a secret society.

This harmless, if slightly ridiculous, fashion gave the opportunity for more clandestine organizations to flourish. Some of these were simply catchpenny organizations giving grandiose initiations into spurious rites for those with sufficient guineas to pay for such a doubtful privilege. Others, such as the notorious Hellfire Club, were a nucleus for degenerate vice with the added piquancy of sacrilegious practices. From this type of organization is derived the tradition of the Black Mass and Satanism, so beloved by writers of occult novels.

The whole hackneyed scenario of naked virgins on altars, the Lord's Prayer being read backwards, the sacrifice of toads and chickens, the officiant being an unfrocked priest, the host being desecrated or made of noxious substances, while being a sordid parade of human viciousness and reaction to organized religion, is hardly typical of the great, broad stream of Neo-Platonic philosophy that is the fount of white magic.

There were also political motives in some of the eighteenth century secret societies. There is some evidence of Jesuit attempts to restore, by these methods, the Roman Catholic Stuart line to the English and Scottish throne. The symbolism of the Hiramic legend was regarded in this case as an allusion to the execution of Charles I. Like the legendary Hiram, both the Old Pretender and the Young Pretender were widow's sons, and the restoration of life to Hiram was likened to the restoration of Bonnie Prince Charlie to the throne. It is possible that this may have been the origin of some Scots Masonry in the British Isles and *Maçonnerie Ecossaise* in France.

More apposite to our main theme, however, is the number of genuine attempts to reconstitute a working equivalent of the ancient mysteries. Such groups tended to form around certain strong intuitive personalities who perhaps also had some penchant for attracting popular attention. In a skeptical yet credulous age (two qualities that paradoxically go together) much of the more colorful stories of their remarkable powers will have been the result of magnified gossip. Yet it should also be said that some of them, such as Emanuel Swedenborg, did undoubtedly have remarkable psychic powers.

Louis Claude de St. Martin (1743–1803) was one of these key figures, the founder of the Martinist Order, and known as *le philosophe inconnu* because he used this phrase as his nom de plume. He was always sympathetic to the Catholic religion, although his books were placed upon the Papal Index, and the general tone of his teaching was that within every human being there is a spiritual quality which at first may not be consciously realized but which can be developed by prolonged intention and effort. He also looked for an ideal society governed by those who had so developed their natural spiritual qualities.

He had himself been initiated into a system of masonry developed by Martines de Pasqually who in 1754 founded the Rite of Elected Cohens. This consisted of seven grades leading to that of Rose Croix and was based on belief in biblical truth together with a general spiritual evolutionary scheme that commenced with man's existence long before the creation story in Genesis. Some of these teachings seem to derive from Jacob Boehme and Dr. John Dee.

A colorful personality of the time was Count Allesandro Cagliostro (1743–1795) who founded the Egyptian Rite of Freemasonry, of which he was the Grand Cophte. There is much controversy about his life and he is often identified with a Sicilian adventurer Giuseppe Balsamo. In the course of his life he took the courts of Europe by storm with a series of faith-healings, prophesies, visions and other wonders. His career came to an end with the cause célèbre of the Queen of France's necklace. He was proved innocent but after some months in the Bastille was banished from France, and in declining health went to Rome with a worthless safe-conduct. Here he was taken by the Inquisition, sentenced to life imprisonment for heresy, and he died incarcerated in St. Angelo.

An even more charismatic figure was that of the Comte de St. Germain. If all that has been claimed of him is true, then he was a living embodiment of the tradition of powerful secret adepts with phenomenal powers. He is reported to have been able to speak eleven languages like a native; to play several musical instruments; to compose music including an opera; to paint strangely luminous pictures; to be completely ambidextrous; to be able to remove flaws from jewels by chemical means; to have profound historical knowledge and also the gift of prophecy. Most remarkable of all, he apparently possessed the elixir of life, for there are reports of his having been active for over a hundred years, from 1710 to 1822. A biographer lists no fewer than nine aliases during this period in various cities of Italy, Germany, France, Russia and England. He is also said to have traveled in the East, being the guest of the Shah in Persia and meeting Clive in India. He is said to have known various famous people such as Frederick the Great, Voltaire, Madame de Pompadour, Rousseau, Chatham, and Horace Walpole.

This tradition of secret adepts of white magic becomes important in the later development of the tradition. Apart from the original implications of the Rosicrucian manifestos the tradition is mentioned in an anonymous work *The Way to Bliss* which was published by Elias Ashmole in 1656, wherein it is said that "There is a Nation of *Wise Men,* dwelling in a soil as much more blessed as yours is than theirs: That is, As they bide under ground, and you upon the face thereof so these Men inhabit the edge and skirt of Heaven; they daily See and Work many wondrous things, which you never saw nor made, because you never mounted so high to come among them." And again in John Heydon's sixth book of *The Holy Guide* (1662) subtitled the "The Rosie Cross Uncovered" he defines them as being "a divine Fraternity that inhabits the Suburbs of Heaven, and those are the Officers of the *Generalissimo* of the World, that are as the eyes and the ears of the great King, seeing and hearing all things."

There is some doubt, then as now, in the tradition, whether such wise men, officers, or secret adepts, walk the world or inhabit part of the creation that is not wholly physical.

Another eighteenth century esoteric group was the Illuminati, founded in 1776 by Adam Weishampt, Professor of Law at the University of Ingolstadt. This organization never grew to encompass large numbers though it exerted a considerable intellectual influence and was favorably regarded by Goethe. Its inception was as a defense of liberal ideas in university education against the ecclesiastical catholic reaction, and it drew its inspiration from the philosophical ideas of Pythagoras and the ancient Eleusinian mysteries.

Paradoxically, in spite of the rationalism of the eighteenth century, masonic and other types of secret society flourished. This was for a variety of reasons, and in a sense represented a secularization of the ancient mystery tradition. Membership of the organization was relatively common and indeed Mozart's opera *The Magic Flute* is a compendium of their symbolism with a Masonic Egyptian flavor. It largely derives in turn from a French symbolic novel of 1731, entitled *The Life of Sethos,* which purports to be the memoirs of an ancient Egyptian.

This book falls within the general tradition of mystical symbolism in fictional guise, or *ludibrium,* that includes *The Chemical Marriage of Christian Rosencreutz*, or the strange Italian tale of an Adept of the Elements *Le Comte de Gabalis*. Thus by derivation Mozart's opera falls within a genre—which later might be said to include Coleridge's *Ancient Mariner* and eventually the novels of Charles Williams, C. S. Lewis, J. R. R. Tolkien, George MacDonald—and even Lewis Carroll.

There were also two religious movements of particular relevance to our theme. Karl von Eckartshausen (1752-1813) wrote a number of works on an esoteric approach to religion and science and contrived to avoid bringing himself into conflict with the Roman Catholic church. The best known of these works is *The Cloud Upon the Sanctuary* which again perpetuates the belief in a secret school of adepts: "It is the most hidden of communities, yet it possesses members gathered from many orders; of such is this School. From all time there has been an exterior school based on the interior one, of which it is but the outer expression. From all time, therefore, there has been a hidden assembly, a society of the Elect, of those who sought for and had capacity for Light, and this interior society was called the interior Sanctuary or Church..."

> The Sanctuary remained changeless, though external religion received in the course of time and circumstances varied modifications, and became divorced from the interior truths...

> This illuminated community has been through time the school of God's spirit...

> Wordly intelligence seeks this Sanctuary in vain; in vain also do the efforts of malice strive to penetrate these great mysteries; all is indecipherable to him who is not prepared; he can see nothing, read nothing in the interior...

In this religious work we seem close to the atmosphere of the ideas of the alchemists. Knowledge is to be gained but only by those who are capable of intuitive and spiritual insights, and who have a high moral intention and deep personal commitment.

The other great unorthodox religious influence was that of Emanuel Swedenborg (1688–1772) who was again a man of many accomplishments. He was primarily a scientist who, having graduated from the Swedish university of Uppsala, studied abroad under famous scientists such as Newton, Flamsteed, Halley and De Lahire. On his return to Sweden he was made Assessor of the Royal College of Mines, and though he was principally a metallurgist and mining engineer he was also learned in astronomy, physics, zoology, anatomy, finance, economics, classics and theology. He was also interested in invention, and made sketches for flying machines, submarines, machine guns and various pumps. He was raised to the nobility by Queen Ulrica but abandoned his highly successful career in mid-course to devote himself to the promulgation of his visions.

He had shown evidence of unusual psychic gifts as a child, going into a trance-like state with no discernible breathing. The philosopher Immanuel Kant investigated and adjudged true the story that he had been clairvoyantly aware of a great fire in Stockholm whilst 300 miles away in Gothenburg. His main work, after 1774, became, however, an intensive investigation into inner worlds, in communication with the spirits of deceased kings, popes, saints and biblical figures.

He was in a sense the first spiritualist, in that he publicly claimed to be in touch with the souls of departed humans. Most attempts to commune with super-terrestrial intelligences had previously been with angelic, elemental, daimonic or even demonic agencies.

Swedenborg's writings fall into two categories, experimental and dogmatic. The first are accounts of what he saw and experienced in the spirit world. The latter are a theological construction upon them.

On the basis of these writings a Swedenborgian Church has been founded, which still survives. They also had a considerable influence on the young William Blake. However, analysis of them indicates the presence of the great bug-bear of all writings of this nature, the difficulties of excluding subjective elements and the preconceptions and prejudices of the seer. Much of Swedenborg's cosmic view seems modeled on Swedish society of the times, with Hell a thinly disguised proletarian world of blackened miners, and Heaven the gentility of Court life.

This notwithstanding, Swedenborg stands as a highly important landmark in the history of inner consciousness in the eighteenth century. He is, as it were, an unorthodox religious pillar that stands opposite an unorthodox scientific pillar, represented by Anton Mesmer and his experiments in "animal magnetism."

Anton Mesmer (1733–1815) graduated as a doctor from the University of Vienna in 1766. He effected cures by applying magnetic plates to the limbs of the afflicted, the theory of which was contained in his thesis *De Planetarum Influxu*. This was to the effect that there exists a subtle universal fluid that is the vehicle for a mutual influence between heavenly bodies, the earth and animate bodies, particularly the human. Its properties are similar to magnetism in its polarity; similar to light in that it can be increased or reflected by mirrors and can also cover a distance without intermediary bodies; and that it can be controlled by means of the human voice.

Mesmer came to Paris where he practiced with enormous success, turning down in 1781 an award of 20,000 livres from the king, together with an annuity of 10,000 livres if he would establish a school to teach his methods. He did however subsequently agree, for 340,000 livres, to give lectures.

His principal means of operation was a *baquet*, or large circular tub of water from which projected iron rods. The patients sat in a circle around this device, holding hands or joined by a cord, and the ends of the rods could be applied to various parts of their bodies. At the same time music was played and an operator walked round and touched patients with another rod at which they fell into hysteric convulsions and were often cured.

Government sponsored committees of the Faculté de Médicine and the Societé Royale de Médicine examined the evidence for a new physical force of "animal magnetism" in 1784, but reported they could find no proof of a magnetic fluid. They thought the cures might be due to vivid imagination. In this they probably spoke more truly than they realized for, as Coleridge was later to point out, the imagination is not necessarily a chimera of fancy to be lightly dismissed. But the physical emphasis in science had already begun to discount as valueless any phenomena that could not be physically weighed, and measured and accounted for with physical laboratory instruments.

In the same year the Marquis de Puysegur began to produce similar effects to Mesmer but without the use of a *baquet*. Instead he used a tree, around which the patients were tied. As a result of his experiments a condition known as the somnambulistic state, or deep hypnotic trance, was discovered. This became the basis for nineteenth century spiritualism.

Chapter 7
The Romantic Rebellion

During the nineteenth century experimentation into somnambulistic phenomena brought many theories and a number of strange discoveries. In this condition a subject was capable of unusual physical and psychological feats, one of the more spectacular being the transposition of senses, where the subject might seem able to see with parts of the body other than the eye.

In 1813 the Abbé Faria echoed the committees of 1784 in emphasizing the role of the imagination in mesmerism rather than the action of subtle physical emanations. This was developed by Alexandre Bertrand's *Traité de Somnambulisme* in 1823, pointing out the hypersensitivity of subjects to the slightest suggestion of the operator, whether by word, gesture, look or even thought. This view was accepted by a committee of the Royal Academy of Medicine in 1831.

In a series of investigations between 1841 and 1845 the British scientist Braid proved the possibility of producing all the phenomena of "magnetism" without the use of magnets or other apparatus and thus brought about the end of mesmerism and the beginnings of modern "hypnotism" with his book *The Power of the Mind over the Body*.

The techniques of mesmerism were used in the 1830s and 40s for the production of anesthesia in surgery until the discovery of the properties of chloroform and ether in 1846. There is a tendency for physical techniques to replace the psychical in all forms of science. Physical methods are more readily controllable, as the subjective, "random" element can be ignored. This usually leads however to the psychical method being forgotten, or thought to be discredited.

The debate over the existence of a subtle physical fluid continued throughout the nineteenth century, leading to the remark by a famous French psychical researcher, that "animal magnetism is a new America which has been alternately lost and found every twenty or thirty years."

Parallel to the scientific and medical interest in these subjective phenomena there was a tendency, not entirely welcomed by the churches, to take these psychical discoveries into the religious orbit. In America a number of new religions came to birth, of which the Mormons, the Seventh Day Adventists, the Jehovah's Witnesses, The Christian Scientists, were principal ones that remain with us today. Spiritualism was one of these and it developed as the main religious offshoot from mesmerism.

This followed upon the discovery that the trance or somnambulistic state might be accompanied by phenomena such as clairvoyance, healing, knocks, levitations, apports of light objects, and phantom forms. All this and more was reported by the French investigator Baron Du Potet between 1836 and 1848 in his *Journal du Magnétisme*. At about the same time in America spirit communications were recorded at Mount Lebanon from 1837-1844; and a semi-literate youth, Andrew Jackson Davis, from 1847 on, produced volumes of abstruse teaching allegedly from the spirit world, and which, whatever their intrinsic merit, seemed far beyond the normal intellectual capacity of the medium.

The beginnings of spiritualism are, however, usually credited to the celebrated case of the Fox sisters at Hydesville, New York, who were plagued by strange rapping noises at their home. They interpreted these as signals and this eventually led to the discovery of the bones of a murdered man buried in the cellar.

The spiritualist movement spread and the early efforts of the Fox sisters were soon eclipsed by the remarkable phenomena produced by professional mediums. These included physical levitation, psychometry (reading the past from an object), phantom hands that could be grasped, spirit photography, spirit impressions in paraffin wax molds, and writings on slates or the skin.

This in turn provoked a reaction of skeptical investigation and the production of similar phenomena by Jasper Maskelyne, the stage illusionist, in an attempt to prove it was all bogus. Eventually there was formed a Society for Psychical Research in both England and America in an attempt to investigate such phenomena in a rational fashion.

From America the spiritualist movement led to Great Britain and a parallel movement in France spread to Italy, and later to Germany. At one point home circles were so popular, it was said, that in polite society one inquired first, not after someone's health, but after the turning and tapping abilities of their table.

In spite of all this activity, not a great deal of wisdom has come from spiritualist communication over the subsequent one hundred and fifty years. Its supporters assert that it proves that there is no death by showing that the personality is not extinguished after physical dissolution. However it is extremely difficult to *prove* the identity of any alleged communicator and the majority of communications are quite banal. It might be said in defense that so are most intimate human communications, particularly in semi-public and through a third party. However, although contact with former famous men and literati has been claimed, there is little that is particularly wise, witty or memorable that is comparable to their observations in life.

This is not to discount the possible genuineness of some communication however, but rather to say that it is rare and and difficult to prove.

There have been consistent scientific efforts to record the phenomena and the Society for Psychical Research holds a great mass of attested documentation. Some of this is impressive and some disconcerting in that on occasion even mediums capable of producing most spectacular phenomena by paranormal means have been caught attempting the most crude of deceptions.

This may well be a result of the extreme suggestibility of a medium in the trance condition. If there is a member of the circle who is a confirmed skeptic, or who has deep religious objections, it can inhibit the production of phenomena. By similar means however, a participant who is convinced that the medium is going to try to cheat may well unknowingly succeed in making her cheat.

If there is any moral danger in the pursuit of spiritualism, as with hypnotism, it lies in the extreme passivity and suggestibility of the medium. It is a temporary complete abrogation of the human will. Those who develop such a high degree of sensibility and suggestibility may be at the mercy of any strong current of thought or general emotional atmosphere about them. This also leads to the evidential difficulty that such a means of communication is likely to play back to others what it feels they want to hear.

The phenomena associated with the somnambulistic state occurs also in other contexts, on the one hand in hauntings, and also associated with the works of saints or holy men of other religious faiths. A common denominator in most types of haunting phenomena is an adolescent youth or girl, which suggests that the motive power comes from a telekinetic misdirection of sexual forces not yet naturally expressed. The intelligence shown by such *poltergeist* manifestations is minimal, at about the level of an infant being violent with its rattle, though the scale and unusual nature of such manifestations can be alarming. There is no record of anyone having been seriously injured by a poltergeist though, even when struck by flying objects.

Such phenomena accompanied the Curé d'Ars, a Catholic priest of considerable reputation as a confessor. A man of deep spirituality, if little learning, he was possessed of clairvoyant gifts that enabled him to see into the hearts of those who came to him. This led to his gaining a national reputation as a confessor. People waited hours, even days, at his confessional. He was plagued by the most violent of *poltergeist* phenomena, which he assumed to be direct attempts at intimidation by the Devil.

We see again that the general structure of belief that surrounds such phenomena gives an interpretation to them and even affects their mode of action.

It seems that we have, at root, split off parts of the human psyche that have a semi-autonomous vitality. The condition is most frequently to be found amongst those who are sufficiently suggestible to be thrown easily into trance; with the high degree of control by other factors and forces that this entails.

All this type of phenomena, it should be said, is for the most part an irrelevance to white magic except in so far as an intimate knowledge of the inner workings of the human mind, which is the province of magic, can throw light on their operation. It is also the province of psychology but the approach of the experimental psychologist tends to be from the outside, in a skeptical fashion which, in this highly suggestible and sensitive area, may materially affect the results.

This is one reason for the religious or quasi-religious ambience to some of these activities. It sets a tone of reverence and respect that is more conducive to a controlled and safer exercise of the faculties, than a spirit of highjinks and skylark that motivates many amateur attempts at spiritualist seances. Although the dangers can be portentously exaggerated, risks certainly do exist if there is anyone present who is naturally psychic or hypnotically suggestible. They could then find themselves open to psychic impulses that they could not understand or control. In most cases this would pass off, provided no further restimulation occurred, though the effect on an immature or neurotic personality could well be more permanently distressing.

The theurgic pursuits of magic are a very different matter from the exploitation of psychism. With the emphasis of magic on the evocation of the spiritual will there can indeed be little common ground with hypnotic or somnambulistic methods.

A similar uncertain area lies in the psycho/physical effects that are associated with certain types of religious experience. There is much attention currently being given to the Pentecostal movement, for example, with its emphasis on speaking in unknown tongues as evidence of direct contact with the Holy Spirit.

Its immediate origins go back to nineteenth century America although there are instances of such phenomena throughout Christian history, commencing, of course, with the events at the original Pentecost. St. Paul, writing to the Corinthians, is concerned to apply some rule and regulations to such manifestations. One could also extend the question to include other "evidences" such as the levitations of St. Teresa d'Avila or the stigmata of St. Francis of Assisi, and many others.

Strictly speaking, this has little to do with magic, although the distinction may easily be blurred. Indeed, the first instance of such lack of distinction was that of Simon Magus, a contemporary wonder worker, who offered money to the disciples for the secrets of their "powers." Confusion also existed in Renaissance times when there was concern as to whether magic, and indeed science as a whole, would enable men to succeed in duplicating the miracles of Jesus, and whether it was impious to do so.

This is all part of a theological problem concerning the merits of the direct experience of mystical religion, which can at times seem indecorous and unrestrained in its worldly enthusiasm, with or without the complication of physical signs following.

Magic is not directly concerned with these matters, except insofar that, like psychology, it may help to throw light from its own experience and thus help to distinguish some wheat from chaff in certain psycho-religious experiences. Thaumaturgy, or wonder working, is no more the main concern of magic, than miracles are the main concern of religion. Both may, however, by virtue of the potencies with which they work, stumble upon little known powers of the mind and unusual physical phenomena.

In its more philosophical aspect magic was influenced at the end of the eighteenth century by a man of singular determination and dedication. This was Thomas Taylor, the English Platonist (1758–1835), who translated into English the works of Plato, the neo-Platonic commentators Plotinus and Proclus, and a variety of other texts of Greek religious philosophy.

His translations have for the most part been superseded but in his day he opened the world of Platonic philosophy, or what is sometimes called "the imaginative tradition," to a whole generation of writers and artists.

Coleridge and Shelley could read Greek themselves, but just as Ficino in the early Renaissance had made the imaginative tradition accessible to Botticelli, Raphael, and Michelangelo, so Thomas Taylor made it available to William Blake, Samuel Palmer, William Wordsworth, John Keats, and others, to name but the greatest in England. His influence also extended to America in Ralph Waldo Emerson and the New England Transcendentalists. Later in the century Taylor's work influenced the Irish movement of W. B. Yeats and A. E. (George Russell) and also Theosophical scholars such as G. R. S. Mead, and John Watkins, the occult bookseller.

With the divorce of the imagination from science by the mechanical philosophy, particularly as expounded by the eighteenth century philosophers Locke and Hartley, and with a corresponding aridity in established religion, a reaction to this rule of barren reason came about through the Romantic poets.

A new theory of the imagination was formulated by Wordsworth and Coleridge and is to be found exemplified in Wordsworth's great autobiography of the growth of the poetic mind, *The Prelude,* and in Coleridge's deeply symbolic ballad of guilt and redemption, *The Rime of the Ancient Mariner*. It is also in Keat's revivification of the Greek myths and in the precise natural symbolism of Shelley, which reflects a world of spiritual forms into the natural order—called by William Blake the "vegetable glass."

William Blake, above all, struck out at the rational mechanical view of the world. Characteristically, like Taylor, he was for the most part ignored or derided within his time. His witness is important however, for his overwhelmingly visionary imagination caused him to make personal mythologies that demonstrate the same lineaments of the imagination as are to be found in the mythologies of races and nations.

In the structure of his imaginative thought a fourfold pattern emerges in four great elemental beings that he called the Four Zoas.

Los, or Urthona, is the Spirit of Prophecy, the divine vision, reminiscent of the classical Phoebus-Apollo. The name derives possibly from Sol (Sun) and/or from "earth-owner."

Urizen, perhaps deriving from "your reason," is the Spirit of Thought, Eternal Mind. His "steeds" are thoughts. The silver mountains of Urizen are where wisdom dwells. He was also a lawgiver, and in some ways similar to Zeus.

Luvah, or Orc, is Prince of Love, Eros, Eternal Youth, sometimes called Red Orc, the fiery boy. The names derive possibly from "lover" and "hawk of May."

Tharmas represents the corporeal Waters of Matter, the fluid matrix of form. He appears as a great daimon of the waters, a Neptune or Poseidon figure.

These four figures have an intriguing parallel with the traditional elements of alchemy and ancient speculative science. They also parallel the four functions of consciousness identified by the psychologist C. G. Jung—Intuition, Thinking, Feeling and Sensation respectively.

In Blake's vision each of these four has an appropriate cardinal point but these have become confused because of strife breaking out between them... "in eternal times the Seat of Urizen is in the South, Urthona in the North, Luvah in the East, Tharmas in West" ("Vala"). Now the appropriate points have become confused as a result of Albion, the Universal Man, in whom the Zoas exist as functions, turning his back upon the Divine Vision and hiding his female counterpart or "Emanation," Jerusalem, who should be the Bride of the Lamb.

There is much that can be elicited in religious, psychological, or magical terms from this symbolism. Once again we see the formulation of a symetrical pattern which acts as model of the universe (the macrocosm) and also the soul of man (the microcosm) in time-honored fashion.

The forerunner of modern playing cards, the Tarot, forms another of these universal patterns. Through the centuries they were the neglected stock-in-trade of fortune telling gypsies. Suddenly, however they became the center of intense interest by virtue of a multi-volume work by Court de Gebelin at the end of the eighteenth century, entitled *Le Monde Primitif.* During this period, following a great interest in Greek antiquities, there was great speculation about Ancient Egypt. Egypt was then, in popular cultural terms, as near and yet so far as some of the planets have become for mankind now. The discovery of the Rosetta Stone enabled Egyptian hieroglyphics at last to be deciphered and so a great period of Egyptian archaeology was opened up. Court de Gebelin fanned interest in the Tarot by advancing the theory, with very little evidence it must be said, that they originated as Egyptian initiatory hieroglyphics.

In this, as with the ancient tradition of Freemasonry, he may have been correct in principle. The psychological dynamics of the Egyptian mysteries would have been much the same as the structure of the Tarot; though claiming a line of continuous historical derivation is another matter.

This stimulation of interest in the Tarot started a vogue in society for fortune telling by cards. Various spurious imitations of symbolic card sets were published backed by the names of well-known society clairvoyants such as "Etteila" and Mne. Le Normand.

At a more philosophical level they were used as the basis of a system of magical exposition by a French Catholic deacon, Alphonse Louis Constant (1810–1875). He wrote, under the Hebraicized pen-name of Eliphas Levi, a series of fascinating but historically imaginative texts on the magical tradition. His influence has been strong in French magical tradition ever since, his main works being *The History of Magic* and *Doctrine and Ritual of Transcendental Magic*.

He is the most enduring of a number of similar savants, with small groups of one kind or another, who formed a reaction to eighteenth century rationalism. They often combined this with a zeal for utopian political reform that could be risky at a time when revolutionary ideas were seething in Europe.

Eliphas Levi's interest in the Tarot encouraged the development of further speculative and esoteric work upon it in France, which culminated in the work of Dr. Gerard Encausse, who published *The Tarot of the Bohemians* under the pseudonym of "Papus" (1889), with a reproduction of the traditional Marseilles Tarot pack and an esoteric version by Oswald Wirth.

A major work of the early nineteenth century was *The Magus* or *Celestial Intelligencer* described as being "A Complete System of Occult Philosophy," by Francis Barrett. Published in 1801, it was a non-fictional equivalent to the Gothic novels rampant at the time and the architectural Gothic structures of Horace Walpole at Strawberry Hill or William Beckford at Bath. Barrett's book was a major compendium after the fashion of Cornelius Agrippa's *De Occulta Philosophia*. It has a certain barbarous air about it, which in common with much modern magical literature, is a result of its being derived from ancient scholarship rather than practical experience.

Half a century later, in 1850, a deeper and more radical book was published, at first anonymously, entitled *A Suggestive Inquiry into the*

Hermetic Mystery. It was described as being "An Attempt towards the Recovery of the Ancient Experiment of Nature, including a Dissertation on the more celebrated of the Alchemical Philosophers."

The work had come about as the result of a long collaboration between a Mary Anne South (later Atwood) and her father, a gentleman of leisure and amateur scholar, who possessed an exceptionally well-stocked library.

Mr. South and his daughter had originally started their investigations into the animal magnetism, animal electricity, mesmerism, hypnotism, somnambulism and spiritism that were so very much the vogue of the day. They had progressed however to a more deeply philosophical approach, the result of which was their book.

Largely quoting from ancient authors, it gives an impression of a very full and even firsthand knowledge of its subject. Having published the book however, they had grave second thoughts about the wisdom of making their researches public, and bought back all the copies that they could find, and burned them. Fortunately, a few survived and editions were later printed from 1918 onward.

An interest in magic and ancient lore was also pursued during the nineteenth century by various small groups and learned societies, though most were theoretical rather than practical. The Rosicrucian Society of England is an example of one. It was founded in 1866 but had little that was Rosicrucian about it except its name. It concerned itself with the investigation of spiritualistic and mesmeric phenomena with occasional lectures on Hermetic subjects. Lord Lytton is also associated with occult interests at this time, using some of his novels, such as *Zanoni,* as a vehicle for his theories.

The great barrier to any practical application of magic was the neglect into which it had fallen. On the one hand was the high Platonic tradition kept alive by the poets; but on the practical side a distorted reflection of a mechanical-scientific approach to the universe, with the psychic phenomena of magnetism and spiritualism being pursued in a disjointed fashion, regarded either as unorthodox science or else as unorthodox religion. The only practicalities of ancient initiation, alchemy or magic were in old manuscripts, inaccurate in their reproduction and barbarous in their application.

A cohesion to the whole subject came about in two ways in the last quarter of the century, with the foundation of two seminal groups that have had an overwhelming influence on the subject during the twentieth century. One of these groups was the Theosophical Society, under the leadership of Madame Blavatsky; the other was the Hermetic Order of the Golden Dawn under the dominating influence of S. L. MacGregor Mathers.

H. P. Blavatsky had originally been a gifted spiritualist medium. A Russian by birth, after many adventures she had, in America, commenced a remarkable corpus of work that was eventually published as the large and influential books *Isis Unveiled* and *The Secret Doctrine*. These constituted a vast body of cosmological theory which sought to delineate the origin and structure of the universe.

Madame Blavatsky's books caught the imagination of a large section of the public which had been spiritually starved in a climate of formalized Victorian Christianity. Madame Blavatsky's teachings were based on the religions of the East, being an amalgam of Buddhism and Hinduism interpreted in the light of a number of traditional neo-Platonic ideas. It was a grand encyclopedic conception that expressed the destiny of man in terms of a *spiritual* form of evolution, perhaps a unique straw to grasp for those whose traditional religious conviction had been badly damaged by Darwinian theories of *physical* evolution.

The philosophy implied a doctrine of reincarnation and also a regulating principle of *karma*. That is, that the deeds of one life would mold the circumstances of a succeeding life. After a series of lives souls would finally achieve liberation from the earthly chain of lives and go on to higher spheres. This was seen as part of an eternal evolution of consciousness in Planetary and stellar evolution. Those who were human today had, previously, through the ages, had the consciousness of minerals, plants and then animals before attaining the human condition. They would eventually evolve to be as gods, citizens of the spiritual starry firmament.

This philosophy was coupled with a belief in a body of "just men made perfect," human beings who had evolved further than the bulk of humanity. These guides were called the Masters or Mahatmas, and their voluntary appointed task was to guide humanity through its current evolutionary problems. And so again we have the idea being promulgated of an "invisible college" of adepts.

Madame Blavatsky attracted round herself a formidable group of strong personalities, and through their propagandizing efforts the Theosophical Society made tremendous strides and became an international organization from which much grew.

In spite of the vicissitudes and splintering of interests to which most religious groups are prone, the sheer synthesizing force of H. P.

Blavatsky's ideas affected almost the whole of twentieth century Western occult thought. With its Eastern bias, reincarnation and *karma* were reintroduced as concepts although they had played a small part down the centuries, in the general tradition of the West, but similar ideas had been current with the Druids and some Ancient Greeks.

The more specifically Western tradition, with its emphasis on the current personality and its physical expression in the world, was nurtured in the Hermetic Order of the Golden Dawn. This was principally through the researches of S. L. MacGregor Mathers at the British Museum. He produced a synthesis of Western traditions and formed a group giving training in practical magic with ceremonies of ritual initiation.

A variety of Knowledge Papers gave elementary instruction in the "alphabet" of symbolism, the astrological and alchemical signs, the Qabalistic Tree of Life, and the Pentagram and Hexagram, which formed the basis of dramatized means of psychic purification. There were, central to the whole system, a series of initiatory rituals which, properly performed, could act as a powerful stimulus to the active imagination and spiritual aspiration of the candidate. These led to admission to an Inner Order of "the Rose of Ruby and the Cross of Gold" which was based on the Christian Rosencreutz mythos, and sought to unite the higher aspects of the initiate's soul with his everyday lower nature.

The initiate was also instructed in the construction and consecration of the various traditional "magical weapons"—the wand, the sword, the cup, the lamen and so on—which represented aspects of the character of the candidate.

We find ourselves in an area of practical psychological dynamics similar to the methods advocated by Marsilio Ficino. Exercises in making talismans concentrated the mind on various archetypal forces of the universe and the soul of man, which were categorized into the twelve types of the zodiacal signs, the seven types of the traditional planets, or the four modes of the elements. There were also instructions on "Scrying in the Spirit Vision," a matter of using the visual imagination in a fashion since exploited to good effect in techniques of psychotherapy. And there was also a philosophical structure based on the symbolism of the Tarot and the Tree of Life, together with much more, including a reconstituted version of Dr. John Dee's system of Elemental Tablets.

This was a perfectly laudable attempt at reconstructing an age-old and valuable system of spiritual growth and self-awareness, although a certain social stigma could attach to it. Thus it was eventually necessary for Dr. Wynn Westcott, a London coroner and one of the founding

Rose Cross Lamen of the Hermetic Order of the Golden Dawn. All members of the higher grades of the Hermetic Order of the Golden Dawn had to make a lamen for themselves, to be worn over their robes on the breast, in accordance with this pattern; personal details were on the reverse. It indicates the synthesizing ideals of this fraternity in its amalgam of magical, alchemical, astrological, Qabalistic and Rosicrucian symbolism. The general tenor is, however, of the equilibration of the fourfold universe or soul leading to a higher quintessence.

members, to withdraw from participation because, as he described in his letter of resignation, of "having recd. an intimation that it had somehow become known to state officers that I was a prominent official of a society in which I was foolishly posturing as one possessed of magical powers and that if this became more public it would not do for a Coroner of the Crown to be made shame of in such a mad way."

This is a far cry from the persecution of former times but serves to emphasize the strong force of social attitudes that enjoined a certain necessity for secrecy about such societies.

There was also in the Golden Dawn, a belief in an invisible college of "secret chiefs" though this was not emphasized to such an extent as in the Theosophical Society. The Golden Dawn, however, did not last in its original form for more than fifteen years.

Gerald Yorke, an authority on the history of the Order, considers that the events of its dissolution are "a fascinating cautionary tale for all who try to develop their latent magical powers without using the protective techniques still taught in all the major religions. From it we see how the majority of those who attempt to tread the occult path of power become the victims of their creative imagination, inflate their egos and fall." The general "protective technique" in the Christian West, to use Gerald Yorke's rather mechanistic terminology, is the assumption that man is fallen from a condition of original grace which can only be remedied by a re-orientation of the will, in repentance and reconciliation, with God. Although some lip service was given to this in certain teachings of the Golden Dawn there was, unfortunately, a general and stronger tacit assumption that members of the Order were somewhat superior to the rest of the human race, and by virtue of secret ceremonies, knowledge and practices could elevate themselves to be considerably more superior.

The result in the case of the Golden Dawn was an inflation of the sense of self-importance of a number of the members, developing a foolish and dangerous pride that led to a humiliating fall.

However, the spark ignited by MacGregor Mathers and the Golden Dawn was sufficient to nourish the poetic genius of W. B. Yeats, and to attract a number of influential people of the day such as Sir Gerald Kelly (later of the Tate Gallery) and Annie Horniman, the tea heiress.

Furthermore the vitality of its vision was so strong that it resulted in the burgeoning of a number of groups, founded by its members, which had a profound effect on twentieth century magical thought and the occult revival of the nineteen sixties and seventies.

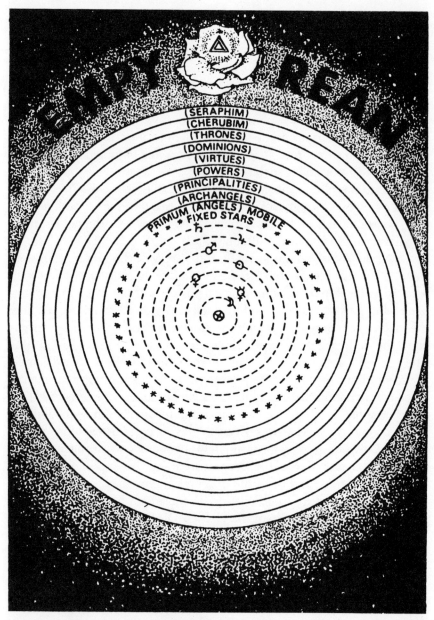

The Crystalline Spheres of the Heavens. Schematic diagram of the crystalline spheres surrounding the Earth upon each of which is a planet, and beyond them the spheres of the Fixed Stars or Zodiac and the Primum Mobile which contains the angels and gives movement to all. The angelic orders are laid out diagramatically in the order given in Pseudo-Dionysius' *The Celestial Hierarchies*. Beyond all in the Empyreum is the Mystic Rose of the Presence of God, the Elect forming the petals with God as a geometric form in the center.

Chapter 8
Toward a Magical Revival

The beginning of the twentieth century saw a consolidation of scholarship in magical matters. If this was not within the bounds of the academic establishment, it was at least the result of reasonably scholarly efforts by a number of responsible writers who were sympathetic to the subject. Certainly such an approach was long overdue.

A number of these works were translations or reprints of ancient works, with a commentary or long introduction by the editor concerned. MacGregor Mathers of the Golden Dawn contributed in this way a fragment of the Qabalistic writings, *The Kabbalah Unveiled*. This had the disadvantage of being a translation of a translation, rendered into English from Knorr von Rosenroth's Latin version of the original Hebrew. Mathers also produced more hair-raising medieval texts such as *The Lesser Key of Solomon* and *The Sacred Magic of Abramelin the Mage*. These were works of more antiquarian than practical usage and with their emphasis on demonology not the best of material with which to encourage a wholesale public rapprochement to the subject. However they caused a *frisson* of excitement through the occult world of the time and much awe was expressed about the possible malignant effects of the magic square to be found on the cover of one of them (see next page). Subsequent cryptographical scholarship has however revealed it to be an early Christian device based on the opening of the Lord's Prayer. It forms the words "Our Father" (*pater noster*) in Latin, together with the ciphers of Alpha and Omega, the "Beginning and the Ending."

S	A	T	O	R
A	R	E	P	O
T	E	N	E	T
O	P	E	R	A
R	O	T	A	S

```
                          P
                          A
              O           T           A
                          E
                          R
          P A T E R N O S T E R
                          O
                          S
              A           T           O
                          E
                          R
```

Magic Square

Another Golden Dawn initiate, A. E. Waite, was responsible for a number of reissues of alchemical and other works, including the writings of Thomas Vaughan, and translations of Eliphas Levi. He was also responsible for a number of weighty volumes on subjects such as the Holy Grail, the Rosicrucians, and the secret traditions in Israel, which attracted reasonably respectful academic notice. He was very conscious of the need to make magic and the more responsible sectors of occult philosophy acceptable to society at large and in his concern for this tended to write in a turgid, verbose and pompous style. This led Aleister Crowley, an *enfant terrible* of twentieth-century occultism, to refer to him as "Dead Weight." However, despite such failings, the tradition owes much to Waite's quite courageous and painstaking work.

W. B. Yeats also participated in this type of scholarly endeavor, and the theosophist scholar G. R. S. Mead did sterling work in the translation of Gnostic manuscripts. Three publishing ventures were also important in this movement. The formation of the Rider imprint devoted exclusively to occult books gave a platform for authors and a small but growing public. Some of the books they published verged on the popular and ephemeral but they produced a number of classic texts of the period. This was paralleled by a long-running journal, *The Occult Review,* under the editorship of the Hon. Ralph Shirley, which met its final demise only with the exigencies of the Second World War. The third important publishing venture was *The Shrine of Wisdom* series which still carries out the aim of making ancient mystical texts available at reasonable prices.

Of considerable embarrassment to those who were seeking to reinstitute the worthy credentials of magic were the antics of Aleister

Crowley, a young man of much promise, brilliant intellect and many social advantages. He played his part in the breakup of the Golden Dawn but went on, as did a number of other former members, to organize his own working groups and system of training.

Unfortunately he was a *farceur* of the *pince sans rire* variety and achieved the distinction of being the first person to be the victim of a press smear campaign. This was at the hands of *John Bull* and the *Sunday Express,* who dubbed him "the wickedest man in the world" on the strength of some political and sexual indiscretions and his avowed interest in magic. Aleister Crowley not only turned the cheek to this assault, but reveled in it. He outgunned his moralist critics by claiming to be no less than "the Beast 666" from the Revelations. How much of this was originally, and eventually, tongue in cheek is difficult to discern. Certainly Crowley was as much sinned against as sinning, although he treated some of his friends and disciples abominably. Some of his original research into magical theory and practice retains the respect of serious practitioners of the subject to this day. Regrettably, his writings are marred by some deliberate efforts to shock. These range from smutty and irreligious jibes of a fourth form variety to the description of sexual acts not aimed at physical reproduction as "child sacrifice." Ironically, this is not far from Roman Catholic religious dogma, a point which would not have been lost upon the malicious wit of Crowley. The additional fact that the society of his times was more likely to be shocked by sex than by murder also no doubt caused him some satirical amusement.

To the informed and intelligent reader, these peccadilloes can be recognized and made allowance for, but there is a danger that some of Crowley's writings, taken literally by the less intelligent and well informed, could lead to some ugly cult beliefs and practices. His main tenets of teaching, taken from Rabelais' Abbey of Thelema, "Do what thou wilt shall be the whole of the Law," is typical of the double meanings involved, for although this phrase at one level might seem the recipe for self-indulgence and anarchy, it is, at another level, an injunction to identify one's actions with the spiritual will, the divine spark of God within, as suggested by his other maxim, "Every man and every woman is a star."

As Gerald Yorke pointed out, there is a great danger in the Golden Dawn system of the inflation of the personality. This seems to have occurred in the case of Aleister Crowley and it remains a danger for any who elect to follow his system. His end was not one to inspire emulation. Having experimented in early years on the effects of drugs upon consciousness, he slipped into addiction, and ended his days as a registered addict.

Like Coleridge, he learned much from bitter experience with drugs, but lacking a deeper religious orientation, was not able to put it to such good effect.

One of the background assumptions of esoteric thought in the twentieth century has been the concept of a new age. Predictions of new ages have always been with us but this particular one is allied to the swing of the Earth's axis which causes a precession of equinoxes, so that the Sun starts the year in the constellation of Aquarius instead of Pisces. As the Zodiacal constellations are not well defined there is considerable latitude in fixing upon the exact date of such an event. As evidence for it, the early Christian symbolism of describing Christ as a fish is invoked, the Piscean Age coincided with the start of the Christian era—the Sun changing sign about every 2,000 years.

Be this as it may, it has, combined with the tendency to personality inflation, led to some claims of a new Messiah, (or *Avatar*, to use an Eastern term), for those whose theology disposes to such a belief. This was reflected in Crowley, for instance, who predicted a new Aeon of Horus, with of course himself as a main protagonist. A similar trend occurred with the Theosophical Society, the other formative influence in twentieth-century occultism.

After the death of its founder, H. P. Blavatsky, the running of the Society fell to the great social reformer Annie Besant, assisted by C. W. Leadbeater. Their propagandizing efforts were powerful and effective and a mass of books, booklets and pamphlets popularizing the "ancient wisdom," interpreted through theosophical eyes, flooded the West.

Mrs. Besant attracted some criticism for involving the Society in Indian politics, though her concern to end the British *raj* was typically within the traditions of her own social conscience, and her views have been justified by subsequent history.

C. W. Leadbeater, perhaps sensing that theosophy lacked something by ignoring Christianity (Madame Blavatsky had been virulently anti-clerical, and not without cause), became a bishop in the Liberal Catholic Church, a small offshoot from the Old Catholic Church of Holland that had split from Rome in the eighteenth century. He also had adopted two Indian boys whom he sensed, by clairvoyant means, were potentially highly gifted spiritual teachers. One of these subsequently became the focus of a movement allied to the Theosophical Society, which had the intention of promoting the young boy as Avatar for the New Age. This movement fell upon disaster when the boy, Krishnamurti, eventually repudiated it.

It is interesting however that Krishnamurti has, none the less, developed a reputation as a spiritual teacher, though by no means on such a universal scale as his disciples originally hoped. His teaching might be described as a type of spiritual existentialism and retains a certain following. Like similar spiritual teachings the intellectual sophistication demanded tends to prevent them from becoming mass movements.

A less radical departure from theosophical principles, and indeed a development of the teachings in some degree of complexity, are to be found in the writings of Alice A. Bailey. *A Treatise on Cosmic Fire,* and a monumental multi-volume *Treatise on the Seven Rays,* are detailed developments of basic theosophical belief from Blavatsky's *Secret Doctrine* and elsewhere. Much has been made in the earlier literature of the "Masters" or "Mahatmas" and the writings of Alice Bailey, for the most part, are stated to be the brainchild of one of these masters, Dwaj Khul, or "The Tibetan."

Although the teachings would eschew much of the Western magical traditions on the grounds that they are the magic of "form," as opposed to a more appropriate concern with higher spiritual forces, an important practical book within this corpus of work is entitled *A Treatise on White Magic.*

The gist of this comprehensive work is concerned with the integration of the elements of human consciousness and embodiment to make a stable and lasting contact with what is called the Soul, an alternative term for the higher self. Much time is given to the correspondences between various levels of bodily activity and consciousness. The teachings state quite categorically that they are monist—that is, that they see God as being embodied in all things—which places a theological and philosophical gap between them and the main traditions of European thought.

A latter-day emphasis has emerged in bringing a Christian element into the teachings, which, as they start from monist assumptions, is not theologically easy. But these considerations aside, the general tendency is for a broad universalism that strives to unite Buddhism and Christianity, at any rate esoterically, and which places emphasis on all human movements towards cultural unity and synthesis, such as for instance the United Nations organization. It is assumed that all mankind is progressing in a general evolution of consciousness, assisted by those already more highly evolved. All men and women of good will are regarded as being in the vanguard of evolution, members of the New Group of World Servers, whether they realize the fact or not, and whatever their field or calling might be.

Another important movement is that which has come to be known as Anthroposophy and is radically concerned with the promulgation of the spiritual dimension in the advancement of science and other forms of human knowledge.

The movement was founded by Dr. Rudolf Steiner, who was born in 1861 in humble circumstances in a border area of Austria that is now part of Yugoslavia. Having worked his way through university to gain a degree in mathematics, physics and chemistry, and a doctorate in philosophy, he made his mark sufficiently well to be asked to edit the scientific section in the complete edition of the works of the great German polymath Johann Wolfgang von Goethe.

Goethe (1749–1832) is something of a transitional figure between the world of the seventeenth century and the burgeoning materialist outlook of the nineteenth century. Universally recognized as a great poet, critic and theatrical director, the author of *Faust* and other major works of German literature also included the sciences in his range of interests.

In this pursuit he was not afraid of attacking the great Newton, particularly on the subject of color and light. He attacked Newton's mathematical bias, which he said had caused Newton to make observational errors in the mater of color. Indeed he went so far as to imply that the whole science of physics had got off on the wrong foot because of the errors of Newton.

Goethe's book, *The Theory of Colors,* appeared in 1810 and caused something of a sensation, and was incorporated by Hegel into his idealist philosophy. An English translation appeared in 1840, which has been reprinted by the Massachusetts Institute of Technology Press as recently as 1970, admittedly as something of a curiosity for students of the history of science and ideas but with an introduction that, while reaffirming the established scientific view that "Goethe's explanation of color makes no physical sense at all" nonetheless concedes that "A reader who attempts to follow the logic of Goethe's explanation and who attempts to compare them with the currently accepted views might, even with the advantage of 1970 sophistication [*sic*], become convinced that Goethe's theory or at least a part of it, has been dismissed too quickly."

This was certainly the conclusion of the young Dr. Rudolf Steiner in the course of his editing the scientific works of Goethe, which are by no means confined to color theory but also covered the morphology of plant growth and the role of the disciplined use of the imaginative faculty in the pursuit of knowledge.

The use of the imagination in this way is no mere subjective fantasy, as is demonstrated by other undisputed contributions that Goethe made to science. He discovered the basic principle in botany that the parts of a plant can be regarded as different forms of the leaf. He also discovered a hitherto unknown bone in the human skeleton—the *os intermaxillare*—through his methods of imaginative investigation.

Steiner felt it incumbent upon himself to pursue the methods of Goethe which the conventional scientific world chose to ignore. This gradually led him into a position of professional isolation and ostracism, particularly after he accepted the public platforms provided for him by the Count and Countess Brockdorff, who were prominent Theosophists. Indeed for a brief period Steiner accepted the presidency of the Theosophical Society in Germany, although his spiritual perceptions and affiliations were more closely concerned with western rather than oriental traditions.

Eventually he found it necessary to found his own movement, from which has grown the Anthroposophical Society and a worldwide network of schools teaching by Steiner's principles. A similar network of schools, homes and residential villages has been developed for handicapped children and adults. Biodynamic agriculture sprang from a course of lectures he gave in 1924 to a group of local farmers who were concerned, even then, about the consequence of "scientific" farming methods. Homeopathic clinics and hospitals have developed from his work with doctors, and his art of eurythmy has attracted much attention in the educational and therapeutic spheres. Training centers for teachers, agriculture, the arts and social work have also been established over the years. The author of many works, Rudolf Steiner's principal works are *Occult Science—An Outline* and *Knowledge of the Higher Worlds*.

An important voice within this movement, which has been more appreciated in the United States than in his native England, has been Owen Barfield, largely through the Wesleyan University of Connecticut. A close friend and intellectual confidant of C. S. Lewis, throughout both their lives, he is another facet of that remarkable group of Oxford University friends known as "the Inklings" which included J. R. R. Tolkien and Charles Williams, who among them have exercised a profound effect upon popular consciousness through their "mythopaeic" approach to fantasy, occult and science fiction. (So much so that I have devoted a whole book to them only, entitled *The Magical World of the Inklings*.)

Barfield's principal work has been on the history and development of language to demonstrate the evolution of the history of human consciousness, which is intimately concerned with the use we make of the imaginative faculty, from primitive "participation mystique" as children of the Great Mother to our current stage of individualized consciousness; the centuries of materialistic emphasis that are now coming to a close being a necessary factor in the development of the human ego to a point when consciousness of the inner dynamics of the group, and the spiritual worlds, can be once more opened up, but on a higher level. The process is paralleled by the evolution of the child from dependence on the womb and then the mother, through burgeoning ego-consciousness through puberty and adolescence to adulthood. This level of responsibility upon a cosmic and spiritual level is what the human race currently aspires to but there is arguably a way to go yet!

A teacher of considerable importance who has very much trod his own furrow is G. I. Gurdjieff, a Russian, like Madame Blavatsky, whose principle disciple was another Russian, P. D. Ouspen-sky. Gurdjieff's major work was comprehensively entitled *All and Everything*, or alternatively *Beelzebub's Tales to his Grandson*. Which, if either, title was chosen tongue in cheek is open to the choice of the reader; Gurdjieff does not make things too easy for the conventional and rational mind.

Much of his teaching is based on a device known as the Enneagram, in appearance somewhat like a nine pointed star within a circle. This he used as a hieroglyph of universal application in much the same way that the mainstream of Western occult tradition uses the tenfold spheres of the Qabalistic Tree of Life.

While he traced the roots of his system as far back as ancient Mesopotamia and through the msytery school of Pythagoras, the immediate antecedent of the enneagram is the mathematical invention of the concept of zero, together with the decimal system, in the 15th century.

It was discovered that if the unity is divided by three then an endless series of threes is generated, (what we learn in school to call a recurring decimal). This also occurs with the six and the nine if the origianl unity is doubled or trebled, thus:

$1/3 = 0.333333\ldots ad\ infinitum$

$2/3 = 0.666666\ldots ad\ infinitum$

$3/3 = 0.999999\ldots ad\ infinitum$ (which is only an infinitude less than the unity itself)

This indicates the importance of the concept of trinity, and the three, six and nine can be graphically expressed as a triangle that is formed in a circle whose circumference has been equally divided by nine points.

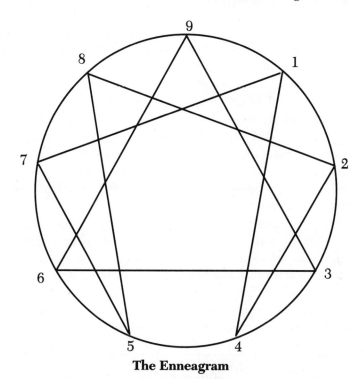

The Enneagram

Another significant result is obtained by dividing the unity by the traditionally mystical number 7. Here we get a recurring sequence of all the remaining digits.

1/7 = 0.142857 142857 142857 . . . etc. *ad infinitum*

These numbers occur in the same sequence in succeeding multiples of sevenths, up toward the unity, thus:

2/7 = 0.285714 285714 285714 . . . etc. *ad infinitum*
3/7 = 0.428571 428571 428571 . . . etc. *ad infinitum*
4/7 = 0.571428 571428 571428 . . . etc. *ad infinitum*
5/7 = 0.714285 714285 714285 . . . etc. *ad infinitum*
6/7 = 0.857142 857142 857142 . . . etc. *ad infinitum*

until one reaches the decimal equivalent of 7/7 which is 0.999999 . . . *ad infinitum.*

This sequence of numbers will complete the enneagram if we join up the appropriate dots around the circle (see Fig. 5).

From this conceptual basis it is possible to build up an awareness of harmonic resonances in the whole of life that extend throughout the physical universe and beyond it into the higher realms that caused its manifestation. Part of this number mysticism is to be developed in its applications to the sevenfold resonances of the spectrum, and of the musical scale, and so forth. Various students of Ouspensky have applied themselves to this system, including the psychologist Maurice Nicoll, whose five volumes of *Psychological Commentaries on the Teaching of Gurdjieff and Ouspensky* is regarded as a classic in this field. Also within this tradition are the books of Rodney Collin, of which *The Theory of Celestial Influence*, for example, embraces the resonances of astronomy, geology, biology, anatomy, psychology and history in an attempt to awaken man to an alternative model of the universe that is perceived by the ordinary logical mind; where the purpose of all and everything in the universe, from star to cell, is seen to be in a process of struggle to the attainment of a higher level of consciousness.

That this is no closed circle of esoteric theorizing is borne out by the adoption of the enneagram system by other schools of thought, including priests and therapists working under the aegis of the Roman Catholic church, where it is used as a system of heart-centered prayer as well as a method of diagnostics for psychological problems, in *The Enneagram and Prayer* by Metz and Burchill, and *The Enneagram, a Journey of Self Discovery* by Beesing, Nogosak and O'Leary. The more esoteric approach is covered by *Enneagram Studies* by Gurdjieff disciple J. G. Bennett.

We must take account of the intellectual climate of the twentieth century as it relates to the dynamics of the human soul. There is no doubt that the major force in this respect is the field of psychology, and in particular that branch of it known to Sigmund Freud as psychoanalysis or to C. G. Jung as analytical psychology. In the earliest decades of the century much attention was given to the powers of suggestion, and Coué's formula of encouraging people to recite "Every day and in every way I am getting better and better" enjoyed a great vogue in what generally came to be called the New Thought movement. This fragmented into various forms of "positive thinking" that still have an appeal to this day, sometimes in the form of manuals for salesmen. The extent of their influence extended even to the religious sphere and it is reported that some nuns preferred to modify Coué's phrase to "Every day and in every way, by the grace of God, I am getting better and better." One of the more successful writers of this genre was W. W. Atkinson with his *Secrets of Mental Magic,* who also wrote a series of books on popularized forms of yoga under the pseudonym of Yogi Ramacharaka.

At a deeper level the psychological thought of the times has outstripped "self help" psychology and is dominated by the depth psychologies of Freud and Jung. Freud can take credit for formulating the theory of the subconscious. This was considerably developed by his pupil Jung, though not in a fashion that Freud approved.

Freud emphasized analysis, in a fashion analogous to the analytic assumptions of physical science—although there are psychologists, of the behaviorist school for instance, who would regard Freud as both unanalytical and unscientifIc. Jung preferred an approach which used a technique of integrating the personality rather than analyzing it. The influence of Jung plays an important part in latter-day magic and occultism, for he seemed to confirm much of what these disciplines had already discovered.

The principal planks of Jung's psychology are the categorization of psychological types, based upon combinations of four psychological functions—intuition, thinking, feeling and sensation—in relation to a general disposition to introversion or extroversion. In this we have a similar pattern to the Pillars of Solomon's Temple and the Four Elements of the ancients.

The four functions have a set relationship, one to another, so that intuition is opposed to sensation, and thinking is opposed to feeling. Each one of us will tend to express himself in relation to the outside world in accordance with one main function, or possibly two. The functions that are unconscious are not well used and can cause uncontrolled reactions. Thus a thinking type will try to control the environment and his reaction thereto by rational thought, but may be prone to sudden reactions of emotion, perhaps manifesting as an altogether unscientifIc bitchiness to rivals, or else as obsessive romantic attachments.

The repressed function tends to express itself in an uncontrolled fashion—although this need not always be the case. If one can come to an understanding with the "unconscious," and allow it to put its point of view forward, as it were, then a process of psychological integration can take place leading to a balanced manifestation of personality traits.

The ways that this integration process may be encouraged are several, the most important of which are probably the recording and analysis of dreams, and the tracing of association chains in free fantasy on the analyst's couch, commencing from dream symbols or from words selected by a word-association test.

In his researches into the unconsciousness, however, Jung came upon a number of major psychological dynamics. These he called *archetypes of the unconscious*. They seemed to be complexes of psychic force grouped around a particular association of ideas that was common to all human experience.

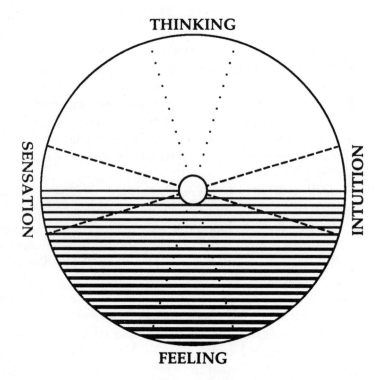

Jungian Functions

In the integration process it was usual to come upon, in turn, figures which he designated the Shadow; the *Animus* or *Anima;* the Wise Old Man or Wise Old Woman; and the Self which might appear as a mandala figure or as a Miraculous Child.

Briefly, the Shadow represents repressed parts of the personality that one does not wish to face as part of oneself. This is often "projected" onto other people, in the form of irrational dislikes.

The Animus or Anima, on the other hand, is a contrasexual image, male (animus) in the case of women and female (anima) in the case of men. These seem to represent the accumulated knowledge and experience of the opposite sex and can also be projected onto another human being, which results in the process known as falling in love.

One can also be possessed temporarily by an archetype, as well as project it. A man possessed by the anima becomes moody and irritable, in short, showing all the adverse reactions of a debased femininity. Conversely a woman possessed by the animus is apt to become bossy and opinionated, a travesty of maleness.

The Wise Old Man and Wise Old Woman tend to be the same sex as the subject and there is an interesting record of Jung's extended conversation with a figure of this nature, whom he called Philemon, in his autobiography *Memories, Dreams, Reflections*.

Finally, the Self archetype represents a complete integration of the personality, and is apt to appear initially as dreams or visions of a balanced fourfold figure, which Jung termed a *mandala*, which translated from Sanskrit into English means "magic circle." This may give place to a kind of religious conversion experience, perhaps allied to a vision of a wonder-working child, such as appears in the Christian nativity story for instance.

Jung found evidence that paralleled much of his clinical experience in folklore, mythology, and religious traditions, and in magical and alchemical symbolism. He therefore developed his theory of the unconscious which states that if one goes deep enough into the unconscious mind then one will go beyond the personal level to depths that one has in common with one's family and racial group, and eventually to a level common to all humanity.

The Jungian theories had a considerable impact upon the mainstream of magical practitioners in the nineteen-thirties who had inherited in one way or another the Golden Dawn tradition. After centuries of scientific neglect they gave a rationale, from a reasonably respectable source, for much of the body of experience and tradition that white magicians had accumulated.

Israel Regardie and Dion Fortune are particularly important figures in this context, during the late 1920s through the 1930s. Although Aleister Crowley had published a fair amount of the Golden Dawn material in his privately published journal, *The Equinox,* in the first decade of the century, it was Israel Regardie who finally arranged the comprehensive publication of the system as a coherent whole in four volumes entitled *The Golden Dawn.* He felt this necessary because the original impetus of the Hermetic Order of the Golden Dawn had petered out. And although its vitality and tradition had been continued by a variety of former members with new groups of their own, he felt it in the public interest to make the original system accessible to all.

Prior to this he published a series of books about the principles of the system, such as *A Garden of Pomegranates*, his notes on the Tree of Life of the Qabalah, and *The Tree of Life*, perhaps his major work, which is an exegesis of magical principles. *The Middle Pillar* also gave details of performing a practical magical exercise, which was an unheard of thing in its day. Of particular importance, in retrospect, are his attempts to relate this knowledge to the new techniques and theories of psychoanalysis; and in some instances he went so far as to suggest that, not only could magic be considered a branch of psychology, but that magical ritual might well be employed in the consulting room. Although this must have seemed a bizarre suggestion at the time there has indeed been a very considerable rapprochement over the years between analytical psychology and occultism.

Dion Fortune, who formed her own magical fraternity, the Society of the Inner Light, also pursued this line of thought. She had previously been a Freudian lay-analyst and one of the reasons she came to occultism was because it seemed to give the answer to a number of phenomena not explained by the psychology of the day. Her major contribution to the literature of the subject is *The Mystical Qabalah*, one of the first texts on the subject which is readily comprehensible. In her books, which ranged from occult novels through a number of popular approaches to magic from various aspects, she generally combined a sound commonsense approach with an awareness of the psychological theories of the times.

Her work has been developed by the present writer and by W. E. Butler, both former members of her society.

W. E. Butler has published a number of texts on the disciplines involved in magical training, of which the most important is perhaps *The Magician: His Training and Work*; and his broad experience in the Theosophical Society in India, in Dion Fortune's Society since the 1920s, as a spiritualist clairvoyant and as a priest in the Liberal Catholic Church, give his works a broad conspectus of the tradition as practiced and developed during the mid-years of the twentieth century.

The Society of the Inner Light still continues and, like some Lodges of the Golden Dawn before it, has been criticized for modifying its magical line towards a more religious and mystical approach. In the light of the strictures already quoted by Gerald Yorke on the Golden Dawn system and its derivatives, this is in some respects understandable, although a sound religious basis to magic does not necessarily imply that the magical work has to be reduced or diluted—rather the reverse in fact.

Of other groups that continued the Golden Dawn tradition in their own fashion, the Builders of the Adytum, founded by the American Paul Foster Case, is important for its emphasis on the Tarot. The Tarot has appeared from time to time in magical history since the fifteenth century. Previously it had been developed as an esoteric system in France by Dr. Gerard Encausse, which he published as *The Tarot of the Bohemians* under the pseudonym of Papus, with a reproduction of the traditional Marseilles Tarot and an esoteric version by Oswald Wirth. A. E. Waite also produced a set of designs, as did Aleister Crowley, and Paul Case. It was not until 1978 that a version of the Golden Dawn set was produced by Israel Regardie and Dr. Robert Wang. From a period when published Tarot cards were great rarities the 1960s and 70s has seen a great spate of their production. Stuart Kaplan's *Tarot Classic* and *Encyclopedia of Tarot* are good reference guides to the subject.

Other American presentations of the magical tradition include re-statements of Rosicrucian principles in line with the culture of the times. One of these was The Rosicrucian Fellowship organized by Max Heindel, author of *The Rosicrucian Cosmo-Conception.* The widespread advertising methods of AMORC, a Rosicrucian organization run on correspondence course lines, also shows a typically American and twentieth-century approach to the tradition. At the other extreme, an American magical fraternity, the Order of the Sacred Word, founded in 1897 by Charles Kingold and George Stanton, only came to public notice recently with the publication of a series of volumes of their teachings by Melita Denning and Osborne Phillips: *The Magical Philosophy* (1974).

It would be impracticable and tedious to record all the groups, many secret, small and ephemeral, that characterize the magical tradition of this time. The scholarship of Manly P. Hall should, however, be noted. He founded the Philosophical Research Society and first came to wide attention in the 1920s with his monumental *Encyclopaedic Outline of Masonic, Hermetic, Qabalistic and Rosicrucian Symbolical Philosophy,* recently re-issued under the less barbarously long title, *The Secret Teachings of All Ages.* His many other works show a responsible and at the same time sympathetic and inclusive view of the esoteric tradition.

There are also individuals and organizations who fall outside the strictly magical tradition but whose techniques or intentions are certainly relevant. One such is Olive Pixley, who evolved a series of exercises of the imagination that might be described as prayer in symbolic pictures. Although magic would probably have been the last thing with which she would wish to be associated, such techniques are nonetheless of the very essence of white magic. In her book *The Armour of Light* and its sequel *The Magnet,* a whole range of these techniques are given that have been found to produce psychic integration and even physical healing.

Of course the whole field of fringe medicine, clairvoyance, and such techniques as water divining, whether with hazel twigs, pendulum, or a "black box," are related to our subject, but we may perhaps confine our attention to one researcher, the American Max Freedom Long, whose book *The Secret Science Behind Miracles,* and others in the same vein, produced a coherent and relatively simple system. His researches commenced in Hawaii, trying to discover the ancient lore of the indigenous miracle workers or medicine men, the Kahunas. This in course of time led him to develop what he called Huna Magic, which for the most part is a coming to terms with the subconscious mind and developing the latent psychic abilities by means of a pendulum. This led him to develop a theory of a "High Self" and a "Low Self" that is similar to the classic more complex formulations of Eastern and Western esoteric traditions.

The expedient of turning to contemporary folk traditions as a way of discovering magical techniques has become a fairly widespread twentieth-century phenomenon. As Max Freedom Long turned to the Kahunas of Hawaii, so contemporaneously has Carlos Castaneda found much to learn from the traditions of the Yaqui Indian, Don Juan.

Castaneda, as a student at the University of California at Berkeley, commenced a research project in anthropology that turned out far differently from his expectations. The Indian whom he approached took him at his word and commenced to initiate him into Indian magic. A first great obstacle to be overcome was his great weight of intellectual preconceptions instilled by higher education, and to do this Don Juan used the somewhat drastic method of strong doses of hallucinogenic mushrooms. In the last book, *Tales of Power,* he states that but for the highly intellectual Castaneda's obtuseness, such methods would have been unnecessary. The first book of the sequence particularly, *The Teachings of Don Juan* (1968), is an object lesson in how the modern mind has manufactured mental blinkers for itself.

A figure who did much to popularize the pagan approaches to magic, particularly in its "witchcraft" nomenclature, was Gerald Brosseau Gardner with his book *The Meaning of Witchcraft.* There is some controversy as to how much Gardner's system of initiation is genuinely traditional and how much his own invention, and with what mixture of motives he produced it, but there is no doubt that the extent of the modern movement owes much to him.

In its more scholarly aspect the tradition is traced by Dr. Margaret Murray in *The Witch-Cult in Western Europe* and *The God of the Witches,* and Robert Graves' speculative book *The White Goddess* is a mine of fascinating information. The folk musician Bob Stewart's book *Where is St. George?* traces old ritual from a selection of folk songs. Perhaps the most consistent, intelligent and well informed modern advocate of the neo-pagan tradition is Frederick McLauren Adams and his organization Feraferia in California.

This country tradition links on to the strong latter-day interest in power centers and "ley-lines" which have been of consuming interest for a number of investigators, a most lucid appreciation of whose efforts are contained in *Earth Magic* (1976) by Francis Hitching. The ley-line theory was formulated by Alfred Watkins, an amateur photographer and archaeologist of Herefordshire in the early years of this century. His ideas were in fact, not particularly occult. He noticed that a number of old churches, earthworks and dew ponds fell in straight lines and developed from this the idea that they were sight-markers for early man transporting commodities across country. This is described in his book *The Old Straight Track* and its practical sequel *The Ley-Hunters Guide*.

Over the years this theory has been overlaid with the more occult theory that many of these sites are in fact psychic power centers, either natural or manmade, with communication lines interlinking them. The theory, even without its occult overlay, has been dismissed by most professional archaeologists who regard such lines as a natural consequence of there being so many such sites in Western Europe of one kind or another. Orthodoxy has been undergoing a certain erosion however by responsible researchers into some of the old stone circles, such as Professor Thom, producing proof that some of them were sophisticated astronomical observatories.

Less academically inhibited enthusiasts have, moreover, embraced related theories and, at Findhorn in Scotland for instance, have succeeded in making the wilderness bloom apparently by communing with natural forces. Other enthusiasts, such as the Aetherius Society, regard certain hills as psycho-spiritual storage batteries utilized by visitors from outer space. This kind of claim of course does not help to reconcile the sceptical to the subject as a whole, but without endorsing every speculation that is made, there may still be stranger things in heaven and earth than are dreamed of in more prosaic philosophy.

The most impressive public evidences of occult or psychic realities are in fact usually from what might be termed psycho-genetic "sports"; that is, occasional individuals with extremely unusual gifts. One such, for instance, Edgar Cayce, was an unassuming man, of conventional, even narrow religious views, who had the unsought ability to fall into trance and give voluminous and usually accurate advice about inquirers' personal or physical problems. There is now a research organization specifically devoted to sorting, collating and publishing the vast amount of information, prophecies and pronouncements that he made during his lifetime. In England, Matthew Manning is another example; a young man with quite abnormal psychic abilities. Examples of such unusual individuals exist through the ages, from political activists and visionaries such as Joan of Arc, to cryptic prophets such as the sixteenth century Nostradamus.

The pursuit of white magic is not however concerned with the production of psychic wonders. Its object is the development of a higher type of awareness, the steady light of the intuition, of pure reason, or the secondary imagination, rather than fleeting and flickering visual or verbal impressions in the fancy. This is a matter which is often misunderstood, particularly in that area popularly known as astral projection. To read accounts of popular occult novelists it might be imagined that magicians spend most of their time engaged in adventures outside their physical bodies in a phantom form called the astral body.

A book which drew wide attention to this subject was *The Projection of the Astral Body* by Sylvan Muldoon, a natural projector, and the psychical researcher Hereward Carrington. Sylvan Muldoon had the advantage, if it might be so expressed, of a sickly physical disposition with, to judge from photographs of him, a certain glandular unbalance. Probably because of this he found he could develop the ability of being conscious outside his own physical body, apparently inhabiting a simulacrum of it.

The phantom body seemed to be connected to the physical one by a silver cord, and the impression was that if this were severed it would result in physical death. The words of the bible "if ever the silver chord be loosed or the golden bowl be broken" were felt to be apposite to this body of light and its thread. When near the physical body the pull of the thread was very considerable, tugging the bodies back together again. When further away this was less noticeable but the cord was infinitely elastic. Muldoon found that with this body he could travel by floating, either slowly, or very fast indeed, and that he could pass through walls and other physical objects. Any real unpleasantness by way of attack or collision was likely to come from other denizens of this "plane," not the physical, although the physical could be observed.

Naturally this aroused great popular interest and a number of books attempted to show ways of emulating this feat; Oliver Fox's *Astral Projection*, Yram's *Practical Astral Projection*, and in latter days Ophiel's *The Art and Practice of Astral Projection* and *Astral Doorways* by J. H. Brennan. It is not however an ability that comes easily. It may demand years of effort and even then may prove physically impossible for those whose psycho-physical constitution is well-knit. W. E. Butler records being forcibly ejected into his astral body by his teacher Robert King, after badgering him to do so, only to be brought back hastily because his heart seemed unlikely to be able to stand the strain.

It is an ability that is recorded of certain yogis, after long, arduous training, but it does not form a part of the essential Western magical curriculum. The function of magic is to bring about a better physical expression of spiritual forces rather than to spend time and effort on an ascetic discipline withdrawn from ordinary life in order to develop the separation of consciousness from the body.

The phenomenon of projection can also occur spontaneously in the occasional individual, even though they may have little interest in such matters. One such was the American businessman Robert A. Monroe who, in his book *Journey Out of the Body,* records finding this happening to him. At first he wondered if he was going mad. He sought psychiatric help but could find no cure or explanation there. In the end he read some occult books which gave him some idea of what was happening to him.

There are many different "regions" that can be experienced by astral projection. At one level is the observation of the physical world from a phantasmal vantage point, but there are other experiences that seem to have no direct physical connection. Some of these may be dream-like and entirely symbolic experiences. Others seem to be earthly experiences in the past or at a distance. In one case recorded by Monroe, he found himself in a civilization with a strange combination of advanced and primitive technology that suggests nothing on this earth, past or present.

Similar visionary experiences may be had by other techniques of magic that are not quite so demanding as full astral projection. It is possible simply to imagine oneself undergoing a journey, and, given the practice that enables persistent strong concentration or subjective visions, an astral awareness that is equally free-ranging may be experienced. Robert Glaskin records experiments along these lines in his book, *Windows of the Mind.*

Both aspects of the subject impinge upon contemporary scientific endeavor. The Society for Psychical Research has painstakingly recorded hundreds of instances of phantasms of the living, many of which appear in Dr. Crookall's *The Study and Practice of Astral Projection* and its sequels.

At the more subjective level the techniques so described are part and parcel of what is more or less common practice in many psychotherapeutic consulting rooms. This is not only the case with Jungian analytical use of free association and creative imaginative techniques. It is also utilized by a number of other practitioners and clinical researchers, whose work has been codified by Dr. Roberto Assagioli and his followers in a book and later journal called *Psychosynthesis.*

Considerable emphasis is placed in these techniques on the visualization of symbols, particularly in significant sequences that imply growth, or the quest of some high ideal or idealized charismatic object.

For instance one exercise described by Assagioli is the visualization of the growth and unfolding of a rose, which is obviously to be taken as a symbol of personal psycho-spiritual unfoldment. This has sympathetic overtones with elements of mystical and magical literature, from the *rosa mystica* of Dante to the rose cross of the Rosicrucians.

The legends of the Holy Grail are also used as individual or group exercises, and sequences from the *Divine Comedy* of Dante. Allied to this is a view of the psyche that posits a super-conscious beyond the range of normal consciousness, as well as a personal subconscious and general objective consciousness. In line with much occult theory it also conceives of a Higher Self which can be brought into contact with normal consciousness.

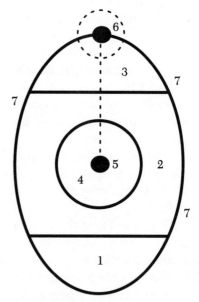

1. The Lower Unconscious
2. The Middle Unconscious
3. The Higher Unconscious or Superconscious
4. The Field of Consciousness
5. The Conscious Self or 'I'
6. The Higher Self
7. The Collective Unconscious

Assagioli's Diagram of the Psyche

In past decades such techniques were almost the exclusive province of magical fraternities. However, since the nineteen-seventies there has been a plethora of books describing them to the general public. Examples of this type of literature are *Seeing with the Mind's Eye* (1975) by Mike and Nancy Samuels, described as "the history, techniques and uses of visualization"; *Getting There without Drugs* (1973) by Buryl Payne, subtitled as techniques and theories for the expansion of consciousness; *Passages* by Marianne S. Anderson and Louis M. Savory, called a guide for pilgrims of the mind; *Mind Games* (1972) by R. E. L. Masters and Jean Houston, called the guide to inner space, a series of carefully developed exercises in self-exploration and education; and *Growth Games* (1970) by Howard R. Lewis and Harold S. Streitfield described in its foreword as "an encyclopedic cook book of the recipes by which the Human Potential Movement seeks to infuse its myriad followers with aliveness, awareness, and sensitivity they do not find elsewhere." Again there are techniques developed and used exclusively by organizations such as L. Ron Hubbard's dianetics and scientology, which are not so readily available to the book-buying general public, the general basics of which are described in his *Dianetics, the Modern Science of Mental Health* (1950).

We live in a period that is indeed almost obsessed with techniques of "blowing the mind," perhaps as a natural reaction to too long a period of rationalist dominance. This has extended to the whole popularity of Eastern meditation techniques adapted to Western usage, such as Transcendental Meditation, and to the practice of elementary forms of yoga, which, from being an exotic eccentricity, has become a suburban commonplace. Real oriental *hatha-yoga*, it should be said, is very much more than simple physical exercises; it involves complex visualizations and then breathing and muscular techniques that intend conscious manipulation of the glandular endocrine balance and the autonomic nervous system. Similarly, Western magic is, in its totality, more than visualization exercises aimed at relieving personal tensions.

All psycho-spiritual endeavors call for considerable investment of time and effort in much the same proportion as the acquisition of any physical or artistic skill. Occultism is no soft option or an easy means of escape from life. This general cultural trend has had its adverse side in the drug culture, which is an attempt to "get there," wherever "there" is conceived to be, without the discipline—though frequently at a terrible ultimate price. Perhaps the only easy way of achieving a degree of spiritual awareness, and even this depends on the individual, is the technique of "having no head" discovered by Douglas Harding and described in his *On Having No Head—a Contribution to Zen in the West*. The technique is better personally demonstrated, however, than described in a book.

In the mainstream of the Western magical tradition, W. G. Gray has done much to give a logical approach to the practice of white magic. In his works *The Ladder of Lights* (1969) and *Magical Ritual Methods* (1970), illustrated by *Seasonal Occult Rituals* (1971), he develops from first principles the fourfold system that we meet time and again in old magical systems and in the Jungian psychology. Gray roots his system in the observation of nature, whose cycles we conceive as being fourfold. This is to be seen in the diurnal cycle of dawn, noon, dusk and midnight, or in the annual cycles of spring, summer, autumn and winter.

Upon this it is possible to overlay a great mass of symbolism, and indeed it is not too much to claim that the whole sum of human experience can be allocated to one quarter or other of this cyclic pattern.

The age-old fourfold symbolism of the traditional magical weapons brings surprising developments of a universal nature. The Tuatha de Danann of ancient Celtic mythology had four most sacred objects—"the living fiery spear of Lugh, the magic ship of Manannan, the sword of Conery Mor which sang, Cuchulain's sword, which spoke, the Lia Fail, Stone of Destiny, which roared for joy beneath the feet of rightful kings." (Mackenzie's *Celtic Myth and Legend*). In the Arthurian and Grail legends they became the Lance and Grail, the Sword and Stone. We find these symbols occurring again in the symbolism of the suits of the Tarot—Swords, Wands, Cups and Disks.

These in turn relate to the traditional Four Elements, Air, Fire, Water and Earth and thence to characteristics of human consciousness, and to the Cardinal Points of East, South, West and North, and their appropriate Archangels. The children's rhyme "Mathew, Mark, Luke and John, bless the bed that I lie on" is a Christianized nursery form of the protective Archangels of the Quarters. The antiquity and depth of the symbolic links can be judged by referral to the traditional signs of the Four Evangelists, the Man, Lion, Ox and Eagle. These are met in the strange Old Testament Vision of Ezekiel and derive ultimately from Babylonian god forms such as the winged lions and bulls to be found in the British Museum, and the four "fixed" signs of the Zodiac, Aquarius, Leo, Taurus and Scorpio.

In the simple circled cross we thus have the foundation for an encyclopedic compendium of symbolism (see figure on next page). This is a rational and intelligent form of magical circle which serves a better purpose than the ill-understood medieval circles blindly copied by novelists, journalistic historians and dabblers in the subject ever since.

The psychological dynamics are best seen by reference to the Four traditional Magical Weapons.

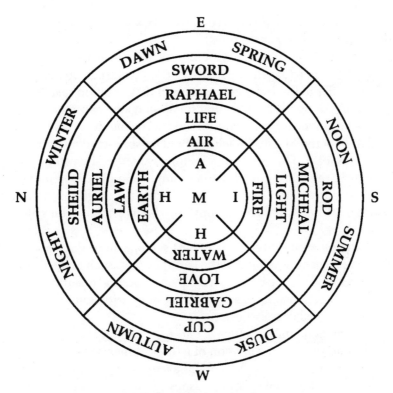

Modern Magic Circle

The Sword or dagger divides, cuts or inscribes.
The Wand points, directs or indicates.
The Cup contains.
The Disc, Coin or Shield is a field upon which information is laid out.

If one looks at any object in the external world it will be found to express one or more of these characteristics.

An electric light bulb for instance has a glass and metal container (Cup principle) in which is a filament that heats and lights up (Rod principle). A direction-finding compass contains all four: a magnetic pointer (rod) on a needle-like pivot (sword) in a circular box (cup) on which directions are inscribed (disc). A telephone consists of mouth and earpiece (cup) joined together (rod) and on a rest (cup) containing a numbered dial (disc) on a spindle (sword), the line going to the exchange being also an extended and flexible rod. An early exercise in developing this system of mind orientation is to devote a day in turn to listing all the cups, rods, swords and discs that one sees in daily life. In a sense these are basic Platonic ideas or archetypes of form.

From these few simple beginnings, as from the few simple axioms of Euclidean geometry, a whole science of the psyche can be built. Insofar that it is similar to the Jungian functions in that intuition relates to East/Air; thinking to South/Fire; feeling to West/Water; sensation to North/Earth we have a means of psychic integration by the steady and persistent formulation of the Magic Circle (or Mandala) and standing in the center as controller of it. This is a form of auto-psychotherapy without the patient-analyst relationship with its tacit implication that one member of the duo is neurotic. In its practical application the magical system works best on a master/apprentice relationship, which certainly seems more appropriate.

In its full application the standard symbolism of the Qabalah, the Tarot, Astrological Signs, and of the natural world, such as the Seasons of the Year, may be used to develop a deep, intricate and beautiful system of personal integration and conscious cooperation with inner dynamics, be they psychological or religious.

The fundamental structure of circled cross may also be regarded as a two-dimensional representation of a three-dimensional figure formed by three interlocking rings (of Time, Space and Event), which together form a sphere, a symbol of consciousness, the universe, and divine perfection, that goes back to Plato and Pythagoras, and which, through Aristotle and Aquinas, played a key part in European culture until the mechanistic philosophy of the seventeenth century. We have in fact a three-dimensional mandala, or symbol of integration and control, a magic sphere as opposed to a magic circle.

The serious magical student will then forge his magical weapons. The sword must be earned as it represents his courage and discernment in the breaking of new ground; the rod must be made according to difficult circumstances and kept secretly as it represents the magician's will; the cup should be given to the magician by one who loves him, for it represents his capacity to give and receive love; and the disc is designed by his own ingenuity as a pattern of his own understanding of how the universe works; it represents his wisdom.

So much for a modern interpretation of classical magical training. There is another synthesizing system of recent formulation that is open to all as a psychotherapy, although the symbols used are entirely magical, and taken directly from the Golden Dawn tradition. This system is known as the Guide Meditation and was developed by Edwin C. Steinbrecher of the D. O. M. E. Foundation, Santa Fe, New Mexico.

It uses a technique of free creative visual imagination in which the subject imagines himself to be in a cave with as great a degree of vivid reality as possible. Then a doorway or outlet is found to the left of the cave which leads eventually upwards and to the right until it breaks into open air. There one waits until an animal is seen to arrive, and leads one to a figure who usually turns out to be one's Guide for subsequent work. This guide may be of any historical period and is never anyone that one knows personally in outer life.

One then asks the guide in a series of meditations to take one to various archetypal figures in turn, commencing with that of the Sun. It is surprising to anyone who tries these techniques of creative visualization how vivid the scenes become, and it soon becomes apparent to most who assay these visualizations that they are dealing with objective realities and not figments of fancy. It is not unknown for tears of joy to overcome those who meet the Sun archetype for the first time, and a great feeling of trust and companionship develops with the guide.

The figures are to a certain extent arbitrary but the Sun obviously represents a central dynamic in consciousness, which some for instance might experience as a form for God. Steinbrecher uses the images of the Trumps of the Tarot although he allows, and indeed encourages, the free adaptation of the traditional images, as long as they do not change to people known in outer daily life.

The Tarot Trumps are as Follows:

0	The Fool	11	Justice
1	The Magician	12	The Hanged Man
2	The High Priestess	13	Death
3	The Empress	14	Temperance
4	The Emperor	15	The Devil
5	The Hierophant	16	The Lightning-Struck Tower
6	The Lovers	17	The Star
7	The Chariot	18	The Moon
8	Strength	19	The Sun
9	The Hermit	20	The Last Judgment
10	The Wheel of Fortune	21	The Universe

Each archetype or trump is approached in turn and a relationship developed with it. This usually takes the form of asking it what one should

A Selection of Tarot Trumps. Trump 1, the Magician, can be regarded as God or the spirit of man, manipulating the forces of creation on the table of manifestation. Trump 6, the Lovers, features the figure of Cupid, a familiar Mystery figure from Apuleius' *The Golden Ass* to the Rosicrucian *Chymical Marriage*. Trump 16, the Lightning Struck Tower, is another symbol that is featured in the *Chymical Marriage* in an alchemical regeneration process. Trump 21, the World, shows a spirit putting on the scarf of the garment of flesh, about to be born into the world, the Four Holy Living Creatures at the corners, representing the Four Elements in their widest context, from the Vision of Ezekiel to the emblems of the Four Gospels. These cards are from the Marseilles Tarot, probably the most accurate of the old packs, from which most modern esoteric versions derive.

be doing to express its principle more fully in outer life; and then taking a symbol from it and imagining this symbol being placed at, in or on a particular part of one's body. This should result in an improvement in one's handling of daily life, and if it does not it is important to confront the relevant archetype again and ask why not.

Extending from this Steinbrecher has found that the psychological dynamics revealed tend to reflect the astrological chart set up for the birth of each subject, with each of the twenty-two trumps being relevant to one of the twelve signs of the Zodiac and ten planets (including Sun and Moon) that appear to orbit the Earth. So impressed is he with this correlation that Steinbrecher is little concerned with working out the astrological chart beforehand as he finds the chart is virtually predicted by the behavior of the archetypes. However, part of his system is to create an astrological chart for those who consult him and to advise that certain of the archetypes be particularly worked upon in meditative work. For instance should Saturn and Venus be badly aspected in the horoscope then, under the direction of the guide, the trump archetypes of the World and the Empress would be particularly worked with to form an amicable and integrated working relationship.

Here we have of course, in twentieth century terms, a direct parallel to the natural magic of Marsilio Ficino in the fifteenth century. It would seem that the techniques work if they survive so long, or are rediscovered anew. It implies that a system of truth is being long neglected first through religious and later through scientific prejudice. For this reason it seems reasonable to assert that magic is a subject that should at last be given some measure of respect, regard and attention.

Chapter 9
Transforming the World

In many respects the attitudes and assumptions of the modern age stem from the ideas of Sir Francis Bacon, later Lord Verulam and Lord Chancellor of England. He consistently spoke out for the scientific method.

He was concerned about the inherent limitations of the scholastic method which argued from the premises of past authority—usually that of Aristotle and the Church Fathers—and tried to explain the workings of the world by referring back to general principles. Bacon argued that knowledge ought to *start* from the observation of the details and only then proceed to general principles.

By these means he intended "a total reconstruction of the sciences, arts, and all human knowledge raised upon the proper foundation."

His aim, in this reconstruction, was also a major departure from past attitudes. It was to be for the benefit of humankind. Thus the acquisition of knowledge was justified for its own sake. It could not be regarded as dangerous and impious, a medieval fear expressed in the legend of Dr. Faustus. The new method was justified in that it might "in some degree subdue the necessities and miseries of humanity."

In *New Atlantis* (1627) he set out the sevenfold process by which such knowledge should be gained. This was:
    (1) the gathering of information and data of all kinds;
    (2) experiments based on the first acquaintance with empirical data;

(3) the arrangement and classification of the findings of these experiments;

(4) their assessment in terms of human benefits and contribution to scientific theory;

(5) the formulation of new experiments that the previous analysis has suggested might be useful;

(6) the performance and reporting of these new experiments;

(7) the enunciation of laws or principles derived from this process.

This program of investigation, which seems no more than systematic common sense now, was revolutionary in its day, and marks a new direction in human thought processes. Professor Herbert Butterfield in *The Origins of Modern Science* 1300-1800, considers that this revolution:

> overturned the authority in science not only of the middle ages but of the ancient world—since it ended not only in the eclipse of scholastic philosophy but in the destruction of Aristotelian physics—it outshines everything since the rise of Christianity and reduces the Renaissance and Reformation to the rank of mere episodes, mere internal displacements, within the system of medieval Christendom. Since it changed the character of men's habitual mental operations even in the conduct of the non-material sciences, while transforming the whole diagram of the physical universe and the very texture of human life itself, it looms so large as the real origin both of the modern world and of the modern mentality that our customary periodization of European history has become an anachronism and an encumbrance.

It was a step so radical that it cannot be credited simply to one man. As in most leaps forward the genius of one man suddenly synthesizes a number of existing growing trends. As Professor Butterfield points out, the scientific revolution, although popularly associated with the sixteenth and seventeenth centuries, reaches back in an unmistakably continuous line to a period much earlier still.

The real beginnings of the scientific method and the ideal that man's destiny is a quest for knowledge lies in the magical and alchemical investigations of a former time, and in men such as Roger Bacon in the thirteenth century, Marsilio Ficino in the fifteenth and Paracelsus in the sixteenth century. It was on the basis of their pioneering that Francis Bacon cleansed the human intellectual critical apparatus as an immediate preparation for a practical advance forward.

In *The Advancement of Learning* (1605) he identified three major vanities or "distempers" that were harmful to learning, together with eleven further unhealthy conditions or "peccant humors."

The three major vanities Bacon warns against are "the first, fantastical learning; the second, contentious learning; and the last delicate learning; vain imaginations, vain altercations, and vain affectations." Of these the first is exemplified in some of the received beliefs of Aristotle; the second in the argumentative logic chopping of scholastic philosophers; and the third in a preoccupation with learned style rather than content.

The eleven "peccant humors" are:

(1) the attraction of either antiquity or novelty;
(2) the assumption that all worthwhile discoveries have already been made;
(3) the assumption that only the best of previous discoveries have prevailed;
(4) the reduction of knowledge into categorized areas so there is no room for expansion;
(5) the abandonment of universal principles that might apply to all knowledge;
(6) too high an opinion of the validity of mental speculation;
(7) predilection for some existing theory or system of ideas;
(8) impatience with the slow amassing of experimental results and observations;
(9) a spurious authoritativeness;
(10) ambitious desire for personal success;
(11) spurious motivation such as idle curiosity, entertainment.

We give these principles in detail, along with the former investigation processes, to draw attention to the fact that they are universally applicable, and can and should be applied to investigation of the "inner worlds" as well, and do not necessarily imply a materialist philosophy. This is a later distortion brought about because some Baconian principles have been ignored, such as the third peccant humor.

From this, in his *New Organon* (1620), Bacon developed the concept of four Idols, to which we have to beware giving undue reverence. He called them Idols of the Tribe, Idols of the Cave, Idols of the Market Place, and Idols of the Theater.

The Idols of the Tribe, which are common to all human nature, are the natural tendency to jump to conclusions, interpreting things in the light of our previous beliefs, seeing those evidences which confirm them and ignoring the minor exceptions and inconsistencies.

The Idols of the Cave differ from individual to individual. They are so called because every man has a certain predisposition to one type of theory or another, idealistic or materialist, optimistic or pessimistic, conservative or radical, which puts him in the position of sitting in an intellectual cave of his own from which he views the world.

The Idols of the Market Place are very difficult to avoid. These are produced by human intercourse and its reliance on the inadequacies of language, which by its very structure can mislead. Words may be coined for concepts which in fact do not exist (e.g. "phlogiston" or "caloric") or for ideas which are muddled or not well defined (e.g. "mysticism" or "the unconscious"—even "gravity"?).

The Idols of the Theatre are false systems of belief which are held to be incontrovertible. Thus Galileo upset some traditionalists because his observation of the Moons of Jupiter upset what seemed to be a rational system of seven planets, so that any extra heavenly bodies seemed an embarrassment.

Bacon has been criticized for putting too materialistic a bias onto his system for a new learning—but this is largely a result of later biased application. For instance the above idols are still as much a feature of established common sense as they were in Bacon's day.

He did make the radical step of excluding theology and all religious questions from the scope of natural philosophy. This was of far-reaching consequence because it once-for-all cut all pretended religious authority from science, although it was to be another 300 years before the disengagement was effected. The bruising confrontations of biblical literalism first with geology and then with Darwin's *Origin of Species* in the nineteenth century finally signaled the armistice for a completely unnecessary involvement.

With this divorce there came however a clouding of issues over the terrain of natural philosophy that lay between—the inner world of the imagination.

This divorce was abetted in an historical sense by the last of the great systematizers, René Descartes (1596–1650), who contemperaneously with Bacon was attempting to construct a complete system of natural philosophy from his own mental speculations. This was finally shattered by the physical observation and scientific method of Newton, whose *Principia* of 1687 established physical science as the only way of investigating and comprehending the physical universe.

There is a certain irony in the fact that Newton's scientific researches were undertaken for theological motives, to prove the existence of God by the evidence of intelligent design in the universe. He was also considerably involved in the intermediate area, between science and religion, with his alchemical interests. But it is subsequent generations that have presumed (and by an abandonment of Baconian principles) that Newton was aberrated in such pursuits. In a similar way it is forgotten that Bacon too was as interested in alchemy, magic and astrology as he was in the "respectable" physical subjects.

We can clarify the problem by recourse to the old tradition of a three-tier universe. In one sector we have the affairs of God and religious questions, in another the investigation of the physical world, and in another that of the "inner" worlds. It is less misleading if instead of ranging the spheres of inquiry into levels, we place them in a circle like a pie chart (see below), for it is not necessary to go "through" the inner world to get to God. Something of this idea is conveyed in certain alchemical and magical diagrams where either the light or the dark side can be conceived as outer or inner world, according to which one the observer is standing within, the heaven world of God being superior to both.

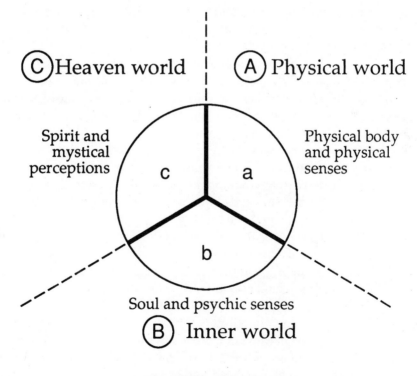

Threefold universe
Heaven of Union with God plus Inner and Outer creation

There will be areas of overlap between all three. Psychical research and types of clairvoyance would be found in the boundary between "inner" and "outer" worlds. Revelations of a mystical nature would be on the border of "inner" and religious. And miracles or events such as the stigmata of Padré Pia are on the boundary between religious and physical.

Our contention is that with the longstanding traditional claims of religion on the one hand, and the ambitious claims of physical science on the other, the "third estate" or "inner earth" tends to be rejected, neglected and even mutually condemned. Small wonder if our understanding of the world seems incomplete.

As a reaction to 300 years suppression of a third of reality there is at the present time an understandable reaction. This manifests in a massive impatience with an institutionalized religious establishment on the one hand, and what has been described as an unscientific "flight from reason" on the other.

We would claim that if due regard is paid to the middle kingdom of the inner universe, there will be an altogether more balanced and wholesome attitude both to religion and to physical science. As things stand at the present modern man not unnaturally feels as if he has been cheated of his soul.

This problem has been ably dramatized in Robert M. Pirsig's modern story of a quest, *Zen and the Art of Motorcycle Maintenance,* which, to judge by its popular success, in spite of its bizarre and quasi-specialist title, struck a nerve in public consciousness. It has been hailed as "a work of great, perhaps urgent, importance" (*The Observer*), "the most explosive detective story of high ideas in years" (*Newsweek*), "a pathfinding attempt to examine our contemporary ills." (*The Guardian*), 'full of insights into our most perplexing contemporary dilemmas" (*New York Times*), "Nothing can affect the weird and wonderful power on the mind that this book has achieved' (*Vogue*); "disturbing, deeply moving, full of insights (*Times Literary Supplement*), "A moving tale of the modern soul, and a fine detective story of a man in search of himself" (*Chicago Daily News*).

It is an account of the author's motorcycle trip across America, accompanied by his son, and also in search of himself or a shadowy figure called Phaedrus who turns out to be himself—or rather the self that he was before undergoing electric shock treatment. The shock treatment had been occasioned because of a breakdown induced by trying to come to terms with the philosophical impasse that our modern civilization has come to. In the finish all ends well, with a re-integration with his old self and a reconciliation of differences with his son.

During the course of the account of the trip the author conducts a long philosophical discussion—called a *chautauqua*, "an old-time series of popular talks intended to edify and entertain, improve the mind and bring culture and enlightenment to the ears and thoughts of the hearer." This is illustrated by events that happen on the journey, the comments and habits of people he meets or knows, and the illustration of many of the high-flying philosophical ideas in terms of the practicalities of maintaining a motorcycle.

Insofar that a long discursive *chautauqua* of this nature can be summed up in a phrase, the substance of the argument is that it is misleading to try to categorize the physical universe about us into objective criteria, for although the world "out there" undoubtedly does have its independent existence, its manifestation is dependent upon our interpretation of it.

A primitive man might experience the world in terms of totems and ancestral ghosts whereas modern man would do so in terms of what he likes to call scientific laws. Scientific laws, however, have no greater or lesser degree of validity than totems and ancestral ghosts. They are simply a different way in which man, in a different time, interprets environmental phenomena.

Reality might therefore be regarded as a meeting point of subjective and objective—each partaking of the other, and Robert Pirsig chooses to describe this by the term *quality*. In fact he defines quality (which in truth is undefinable) as "the parent of mind and matter, that event which gives birth to mind and matter," for it occurs a fraction of a second before intellectualized consciousness has registered its perceptions. This means that "*any* intellectually conceived object is always in the past and therefore *unreal*. Reality is always the moment of vision *before* the intellectualization takes place. *There is no other reality*."

Insofar that it is so simple, immediate, direct and pre-intellectual, quality is undefinable. Though as most modern people are conditioned to think in terms of subject/object or stimulus-response behavior theory, the easiest way to define it is: "Quality is the response of an organism to its environment." This is in fact less accurate than the definition given above, though initially more readily understandable.

Pirsig takes as an example an amoeba which, if placed near a drop of acid, will automatically pull away from it. If the amoeba could be asked why it did so it might, without knowing anything about chemistry, simply say that the environment near it had a poor quality. A more complex organism would seek analogs from previous experience to explain why it thought the environment was of poor quality; for to understand the environment is a means of survival.

He then applies this situation to a human being.

> In our highly complex organic state we advanced organisms respond to our environment with an invention of many marvelous analogs. We invent earth and heavens, trees, stones and oceans, gods, music, arts, language, philosophy, engineering, civilization and science. We call these analogs reality. And they *are* reality. We mesmerize our children in the name of truth without knowing that they *are* reality. We throw anyone who does not accept these analogues into an asylum. But that which causes us to invent the analogues is Quality. Quality is the continuing stimulus which our environment puts upon us to create the world in which we live. All of it. Every last bit of it.

Having come to this realization in purely philosophical terms Pirsig then records comparing it with the description of the Tao, in the 2,400 years old *Tao Te Ching* of Lao Tzu.

"He read on. Line after line. Page after page. Not a discrepancy. What he had been talking about all the time as Quality was here the Tao, the great central generating force of all religions, Oriental and Occidental, past and present, all knowledge, everything."

From this all-embracing realization Pirsig takes the view that it should provide the basis for unifying three areas of human experience that are at present disunified. He calls these Religion, Art and Science. These correspond to the three-tier or three-segment universe that we have already described, for Art is one of the principal ways into the "inner" equivalent of physical phenomena.

Pirsig continues in his book with an analysis of quality in these three areas, with the least emphasis on the middle area, which he approaches in terms of aesthetics. As this is central to our current inquiry we may find it fruitful to branch off at this point, to consider Coleridge's theory of the Imagination. He conceived the function of the Primary Imagination to be the means by which we build up our awareness of a surrounding universe. Thus there is a correlation between Pirsig's Quality and Coleridge's Primary Imagination.

This is rendered more intriguing in the testimony of two other thinkers in this field. The one, Anthony Duncan, the author of a perceptive book on the relationship between religion and the "inner worlds," *The Christ, Psychotherapy and Magic,* has stated that in reading the *Tao Te Ching*, the word Tao might be interchanged for that of Jesus Christ and make inspiring religious sense. The other is William Blake's otherwise somewhat cryptic statement identifying the imagination with Jesus.

The dualist subject-object conception of perception was very much an eighteenth-century invention of the philosophers Hartley and Locke. They tended to see the human mind as a *tabula rasa,* or a blank sheet, upon which environmental experience produced reactions, and therefore character, in a quite mechanical fashion. The environment was therefore *all,* and Rousseau formulated his educational theories upon their concept, believing that a totally controlled educational environment could produce a virtually perfect student; a view which has political and educational reverberations to this day.

Although the eighteenth-century psychologists no doubt felt themselves to be in the vanguard of enlightened scientific endeavor, their views are considerably at variance with the wiser Francis Bacon; who stated that "the mind of man is far from the nature of a clear and equal glass, wherein the beams of things should reflect according to their true incidence; nay, it is rather like an enchanted glass, full of superstition and imposture, if it be not delivered and reduced."

In the function of perception, in the subjective result of quality, in the continuous creation of the primary imagination, there is a dual, reflective action which Coleridge exemplified in a number of illuminating poetic images. These are the well at Upper Stowey; the observer and the chameleon; the blind man and the Moon; and the Brocken Spectre.

A note of Coleridge's in 1805 concludes:

> Thought and Reality two distinct corresponding Sounds, of which no man can say positively which is the Voice and which the Echo. O the beautiful Fountain or natural Well at Upper Stowey . . . The images of the weeds which hung down from its sides, appeared as plants growing up, straight and upright, among the water weeds that really grew from the bottom and so vivid was the Image, that for some moments and not until after I had disturbed the water, did I perceive that their roots were not neighbors, and they side-by-side companions. So— even then I said—so are the happy man's *Thoughts* and *Things.*" (*Anima Poetae* and *Notebooks* Vol. 2).

From what we have said it may be realized that a poetic image may be a more adequate means of approaching the truth than an attempt at verbal definition. The above note, which was written in Malta, is also an example of one of those "images recollected in tranquility" the mechanics of which are explained in Wordsworth's poem about the daffodils. It is worth therefore contemplating Coleridge's image of the well. It applies not only to our perceptions and ideas of the physical world, but also, and to a greater degree even, to our perceptions of the inner worlds. These have a reflective life of their own and in Coleridge's image in *Aids to Reflection:* "The Chameleon darkens in the shade of him who bends over it to ascertain its colors." This is a problem which has recently been met even in physical science where attempts to observe the subatomic quanta affect their behavior.

The feeling of quality is all, as Pirsig says. And an unfeeling "objectivity" is one reason why both Pirsig and Coleridge felt the otherwise relevant philosophy of Immanuel Kant to be inadequate. In a letter of 1817 Coleridge writes "I reject Kant's *stoic* principles, as false, unnatural, and even immoral, where in his *Critik der Practischen Vernunft* he treats the affections as indifferent . . . in ethics, and would persuade us that a man who disliking, and without any feeling of love for, Virtue, yet *acted* virtuously, because and only because it was his *Duty,* is more worthy of our esteem, than the man whose *affections* were evident to, and congruous with, his Conscience."

Colerige summarized the Kantian philosophic view in a poem called *Limbo,* using the image of a blind man looking at the Moon, each appearing to gaze upon the other, yet actually in mutual blindness:

An Old Man with a steady look sublime,
That stops his earthly task to watch the skies;
But he is blind—a Statue hath such eyes;—
Yet having moonward turn'd his face by chance,
Gazes the orb with moon-like countenance,
With scant white hairs, with foretop bald and high,
He gazes still,—his eyeless face all eye;—
As 'twere an organ full of silent sight,
His whole face seemeth to rejoice in light!
Lip touching lip, all moveless, bust and limb—
He seems to gaze at that which seems to gaze on him!

This meaningless void is the condition which would operate without any meaningful resonance between the projection and reception of the human mind. It is, as Stephen Prickett points out in his highly perceptive *Coleridge and Wordsworth: The Poetry of Growth,* the philosophic paradox of Kant's doctrine of the unknowability of things-in-themselves taken to its logical conclusion.

More accurate is the portrayal of the human condition in terms of the Brocken Spectre. This is a famous phenomenon of light on the Hartz

Mountains in Germany, where a shadow of a man is cast by the rising Sun behind him onto a bank of mist. This gives the appearance not merely of a shadow, but of a giant figure surrounded by a halo of glory. It is sometimes possible to see a similar effect from an aircraft when flying between the Sun and a cloud bank. The image of the aircraft is seen in the center of a brilliant white light, and as many as three full concentric rainbows.

To Coleridge this was an apt image of the human condition—the interpenetration of man and nature which is both perception and creation, for man by his own pursuit of quality throws his own image onto the snow-mist which throws it back with "a glory round its head," giving to the pursuer of quality both growth and value.

In his *Constancy to an Ideal Object* Coleridge asks of "the ideal':

And art thou nothing? Such thou art, as when
The woodman winding westward up the glen
At wintry dawn, where oer the sheep-tracks maze
The viewless snow-mist weaves a glistening haze,
Sees full before him, gliding without tread,
An image with a glory round its head;
The enamored rustic worships its fair hues,
Nor knows he makes the shadow, he pursues!

This is the Brocken Spectre. The conception is expanded in some lines from *Dejection:*

O Lady! We receive but what we give,
 And in our life alone does nature live:
 Ours is her wedding-garment, ours her shroud!
And would we aught behold of higher worth,
Than the inanimate cold world allowed
To the poor loveless ever-anxious crowd,
Ah! from the soul itself must issue forth,
A light, a glory, a fair luminous cloud
Enveloping the earth—

This stresses the point that the things we perceive are neither "out there" in a material world, nor "in here" in a subjective mind, but a fusion of both, a union of perceiver and perceived. These are the mechanics of *physical* perception. They are also the mechanics of *interior* perception.

The imagination which is the relationship between man and nature which scientists call sense-perception, is also to be found in the relationship between what psychologists now call the conscious and the unconscious. In days long before such psychological terms were coined

Wordsworth gave the image in the description of a moonlight ascent of Snowdon in Book XIII of *The Prelude* (1805):

Meanwhile, the Moon look'd down upon this show
In simple glory, and we stood, the mist
Touching our very feet; and from the shore
At distance not the third part of a mile
Was a blue chasm; a fracture in the vapour,
A deep and gloomy breathing-place through which
Mounted the roar of water, torrents, streams
Innumerable, roaring with one voice,
The universal spectacle throughout
Was shaped for admiration and delight,
Grand in itself alone, but in the breach
Through which the homeless voice of waters rose,
That deep dark thoroughfare had Nature lodg'd
The Soul, the Imagination of the whole.

Here are what in modern intellectual terms we would call the conscious (the mountaintop), the unconscious (the deeps below), and the imagination as the "deep dark thoroughfare" of the "fracture in the vapour," when applied to the inner worlds.

This is the realm of the third estate, between Heaven and Earth, which we should now investigate. There are three disciplinary areas to which this investigation could fall, the psychological, the aesthetic, or the magical.

It is not the prime concern either of religion or of material science, although each has marginal interests in it—which may however in certain contexts be quite important.

Prior to Francis Bacon religion tried to dominate all knowledge. Since Bacon physical science has tended to dominate it. With a proper definition of boundaries there should be an opportunity for balanced growth that is without the faults of either unbalanced usurpation of knowledge. Both a theocratic society and a technological one have been tried in the West and both have been found wanting.

Since a more general realization of the magical element in reality, that has occurred since the watershed decade of the 1960s, there has been a gradual increase in *planetary* awareness. That is, a realization of our responsibilities towards the Earth as an organism within whose substance and *consciousness* we live and move and have our being.

At its most material level this concern for the Earth may be expressed and motivated solely by simple self-interest in self-survival; we cannot go on treating our small island in space like a toxic rubbish dump or as an inexhaustible repository of mineral and organic loot.

The cosmic side of the enlightened self-interest equation is seen in concern for the ozone layer, and the development of satellite technology as an aid to communication, and beyond this, dreams of opening up human access to other celestial bodies within the solar system. The flip side of this is of course the possible use of such technology for harmful purposes, whether of warfare or greedy exploitation.

More hopefully, and indeed more significantly, has been an increasing realization of the inner powers that lie *within* the Earth, unsuspected by materialist vision. And in the cosmic context this is accompanied by a realization of the place of Earth itself as a cosmic entity within "the company of heaven." This has been called in modern mystical terms the Earth being raised to the status of a "sacred plane," although the more traditional symbolic expression of such a process is couched in terms of a New Age or a New Jerusalem, or the return to the golden age of an Earthly Paradise.

These trends in thought and belief have shown their presence in various ways. There is no vast organization that is orchestrating them, at any rate in the physical politico-social world. It is more in the nature of a general psychic and spiritual pressure from inner sources, that find their expression in a myriad ways, through individuals and small groups.

Perhaps one element in this expression was allied to the fall of Llasa when the communist Chinese oppressors of Tibet precipitated the flight of the Dalai Lama and a number of his monks who have since set up various centers throughout the world, and unleashed a pent-up dam of ancient spirituality preserved on the remote "roof of the world" since at least medieval times, which has strange resonances with Western esoteric traditions. The fourfold structures of the mandalas to be found in the *Tibetan Book of the Dead* and in the related literature have a curious concordance with the Celtic magic circle or the Amerindian medicine wheel.

It must also be said that the current wide public concern for ecological issues started in the modern mystery lodges. In the late 1950s the beginnings of it were to be found in the teachings of the Society of the Inner Light, based upon wisdom teachings penned by Dion Fortune at Glastonbury as far back as 1922, and published as *The Cosmic Doctrine*. Concern was particularly expressed for what it described in this volume as "the Planetary Being." A similar concept is also to be found in one of Alice Bailey's early works in *A Treatise on Cosmic Fire* (1925), described as the Planetary Entity. This once somewhat recherché esoteric concept has come to unbelievable prominence in the intervening years.

This does not necessarily mean that magical groups or esoteric societies bring these things about, but that there is evidence to suggest that they have the antennae needed to pick up the need for changes in human awareness and consciousness more quickly than most other sectors of society. The ultimate source of such major changes in human consciousness and ideas may be regarded as somewhat beyond the power and wisdom of the average member or leader of such groups, but rather in the hierarchical spiritual powers that surround the burgeoning planet. We can envisage these powers in whatever form we like—as choirs of angels, or higher intelligences in space, or the brooding presence of the Holy Spirit or the Shekinah. For all our assumed superiority in knowledge and wisdom we moderns do occupy a very narrow window in time when it comes to the realization or recognition of such superior powers. Our intellectual establishment is considerably in the minority in the annals of human history in choosing to ignore or deny the psychic and spiritual worlds.

It can also be surprising how that which seems obvious in one decade seemed impossible, unthinkable or at least highly unlikely in another. For instance in the 1930s Dion Fortune opined that the American Indian held the key to the mysteries of the New World. And over subsequent years many interested American citizens inquired how this could possibly be so. However, in the current wave of expanded awareness it is becoming abundantly clear that the American Indian does have, in some subtle way, the custodianship of the deep powers of the Earth, and through the years of neglect and persecution these have been guarded until such time as the waves of European immigrants shall have passed their phase of preoccupation with land and money and material exploitation. Only now that there is a genuine seeking for a deeper spiritual meaning are these secrets being realized. Along with them too is the discovery of ancient megalithic sites within the New World that rival anything that is to be found in the Old.

However, this is only part of a worldwide dawn of realization about the inner powers inherent within the Earth, and the role of custodianship played by hitherto often despised indigenous peoples, who, in their culture and shamanistic practices, have preserved this wisdom. This applies as much to the Aboriginals of Australia as to the Indian races of the Americas, and is to be found too even in the less accessible native traditions of Europe.

The author and composer Bob Stewart has done much to uncover such material. Commencing his career as a folk musician he discovered fascinating insights into pagan imagery in the lyrics of folksongs and ballads,which showed that, far from the inner-world dynamics being the prerogative of secret magical societies or fraternities, very powerful transformative symbolism was to be found in these popular songs, upthrust from the deep consciousness of the race itself, particularly when it was close to the land.

In a series of books of seminal importance, including *The UnderWorld Initiation, Living Magical Arts* and *Advanced Magical Arts*, he laid out a ground plan for a natural system of magical development, including a tentative list of objectives of what magic should be all about.

To summarize, these are:

a) an increased consciousness by human beings of the role of the land and of the Earth itself;
b) the conscious regeneration of imaginative forms for the purpose of rebalancing consciousness, both on an individual and a collective basis;
c) deeper association with the inner worlds in pursuit of knowledge and enlightenment.

This implies the restatement of primal mythical themes within the imagination, developing appropriate forms of expression for these themes, and associating them with the opening up and restoration of natural power sites, both minor ones locally and major ones around the world.

And he personally develops, as a means of exegesis, five typical mystery systems which are, by definition, a pattern of images that can teach, enliven and transform the consciousness of those who take part in them.

Those he cites are those of the Weaver; the Son of Light; the UnderWorld; the Vault; and Merlin.

Briefly, the Weaver represents the originative power of being, working through the form of a Great Mother, both above and below, of stars and under-Earth.

The Son (or Daughter) of Light is an image incorporating all historical, religious or mythical heroes, saviors, redeemers, sacred kings and the like. Strictly speaking this is, in essence, an androgynous being.

The UnderWorld represents the deep powers of the Earth itself, which are not evil, but reflections of the spiritual and cosmic powers within the heart of the Earth itself. Without contact with it, any magical or regenerative works will tend to be nebulous and cut off from essential roots—idealism without practicality.

The Vault is a transitional state of consciousness, a threshold between worlds in the process of transformation or spiritual growth. Examples of it are to be found in Rosicrucian symbolism, but it includes much more than this, from the pyramids of ancient Egypt to the burial and oracular mounds of neolithic times.

Finally Merlin, who is an entirely human archetype, not only of the wise old man or magical elder, but in his traditional life as recorded by Geoffrey of Monmouth in the *Vita Merlini* as exemplar in all the stages of human life.

This is very much a grafting of Western inner world and spiritual aspirations back on to their natural roots, from which, in centuries past they have, for various cultural and social reasons, tended to have been divorced. It provides a salutary balance to the intellectual systems epitomized by the Golden Dawn and the Western adaptations of Eastern systems, as well as some of the more atavistic leanings of certain of the neopagan revivalists. And it also means a considerable relaxation of unnecessary secrecy and sectarianism in the pursuit of mystery traditions.

An example of this may be found in the work of John and Caitlin Matthews, whose exposition of the dynamics of western magical traditions in *The Western Way* embraces, in its two volumes, both "the Native Tradition" and "The Hermetic Tradition," demonstrating that the Western Mystery Tradition in all its ramifications is at root one unified path.

This does not imply a compote of bland assimilation of disparate elements, either, for in other works they have explored the specialized branches that might be regarded as individual leaves on the miraculous Tree of Life "whose leaves are for the healing of all nations." These included investigations of the Holy Graal tradition and the fragmented mystery of the Mother and Son (Modron and Mabon) in the Welsh stories of *The Mabinogion*. And thus incidentally demonstrating that there is no unnecessary antagonism between the spiritual heights of esoteric Christian tradition and the profound deeps of our pagan heritage.

Other neglected areas of the magical tradition have also been brought to light in the general restimulation of the magical imagination, some of them hardly touched since the researches of the Elizabethan magus Dr. John Dee into the sacred sites, crystal lore and the dynamics of magical or "angelic" languages.

And although the Celtic legendary tradition has rightly been a focus of particular attention, other systems such as the Anglo-Saxon and the Norse have been realized to have much to contribute, and rune lore has been revived to take its place alongside popular oracular devices such as the Tarot, which itself has shown incredible growth in public attention. In the late 1950s, when researching a book on the subject, I found it impossible to obtain a set of Tarot cards in the whole of London. A card manufacturer's catalog which has just arrived on my desk now lists no less than 175 different sets!

It is not only in divination systems however that these magical dynamics have been breaking out into wider public consciousness. As, for example, the explosion of interest in the hitherto personal speculations of the artist and writer José Argüelles that blew up into the worldwide Harmonic Convergence event of August 16-17, 1987.

Developed from his personal meditations upon Mayan traditions and the prophecies of several North American Indian tribes as a point in time when concentration upon certain planetary force patterns would be propitious, the media got hold of it, and despite their portrayal of it as a semi-lunatic New Age folly, it attracted many sane, normal people around the world, who were grateful for some lead in how to express a deep-felt need to do something for the peace and welfare of the world on an inner level.

Despite the ridicule that may be leveled at private or popular manifestations of New Age idealism (sometimes with justification), the concerted action of so many people, motivated by an inward impulse, is not without effect. It is, in essence, an act of talismanic magic on a wide scale—the earthing of spiritual and inner realities, contributed to by ordinary people within their own homes, and by the action of celebrities such as Shirley MacLaine flying to the sacred site of Lake Baikal in Soviet Siberia. Who is to say that the church bells ringing in Russia for the first time in seventy years and other remarkable changes in the confrontational politics of the world were not, to some degree, influenced by such an event?

Soon after this event, José Argüelles was overtaken by personal tragedy in the loss of his son in a road accident. After a period of deep mourning he emerged with a book written in a racy style to capture the imagination of the younger generation to which his son belonged. This he called *Surfers of the Zuvaya,* which is almost as off-beat a title as Pirsig's *Zen and the Art of Motorcycle Maintenance,* and it is interesting to note the resonance between the two books, of a father trying to communicate with his son. Perhaps there is a cosmic parable to be read into this, with modern humanity in the role of the son.

Underneath its racy language, which makes it read at times much like pulp science fiction, one finds however the same deep dynamics that are to be found in the serious works of magical writers, including a journey to the center of the Earth, in vision, to make the necessary connection with the extraterrestrial contacts of "the starry wisdom." And "Uncle Joe," despite his extravagant language and whacky vision journeys, is of the same genus as those whom the poet Shelley described when he wrote:

> From unremembered ages we
> Gentle guides and guardians be
> Of heaven-oppressed mortality;
> and we breathe and sicken not
> the atmosphere of human thought . . .

He is an exuberant modern expression of a long line of tradition that is perhaps first referred to in ancient Greece as Socrates' *daimon*, and in seventeenth-century Rosicrucian literature as "a divine Fraternity that inhabits the Suburbs of Heaven . . . officers of the *Generalissimo* of the world," and more recently the "Secret Chiefs" of the Golden Dawn and the "Planetary Hierarchy" of Alice Baily, the "inner plane adepti" of Dion Fortune, or the "inner guide" of Edwin Steinbrecher. The only guide to truth in all of this, as in religious faith, lies in first-hand experience. The Rosicrucian *Fama Fraternitatis* invited like-minded people to join them but gave no forwarding address. They simply stated that the Brothers would be aware of anyone who evinced a true desire.

"Uncle Joe" combines concepts of a personal higher self with that of a spokesman of the Ancestors (in Argüelles' case Mayan/Mexican), and demonstrates that by attunement of consciousness through various visualizations an awareness of multi-dimensional reality can be attained, through time and through space and beyond them.

And despite the strong emphasis on Mayan traditions we find that the book concludes with an invocatory poem devoted to the archetypal figure of Merlin.

This figure shows every sign of taking on a universal significance. From obscure and disputed oral Celtic origins, Merlin is accorded a full biography and set of prophecies by the twelfth century Geoffrey of Monmouth, which have been ably made accessible by Bob Stewart's *The Prophetic Vision of Merlin* and *The Mystic Life of Merlin*. And he occurs in practical communicable form in modern times to whomever seems attuned to him. Alan Richardson and Geoff Hughes in their *Ancient Magicks for a New Age* give detailed records of two such instances, experienced by two small groups separated by a term of half a century. And these are by no means unique instances of the vitality of this important and increasingly ubiquitous figure. One could include the work of Dion Fortune (largely written up in my own *Secret Tradition in Arthurian Leg-*

end), and a direct contact with the figure was also responsible for much of the material in the first section of my *The Rose Cross and the Goddess*. There have also been a variety of New Age interpretations through mediators of varied ability, to say nothing of a considerable amount of "channeling" on the quality of some of which perhaps, the less that is said the better.

At the first of a series of conferences on Merlin that Bob Stewart organized in London from 1986–1989, John Matthews produced a list of 39 modern fictional works that feature Merlin, and reviewed some of them; while another 35 titles could be cited of works relating to Merlin between AD 900 to 1857, from early poems attributed to him through Geoffrey of Monmouth, Sir Thomas Malory, Edmund Spenser to Alfred Tennyson. There is even now a Merlin Tarot!

The lively and universal interest in the archetypal figure of the magician would seem to indicate that someone somewhere is trying to get a message across with an increasing sense of urgency!

And this in turn suggests that there is a growing and urgent need for a true appreciation of the significance of Magic for the Western mind.

BIBLIOGRAPHICAL INDEX

AGRIPPA, Cornelius, De Occulta Philosophia, 90, 144

ANDERSON, Constitutions, 129

ANDERSON, B. W., The Living World of the Old Testament, 38

ANDERSON, M. & SAVORY, L. M., Passages 171

ANON. Book of Enoch, 54

ANON. The Tibetan Book of the Dead, 191

ANON. Book of Splendor (The Zohar) 78-79

ANON. The Chemical Wedding of Christian Rosencreutz, 103, 106, 107, 110, 133

ANON. The Cloud of Unknowing, 48, 77, 78

ANON. Le Comte de Gabalis, 133

ANON. Confessio Fraternitatis, 103, 106, 107, 115

ANON. The Dead Sea Scrolls, 39

ANON. Fama Fraternitatis, 103-106, 107, 110, 115, 196

ANON. The Life of Sethos, 133

ANON. The Mabinogion, 194

ANON. The Picatrix, 85, 98

ANON. The Way to Bliss, 132

APULEIUS, Metamorphoses, or the Golden Ass, 28, 37-36

ARGÜELLES, José, Surfers of the Zuvaya, 195

ASSAGIOLI, Roberto, Psychosynthesis, 169-170

ARNOLD, Paul, Historie des Rose-croix, 107

ATKINSON, W. W., Secrets of Mental Magic, 160

ATWOOD, M. A., A Suggestive Enquiry into the Hermetic Mystery, 144-145

BACON, Francis, The Advancement of Learning, 111, 180-181

BACON, Francis, New Atlantis, 111, 179

BACON, Francis, New Organon, 181-182

BAILEY, ALICE A., A Treatise on Cosmic Fire, 155, 191-192

BAILEY, Alice A., A Treatise on the Seven Rays, 155

BAILEY, Alice A., A Treatise on White Magic, 155

BARFIELD, Owen, Saving the Appearances, 9

BARRETT, Francis, The Magus, Or Celestial Intelligencer, 144

BEESING, Maria, NOGOSEK, Robert, & O'LEARY, Patrick, The Enneagram, 160

BENNETT, J. G., Enneagram Studies, 160

BERTRAND, Alexandre, Traité de Somnambulisme, 137

BLAKE, William, Vala, 143

BLAVATSKY, H. P., Isis Unveiled, 146

BLAVATSKY, H. P., The Secret Doctrine, 146, 155

BOEHME, Jacob, Aurora, 118

BRAID, The Power of the Mind over the Body, 137

BUDGE, E. A. Wallis, The Book of the Dead (Book of Coming Forth by Day), 30-32

BRENNAN, J. H., Astral Doorways, 168

BUTLER, W. E., The Magician, His Training and Work, 164

BUTTERFIELD, H., The Origins of Modern Science, 180

INDEX

205

Holy Grail, 57, 60, 64, 65, 67, 68, 69, 78, 152, 170
Holy Spirit, 192
Homeopathy, 102, 157
Hopkins, Gerard Manley, 21
Horniman, Annie, 149
Horror Books and Films, 124
Horus, 20, 21, 22, 33
House of the Holy Spirit, 104
Houston, Jean, 171
Hubbard, J. Ron, 171
Hughes, Geoff, 196
Human Potential Movement, 171
Human Sacrifice, 37, 55
Huna Magic, 166
Huxley, Aldous, 50
Hypnotism, 23, 77, 135, 137, 139, 145
Hysteria, 77, 135

I

Iamblichus, 51
Ideas, Platonic, 48, 49
Ignatius of Loyola, 119, 120
Illuminati, 132
Imagination, 93, 103, 119, 135, 182, 186, 187, 189, 190, 193, 194, 195
Imaginative Tradition, 142
Inferior Governors, 105
Ingolstadt, University of, 132
Initiation, 30, 34, 38, 44, 62, 96, 106, 145, 147
Inner Earth, 184
Inner Guide, 196
Inner Plane Adepti, 196
Inner Worlds, 114, 117, 134, 181, 186, 188, 190, 193
Inquisition, 91, 109, 131
Introversion, 161
Intuition, 143, 161, 168, 174
Invisible College, 117, 118, 146, 149
Isaac the Blind, 79
Ishtar, 17, 21, 30, 69
Isis, 18, 20, 21, 22, 28, 29, 30, 33, 64

Islam, 59, 60, 61, 62, 104, 106
Isles of the Blessed, 57, 59

J

James I, 107, 111
Jehova's Witnesses, 138
Jehovah, 16, 111, 128
Jerusalem, 15, 20, 29, 58, 60, 61, 97, 103, 128
Jesuits, 115, 119, 120, 130
Jesus, 12, 37, 40, 41, 50, 59, 62, 63, 64, 68, 69, 70, 73, 77, 92, 105, 106, 119, 141, 186
Jesus Prayer, 78
Jews, 11, 15, 16, 17, 18, 22, 24, 25, 26, 29, 37, 39, 40, 47, 53, 78, 79, 81, 82, 91, 128
Joachim de Fiore, 79
Joan of Arc, 168
John Bull, 153
Jonqleurs, 58
Joseph of Arimathea, 64, 65, 67, 70
Jungian Psychology, 9, 12, 53, 64, 80, 143, 160, 161, 169, 172

K

Kabyric Mysteries, 65
Kahunas, 166
Kant, Immanuel, 5, 134, 188
Karma, 50, 146, 147
Keats, John, 142
Keller, Werner, 38
Kelley, Edward, 102
Kelly, Sir Gerald, 149
Kempis, Thomas, 119
Kepler, Johannes, 2, 15, 100, 102, 114, 115, 117
Khunrath, Heinrich, 110
King, Robert, 168
Kingold, Charles, 165
Kircher, Athanasius, 115
Knights of the Golden Stone, 107
Knights Templar, 28
Krishnamurti, J.J., 154

S

Samuels, Mile and DNancy, 171
Sancho IV of Castile, 79
Satanism, 130
Savory, Louis M., 171
Schlieman, Heinrich, 23
Schweighardt, Theophilus, 119
Science, 90, 93, 95, 96, 97, 100, 102,
    109, 110, 111, 113, 114, 123,
    133, 135, 180, 182, 183, 184,
    186, 188, 190
Science Fiction, 48
Scientology, 171
Secondary Imagination, 3, 4, 5, 6, 7,
    63, 168
Secret Chiefs, 196
Seventh Day Adventists, 138
Shah of Persia, 132
Shekinah, 192
Shelley, Mary, 124
Shelley, P. B., 142, 196
Shrine of Wisdom, 152
Siberia, 195
Sidney, Sir Philip, 109
Siena Cathedral, 89
Simon Magus, 141
Sirius, 29, 64
Sky Father, 11, 16
Snowdon, 190
Society for Psychical Research, 138,
    169
Society of the Inner Light, 164, 191
Socrates, 196
Solomon, 26, 27, 28, 125
Solomon's House, 111
Somnambulism, 135, 137, 138, 139,
    141, 145
Son of Light, 193
Soul of the World, 100
Spenser, Edmund, 107, 197
Spiritualism, 134, 135, 138, 139, 145
Sprat, Thomas, 117
Stanton, George, 165
St. Angelo Prison, 131
St. Anne, 63
St. Bernard of Clairvaux, 74

St. Brendan, 57, 59
St. Eustace, 76
St. Francis, 141
St. George, 57, 58
St. Germain, Comte de, 131
St. James, 73
St. John the Divine, 46
St. John the Evamngelist, 172
St. Martin, Louis Claude de, 131
St. Paul, 11, 31, 38, 40, 141
St. Peter, 12, 41, 73
St. Teresa, 141
Starry Wisdomx, 196
Steinbrecher, Edwin C., 174, 175,
    177, 196
Steiner, Rudolf, 156, 157
Stewart, Bob, 166, 192, 196, 197
Stoicism, 48
Stone of Destiny, 172
Strawberry Hill, 144
Streitfield, Harold S., 171
Stuart, Elizabeth, 107
Stuarts, 109, 130
Sublunary World, 128
Subconscious, 161, 166, 170
Sufism, 62
Sun, 73, 90, 96, 97, 98, 100, 105,
    107, 123, 128, 143, 154, 175,
    189
Sun Priest, 97
Swedenborg, Emmanuel, 131, 133,
    134
Symbolism, 98, 110, 118, 124, 125,
    128, 129, 130, 133

T

Talismans, 91, 94
Tammuz, 21, 30, 69
Tao, 186
Tarot, 107, 143, 144, 147, 164, 172,
    174, 175, 194
Tauler, John, 119
Taylor, Thomas, 142
Temple of Solomon, 26, 82, 125,
    128, 129
Tennyson, Affred Lord, 197